北大版 新HSK 应试辅导丛书

新HSK词汇精讲精练

四级

刘云 姜安 主编

根据2013年最新词汇大纲编写

含MP3光盘

北京大学出版社
PEKING UNIVERSITY PRESS

图书在版编目（CIP）数据

新 HSK 词汇精讲精练（四级）/ 刘云，姜安主编 . —北京：北京大学出版社，2013.7
（北大版新 HSK 应试辅导丛书）
ISBN 978-7-301-21895-2

Ⅰ . 新⋯ Ⅱ . ① 刘⋯ ② 姜⋯ Ⅲ . 汉语－词汇－对外汉语教学－水平考试－自学参考资料 Ⅳ . H195.4

中国版本图书馆 CIP 数据核字（2012）第 316264 号

书　　　　名：	新 HSK 词汇精讲精练（四级）
著作责任者：	刘　云　姜　安　主编
责 任 编 辑：	欧慧英
标 准 书 号：	ISBN 978-7-301-21895-2/H・3222
出 版 发 行：	北京大学出版社
地　　　　址：	北京市海淀区成府路 205 号　100871
网　　　　址：	http://www.pup.cn　　新浪官方微博：@北京大学出版社
电 子 信 箱：	zpup@pup.cn
电　　　　话：	邮购部 62752015　发行部 62750672　编辑部 62752028　出版部 62754962
印 　刷　 者：	天津中印联印务有限公司
经 　销　 者：	新华书店
	787 毫米 ×1092 毫米　16 开本　17.75 印张　320 千字
	2013 年 7 月第 1 版　2020 年 4 月第 4 次印刷
定　　　　价：	49.00 元（含 MP3 盘 1 张）

未经许可，不得以任何方式复制或抄袭本书之部分或全部内容。
版权所有，侵权必究
举报电话：010-62752024　　　电子信箱：fd@pup.pku.edu.cn

目录

Contents

Unit 01（爱情 ~ 抱歉）... 1
Unit 02（报名 ~ 表扬）... 6
Unit 03（饼干 ~ 参观）.. 11
Unit 04（餐厅 ~ 乘坐）.. 16
Unit 05（吃惊 ~ 从来）.. 21
Unit 06（粗心 ~ 大使馆）... 26
Unit 07（大约 ~ 得意）.. 31
Unit 08（得 ~ 动作）... 36
Unit 09（堵车 ~ 翻译）.. 41
Unit 10（烦恼 ~ 否则）.. 46
Unit 11（符合 ~ 感动）.. 51
Unit 12（感觉 ~ 共同）.. 56
Unit 13（购物 ~ 广播）.. 61
Unit 14（广告 ~ 航班）.. 66
Unit 15（好处 ~ 怀疑）.. 71
Unit 16（回忆 ~ 寄）.. 76
Unit 17（记者 ~ 减肥）.. 81
Unit 18（减少 ~ 饺子）.. 86
Unit 19（教授 ~ 禁止）.. 91
Unit 20（京剧 ~ 举）.. 96

Unit 21（举办～棵）.. 101
Unit 22（咳嗽～困）.. 106
Unit 23（困难～冷静）.. 111
Unit 24（礼拜天～凉快）.. 116
Unit 25（零钱～毛）.. 121
Unit 26（毛巾～难道）.. 126
Unit 27（难受～陪）.. 131
Unit 28（批评～其次）.. 136
Unit 29（其中～穷）.. 141
Unit 30（区别～扔）.. 146
Unit 31（仍然～申请）.. 151
Unit 32（深～实际）.. 156
Unit 33（实在～首先）.. 161
Unit 34（受不了～说明）.. 166
Unit 35（硕士～态度）.. 171
Unit 36（谈～提前）.. 176
Unit 37（提醒～脱）.. 181
Unit 38（袜子～无）.. 186
Unit 39（无聊～详细）.. 191
Unit 40（响～信息）.. 196
Unit 41（信心～牙膏）.. 201
Unit 42（亚洲～样子）.. 206
Unit 43（邀请～因此）.. 211
Unit 44（引起～由于）.. 216
Unit 45（邮局～原来）.. 221
Unit 46（原谅～增加）.. 226
Unit 47（占线～支持）.. 231
Unit 48（知识～重点）.. 236
Unit 49（重视～仔细）.. 241
Unit 50（自然～座位）.. 246
Keys & Listening Script 答案及听力文本 251

Unit 01

爱情	棒
安排	包子
安全	保护
按时	保证
按照	抱
百分之	抱歉

1 爱情 àiqíng 名 (n.) love

搭配：爱情电影 a love movie；爱情故事 a love story

例句：我希望得到一份真正的爱情。I hope I can get a true love.
她想和男朋友一起看这部爱情电影。She wants to watch this love movie with her boyfriend.

2 安排 ānpái 动 (v.) arrange

搭配：安排工作 to arrange some work；节目安排 to arrange a program

例句：她安排小王去机场接北京来的客人。She arranged Xiao Wang to pick up guests from Beijing at the airport.
王玲的表演安排在第二个，你看可以吗？Wang Ling's performance is arranged as the second. How do you like it?

3 安全 ānquán 形 (adj.) safe

搭配：注意安全 be safe；交通安全 road safety

例句：食品安全非常重要。Food security is extremely important.
你一定要注意安全，保护好自己。Be careful and take good care of yourself.

4 按时 ànshí 副 (adv.) on time, on schedule

搭配：按时完成 to finish sth on schedule；按时吃药 to take medicine on time

例句：老师要求我们按时到校，不要迟到。The teacher asks us to arrive at school on time and not to be late.
运动会的所有准备工作都会按时完成。All preparations for the sports meeting will be finished on schedule.

5 按照 ànzhào 介 (prep.) according to

搭配：按照规定 according to the rules；按照计划 according to the plan

例句：按照公司安排，赵强明天要去北京参加会议。According to the company's arrangement, Zhao Qiang will go to Beijing to attend the meeting tomorrow.
按照计划，我今天本来应该在家休息的。According to the plan, I should have had a rest at home today.

6 百分之 bǎifēnzhī percent

搭配：百分之十 ten percent；百分之百 100 percent

例句：谁也不能百分之百保证，王东今天一定来。Nobody can be 100 percent sure that Wang Dong will come today.
她大约只有百分之一的机会可以活下去。She perhaps only has a slim chance to survive.

Unit 01

7 棒 bàng 形 (adj.) excellent, good, nice

搭配：太棒了！ Terrific; Great; Lovely!；真棒！ Well done; That's great!

例句：你的办法太棒了。Your idea is so great.

真棒！你又得了第一。Nice! You've got the first prize one more time.

8 包子 bāozi 名 (n.) steamed stuffed bun

搭配：菜包子 vegetable-stuffed buns；肉包子 meat-stuffed buns

例句：我买两个菜包子和四个肉包子。I've bought two vegetable-stuffed buns and four meat-stuffed buns.

这家饭店的包子味道很不错。The stuffed buns in this restaurant are tasty.

9 保护 bǎohù 动 (v.) protect

搭配：保护措施 protection measures；保护眼睛 to protect one's eyes

例句：保护眼睛要从小做起。We should start to protect our eyes from childhood.

保护环境是我们的责任。It is our duty to protect the environment.

10 保证 bǎozhèng 动 (v.) guarantee, assure

搭配：保证质量 to guarantee the quality of sth；保证完成 to guarantee the completion of

例句：他向老师保证，以后一定会认真完成作业。He assures the teacher that he will finish his work carefully from now on.

你看到桌上的那张质量保证书了吗？Did you see that quality certificate on the desk?

11 抱 bào 动 (v.) hold/ carry in the arms, embrace, hug

搭配：抱着孩子 to hold the child in the arms；抱着书 to hold some books

例句：她抱着几本书，低着头进了教室。She was holding some books, kept her head down and went into the classroom.

你去办公室，把作业本都抱过来。Go to the office and bring the workbooks for me, please.

12 抱歉 bàoqiàn 形 (adj.) sorry

搭配：十分抱歉 be very sorry about sth；非常抱歉 be extremely sorry about sth

例句：对于今天的事情，她觉得很抱歉。She is very sorry about what happened today.

我真是抱歉，这么晚了才打电话给你。I'm very sorry for calling you so late.

实战练习（一）

一、听对话，选择正确答案

1. A. 男的　　　　B. 女的　　　　C. 男的和女的　　　D. 女的和李明
2. A. 正在接电话　　B. 身体不太好　　C. 是一个医生　　　D. 很害怕吃药

二、选词填空

　　　　A 爱情　B 安排　C 安全　D 按时　E 按照　F 百分之

1. 张红第一次出远门，妈妈很不放心，让她路上一定要注意（　　）。
2. 她喜欢看（　　）电影。
3. （　　）王玲的要求，校长安排她去教三年级的数学。
4. 他放假前已经把自己的工作全都（　　）好了。
5. A：我们终于（　　）完成了这么多的工作，真是不容易啊。
   B：这和大家的努力是分不开的。
6. A：这次希望大吗？
   B：不大，（　　）一的可能性都没有。

　　　　A 包子　B 保护　C 保证　D 棒　E 抱歉　F 抱

7. 她刚（　　）着孩子上楼去了。
8. 动物是人类的好朋友，我们要（　　）它们。
9. 他的汉语非常（　　），常有人请他当翻译。
10. 真是非常（　　），我今天还有其他的事情。
11. A：这么远的路，你一个人开车行吗？还是让小李和你一起去吧。
    B：你放心，我（　　）会安全到那儿的。
12. A：你吃的是什么？
    B：（　　），这是中国的传统美食。

三、排列顺序

1. A. 不能再工作了　　　B. 按照医生的安排　　　C. 他现在必须好好儿休息
2. A. 他们公司最近很忙　　B. 所以没法按时休息
   C. 几乎每天晚上都要加班

四、完成句子

1. 可以　作用　安全带　保护的　起到 _____
2. 二十分钟　保证　我　到公司　提前 _____
3. 你应该　说一声　向他　我觉得　抱歉 _____
4. 经理的　不太满意　王红　对　这种安排 _____
5. 来了　怎么　你　一个篮球　抱着 _____

五、看图，用词造句

1. 爱情

2. 棒

Unit 02

报名	遍
倍	标准
本来	表格
笨	表示
比如	表演
毕业	表扬

Unit 02

13 报名 bàomíng (v.) enroll in/on, enlist

搭配：报名上学 to enroll in school；报名参加比赛 to enlist for a competition

例句：他已经去报名参加那个节目了。He has entered for that programme.

这两天来报名的人很少。We had few enlistees these two days.

14 倍 bèi (m.w.) time, fold

搭配：提高两倍 to increase two times；扩大一倍 to expand one time

例句：公司今年的销售量比去年提高了一倍。This year the company's sales volume increased one time than last year.

15 是 5 的 3 倍。Fifteen is three times as much as five.

15 本来 běnlái (adj./adv.) original, at first; originally

例句：我想你误会了他本来的意思。I think you misunderstood his original meaning.

李红本来是打算今天去报名的。At first, Li Hong planned to sign up today.

我本来不知道这件事，到了这里才听说了。I didn't know that originally, and heard of it here.

16 笨 bèn (adj.) dull, foolish, stupid

搭配：笨重 heavy；嘴笨 clumsy

例句：他不希望自己被别人看成是一个笨学生。He doesn't want to be treated as a slow student.

这双鞋子看起来很笨重。This pair of shoes looks heavy on me.

他笨手笨脚的。He is clumsy.

17 比如 bǐrú (v.) for example, for instance, suppose, such as

搭配：比如说 for example; for instance

例句：汉语中有很多词意思差不多，比如保留和保存。Many Chinese words are similar in meaning, for example, "reserve" and "preserve".

不是每个人都喜欢花，比如说，我就不喜欢。Not everyone likes flowers, such as me.

18 毕业 bìyè (v.) graduate

搭配：大学毕业 to graduate from college；毕业论文 thesis

例句：我儿子已经毕业两年了。My son had graduated for two years.

她毕业后就去了北京。She went to Beijing after graduation.

⑲ 遍 biàn 量 (m.w.) one time

搭配：一遍 one time；好几遍 several/ many times

例句：我再给你讲一遍，你可要认真听。I'll explain it to you one more time, and you should listen carefully.

这些我都已经复习好几遍了。I have reviewed these materials many times.

⑳ 标准 biāozhǔn 名 (n.) standard, criterion

搭配：卫生标准 hygiene/ health standard；标准时间 standard time

例句：这一题的标准答案是什么？What is the correct answer to this question?

她的普通话不太标准。Her mandarin is not good enough.

㉑ 表格 biǎogé 名 (n.) form, list, table

搭配：一张表格 a form；电子表格 a spreadsheet

例句：你帮我把这张表格送到经理室，好吗？Would you please bring this form to the manager's office for me?

把这张表格里的信息填完后交给老师。Fill in the form and hand it in to the teacher.

㉒ 表示 biǎoshì 动 (v.) express, show

搭配：表示喜欢 to show one's interests in；表示欢迎 to extend a welcome to；没有表示 have no expression

例句：我问他，他表示不知道。I asked him but he said he did not know.

老师没有高兴的表示。The teacher didn't show any sign of happiness.

我们对于他的到来表示了欢迎。He was welcome by us.

㉓ 表演 biǎoyǎn 动 (v.) perform, act, play

搭配：唱歌表演 a singing performance；跳舞表演 a dancing performance；看表演 to watch a performance

例句：他表演得很好。He performed well.

我们看了跳舞表演。We watched a dancing performance.

㉔ 表扬 biǎoyáng 动 (v.) praise, commend

搭配：表扬信 a letter of commendation；受到表扬 to receive a praise

例句：老师表扬王东学习认真。The teacher praised Wang Dong's diligence.

今天终于得到了老师的表扬，他非常高兴。He is very glad about being praised by the teacher today.

实战练习（二）

一、听对话，选择正确答案

1. A. 公司　　　　B. 机场　　　C. 宾馆　　D. 会议室
2. A. 女的对小王很满意　　　　B. 男的刚刚参加工作
   C. 小王现在正在开会　　　　D. 小王和男的一个组

二、选词填空

A 报名　B 倍　C 本来　D 笨　E 比如　F 毕业

1. 我六月份就（　　）了，现在正在找工作。
2. 这些事情（　　）都是安排给王刚做的。
3. 你再说我（　　），我可要生气了。
4. 小王已经（　　）参加这次比赛了。
5. A：你以后有什么打算？
   B：我想从事教育工作，（　　）中学老师什么的。
6. A：这个李红还真是不简单，销售量比去年提高了一（　　），这不是谁都能做到的。
   B：是啊，这样的成绩，整个公司也只有她一个。

A 遍　B 标准　C 表演　D 表格　E 表扬　F 表示

7. 女朋友（　　）了你一下，你就这么高兴？
8. 这些（　　）要在明天下午一点前送到办公室。
9. 摇头（　　）不同意或不满意。
10. 这件衣服没有洗干净，要再洗一（　　）。
11. A：这次的（　　）是不是有些太高了？
    B：是啊，公司里大多数人都这样觉得。
12. A：你的要求也太高了吧？这么多演员，居然没有能让你满意的。
    B：没有一个人会（　　）。

三、排列顺序

1. A. 可刚接到通知　　　　B 我本来打算今天下班后去看电影的
   C. 晚上又要加班

2. A. 大学不知怎么毕业的　　　　　　B. 他真笨
   C. 连表格都不会弄

四、完成句子

1. 就已经　这次活动　昨天　结束了　报名 _____
2. 表扬　他　能得到　希望　老师的 _____
3. 饼干　觉得　太甜了　我　这个 _____
4. 表示　同意　点头　或满意　一般 _____
5. 正在　怎么做　学习　电子表格　我 _____

五、看图，用词造句

1. 饼干

2. 表演

Unit 03

饼干　　　　　不仅
并且　　　　　部分
博士　　　　　擦
不过　　　　　猜
不得不　　　　材料
不管　　　　　参观

㉕ 饼干 bǐnggān (名) (n.) biscuit, cracker

搭配：几块饼干 some biscuits；低糖饼干 biscuits with low sugar

例句：真抱歉，这种饼干已经卖完了。We're very sorry that this kind of biscuits were sold out.

她早饭只吃了几块饼干。She took some biscuits as breakfast.

㉖ 并且 bìngqiě (连) (conj.) and, also

例句：她很快做完了作业，并且检查了一遍。She finished the work quickly, and checked it again.

我们讨论并且通过了一项计划。We discussed and approved a plan.

我觉得这个房子租金不贵，并且环境、交通都很好。The rent of this house is low and the traffic is very good.

㉗ 博士 bóshì (名) (n.) doctor

搭配：博士帽 doctoral cap；博士研究生 doctoral candidate

例句：他博士生毕业以后就进了这家公司。He entered this company after getting the doctoral degree.

王东想去国外读博士。Wang Dong wants to pursue a doctorate abroad.

㉘ 不过 búguò (副/连) (adv./conj.) only, no more than; but, yet, however

例句：我猜她不过三十岁。I guess she is at most 30 years old.

小王认为这不过是个游戏，不用太认真的。Xiao Wang thinks that this is merely a game, do not take it too seriously.

这个笔记本挺好看，不过价格有点贵。This notebook looks good, but it is a bit expensive.

㉙ 不得不 bùdébù have no choice/ option... but to..., have to...

例句：因为没有工作，他不得不靠父母生活。He has to live on his parents because of his unemployment.

我不得不说，你的方法更好。I have to admit that your method is better than mine.

在事实面前，他不得不说真话。In the face of the facts, he had to tell the truth.

㉚ 不管 bùguǎn (连) (conj.) no matter, despite

例句：不管遇到什么问题，我们都要按时完成任务。No matter what will happen, we must finish the work on schedule.

不管天晴还是下雨，我明天都会来。I shall come tomorrow, rainy or sunny.

不管他说什么，我就是不生气。Whatever he said, I would not get mad.

31 不仅 bùjǐn (conj./adv.) not only (... but also...)

搭配：不仅如此 moreover；不仅……还…… not only ... but; both；不仅……而且…… not only... but also...

例句：李红不仅没给他打电话，还把手机也关了。Li Hong didn't call him, but also turned off her mobile phone.

他不仅在工作上给我帮助，而且在生活上也很关心我。He helps me not only in my work, but also in my life.

这不仅是我一个人的意见。It's not my personal opinion.

32 部分 bùfen (n.) part, section, portion

搭配：大部分 a large portion；第一部分 the first part

例句：大部分的词语她都没写出来。She can't write out most of the words.

这本书的上半部分我已经看完了。I have finished reading the first half of this book.

33 擦 cā (v.) wipe, clean, polish

搭配：擦鞋 to polish shoes；擦桌子 to clean the desk；擦窗户 to clean the window

例句：她吃过饭后把桌子擦得干干净净。She cleaned the table thoroughly after dinner.

你把窗户擦擦。Please clean the window.

34 猜 cāi (v.) guess, suspect

搭配：猜谜语 to guess a riddle；猜不出 to miss one's guess；猜对 to guess right；猜错 to make a bad guess

例句：你猜不到她最后做了些什么。You cannot guess what she has done at last.

王红猜了半天，也不知道是谁送她的花。Wang Hong guessed for a long time, but still couldn't figure out who had given the flower to her.

35 材料 cáiliào (n.) material, data, reference material

搭配：写作材料 writing materials；重要材料 important materials

例句：对王红来说，这些材料非常重要。These materials are very important to Wang Hong.

王先生去买学习材料了，一会儿就回来。Mr. Wang was out to buy some learning materials and would be back soon.

36 参观 cānguān (v.) visit, look around

搭配：参观学习 a studying tour；参观故宫 to visit the Forbidden City

例句：你们明天要去哪儿参观？Where will you visit tomorrow?

你先随便参观一下，我去看看李经理在不在。Please take a casual visit around. I will check whether Manager Li is available.

实战练习(三)

一、听对话,选择正确答案

1. A. 自己现在没时间　　B. 想再去买点东西
   C. 想找人帮忙打扫　　D. 欢迎大家去做客
2. A. 逛街　　B. 买电脑　　C. 看电影　　D. 在家休息

二、选词填空

A 并且　B 博士　C 饼干　D 不得不　E 不管　F 不过

1. 因为怎么都找不到李红,我(　　)给赵刚打了一个电话。
2. 她昨天来公司找我了,(　　)没和我说这件事。
3. 我们做自己喜欢的事,(　　)努力把它做好。
4. 按照小王现在的能力,考上(　　)是没有问题的。
5. 女:怎么样,有问题吗?
   男:您放心吧,(　　)今天做到几点,我保证在明天会议前把表格送过去。
6. 马上就要吃饭了,你少吃点儿(　　)。

A 不仅　B 部分　C 擦　D 猜　E 材料　F 参观

7. 她没有想到,前来(　　)的游客会这么多。
8. 窗户不太干净,你用水(　　)一遍。
9. 他这次去北京,(　　)见到了老同学,还参观了以前的中学。
10. 按照经理的要求,我不得不重新整理这些(　　)。
11. 男:你(　　),我这次给你带了什么礼物?
    女:快拿出来让我看看。
12. 女:明天是周末了,你还不能休息?
    男:我打算带我们班一(　　)学生去北京大学参观一下。

三、排列顺序

1. A. 王东的成绩不仅是全班最高　　B. 在这次考试中　　C. 并且是全年级第一名
2. A. 才能让大部分的人都满意　　B. 我怎么也猜不到　　C. 他要如何安排

四、完成句子

1. 二十分钟 现在 参观时间 离 还有 _____
2. 一部分 他在 上海 还有 朋友 _____
3. 妈妈的鞋子 擦得 她 干干净净 把 _____
4. 回家的路上 小王现在 一定 我猜 在 _____
5. 留在 照顾妹妹 王玲 家里 不得不 _____

五、看图，用词造句

1. 擦

2. 参观

Unit 04

餐厅	场
厕所	超过
差不多	成功
长城	成为
长江	诚实
尝	乘坐

Unit 04

37　餐厅 cāntīng　名 (n.)　restaurant, dining room, dining hall

搭配：学校餐厅 dining hall；餐厅服务员 waiter; restaurant staff

例句：新餐厅什么时候开始营业？ When will the new restaurant open?

　　　我们去留学生餐厅吃吧。Let's have a meal in the dining hall for international students.

38　厕所 cèsuǒ　名 (n.)　toilet, wash room

搭配：公共厕所 communal toilet; comfort station；上厕所 to go to the bathroom

例句：北京的公共厕所免费。The public toilets in Beijing are free.

　　　我拉肚子了，一小时上了五次厕所。I had a diarrhea, and went to the toilet five times in one hour.

39　差不多 chàbuduō　形/副 (adj./adv.)　almost; nearly, just about right

例句：王红差不多也该到了，我们去办公室等她。Wang Hong will be arriving in soon. Let's go and wait her in the office.

　　　他那边的情况和这儿也差不多。He has almost the same situation there.

　　　这两个足球队的水平差不多。The two teams are almost the same in performance.

40　长城 Chángchéng　名 (n.)　Great Wall

搭配：万里长城 the Great Wall

例句：我喜欢长城、故宫、中国电影和中国的一切。I like the Great Wall, the Forbidden City, Chinese movies and everything about China.

　　　我们班同学打算明天去爬长城。Our classmates plan to climb the Great Wall tomorrow.

　　　不到长城非好汉。He who has never been to the Great Wall is not a true man.

41　长江 ChángJiāng　名 (n.)　Yangtze River

搭配：长江大桥 the Yangtze River Bridge

例句：长江是世界第三长河。The Yangtze River is the third longest river in the world.

　　　长江和黄河是中国两大河流。The Yangtze River and the Yellow River are the two major rivers in China.

42　尝 cháng　动 (v.)　taste, try

搭配：尝尝 to have a taste；尝一尝 to try the flavor of sth

例句：你来尝一下，这菜是不是有些太甜了？ Try this dish and tell me whether it is too sweet or not.

　　　尝尝这瓜怎么样？ Come here and try this melon.

43 场 chǎng 名/量 (n./m.w.) place used for a particular purpose; used for sports and recreation

搭配：会场 meeting place；飞机场 airport；一场电影 a movie

例句：他在机场已经等了两个多小时了。He has been waiting for two hours at the airport.
我想请你去看晚上八点的那场电影。I want to invite you to watch the movie at 8:00 pm.

44 超过 chāoguò 动 (v.) excel, surpass, exceed

搭配：超过标准 to exceed the standard；超过时间 overtime

例句：这个温度已经超过了历史最高水平。The temperature ranked the highest in history.
这儿的字数不能超过三十个。No more than thirty words are allowed here.

45 成功 chénggōng 形/动 (adj./v.) successful; succeed (in)

搭配：非常成功 be very successful；成功的画家 a successful painter

例句：经过这么多年的努力，他终于成为一位成功的作家。After so many years of efforts, he finally becomes a successful writer.
我相信，如果我坚持下去，就一定会成功。I believe that I will gain success with my persistence.

46 成为 chéngwéi 动 (v.) become, turn into

搭配：成为朋友 to become friends；成为老师 to become a teacher；成为经理 to become a manager

例句：他希望自己可以成为这个学校的学生。He hopes to become a student of this school.
经过那件事以后，我们就成为了好朋友。After that, we became good friends.

47 诚实 chéngshí 形 (adj.) honest, sincere

搭配：诚实的人 an honest person；非常诚实 be very honest

例句：这是一个非常诚实的孩子。This is a very honest child.
他非常诚实地把事情的经过告诉了我。He told me the whole thing honestly.

48 乘坐 chéngzuò 动 (v.) take

搭配：乘坐飞机 to take a plane；乘坐火车 to take a train

例句：这个车太小了，最多只能乘坐四个人。This vehicle is too small to take more than four people.
公司安排小王乘坐汽车去北京。The company arranged Xiao Wang to travel to Beijing by car.

实战练习（四）

一、听对话，选择正确答案

1. A. 医院　　　B. 超市　　　C. 家里　　　D. 饭店
2. A. 要开会　　B. 不舒服　　C. 觉得累　　D. 没时间

二、选词填空

A 差不多　B 尝　C 长城　D 场　E 超过　F 餐厅

1. 到了北京，怎么可能不去爬（　　　）？
2. 你们先去（　　　）点菜，我一会儿就到。
3. 这西瓜甜不甜，您得自己（　　　）一下才知道。
4. 你放心吧，他不可能（　　　）我们的。
5. A：你昨天怎么回来得那么晚？
   B：我和李红一起吃饭，然后又去看了（　　　）电影。
6. A：时间（　　　）了，我们现在去机场吧。
   B：再等一下，我去和小李说一声。

A 成功　B 厕所　C 成为　D 诚实　E 乘坐　F 长江

7. 为了能（　　　）你的男朋友，我一直在努力。
8. 老师教育我们要做一个（　　　）的人，不能骗人。
9. 李强要（　　　）明天晚上九点的火车去上海。
10. 王玲的家住在（　　　）边上。
11. A：李丽，谢谢你，没有你的帮助我不可能（　　　）。
    B：别这样说，这是你自己努力的结果。
12. A：外出旅游时你最担心什么？
    B：找不到（　　　）！

三、排列顺序

1. A. 所以考博士没有成功　　B. 本来李明的成绩和王红是差不多的
   C. 不过最近他爱上了玩游戏
2. A. 不过我最近工作很忙　　B. 王红很想来尝尝我做的饭　　C. 所以一直没有机会

四、完成句子

1. 已经　他的　超过了　身高　两米　_____
2. 小王　工作　到北京　差不多　有半年了　_____
3. 要　去海南吗　我们　乘坐　飞机　_____
4. 这家餐厅的　非常　经理　诚实　_____
5. 我觉得　这场　很没意思　比赛　_____

五、看图，用词造句

1. 尝

2. 成功

Unit 05

吃惊	出现
重新	厨房
抽烟	传真
出差	窗户
出发	词语
出生	从来

49 吃惊 chījīng 动 (v.) surprise, astonish, shock
搭配：大吃一惊 be very surprised；吃惊的样子 a surprised look
例句：她非常吃惊地看着我。She is surprised and staring at me.
看到小王吃惊的样子，我相信他也不知道这件事。By Xiao Wang's surprised look, I believe that he didn't know the matter either.

50 重新 chóngxīn 副 (adv.) again, anew, afresh
搭配：重新安排 to rearrange；重新开始 to restart
例句：李红不得不重新安排明天的工作。Li Hong has to rearrange tomorrow's work.
经理告诉我，这份材料要重新再写一遍。The manager asked me to rewrite this material.

51 抽烟 chōu yān smoke (a cigarette)
搭配：禁止抽烟 no smoking；抽烟有害健康 smoking is hazardous to health
例句：对不起，先生，这儿禁止抽烟。Sorry, sir, no smoking here.
抽烟对身体不好，你怎么就是不听呢？I've told you that smoking is bad for your health. Why don't you just listen to me?

52 出差 chūchāi 动 (v.) go/ be away on a business trip
例句：小王去北京出差还没回来呢。Xiao Wang was away on a business trip to Beijing and not back yet.
他这次出差差不多要半个月。His business trip will last nearly a half month.
我出了一个月的差。I was on a business trip for a month.

53 出发 chūfā 动 (v.) depart, leave
搭配：出发时间 departure time；出发地点 departure place
例句：你告诉李红明天的出发时间没有？Did you tell Li Hong tomorrow's departure time?
我们开车从上海出发，差不多三个小时就到了。It will take about three hours to get there by driving from Shanghai.

54 出生 chūshēng 动 (v.) be born
搭配：出生证明 a birth certificate；出生地点 the place of birth
例句：你是几月出生的？Which month were you born?
妈妈告诉他，他出生在中国。His mother told him that he was born in China.

Unit 05

55　出现 chūxiàn　(v.)　appear, turn up

搭配：出现问题 to go wrong；出现变化 changes begin to emerge

例句：他的身体出现了问题。He has some health problems.

这两年出现了很多新的电子产品。Many new electronic products have emerged in the past two years.

56　厨房 chúfáng　(n.)　kitchen

搭配：打扫厨房 to clean up a kitchen；干净的厨房 a clean kitchen；大厨房 a big kitchen

例句：妈妈在厨房做饭。My mother is cooking in the kitchen.

这家饭店的厨房很干净。The kitchen of the restaurant is very clean.

57　传真 chuánzhēn　(n./v.)　fax; send sb a fax

搭配：发传真 send (sb) a fax；传真纸 fax paper；传真机 a fax machine

例句：你打电话问一下，怎么传真还没有发过来？Please make a phone call to ask them why the fax hasn't been sent yet.

公司又重新买了一台传真机。The company bought a new fax machine again.

我已经答应明天把计划给他们传真过去。I've agreed to fax them our plan tomorrow.

58　窗户 chuānghu　(n.)　window

搭配：关窗户 to close the window；开窗户 to open the window；窗户外面 outside the window

例句：这边的窗户怎么打不开了？ Why this side of the window can't be opened?

李红把窗户擦得非常干净。Li Hong cleaned the windows.

59　词语 cíyǔ　(n.)　word, term

搭配：新词语 a new word；学习词语 to learn words；复习词语 to review words；练习词语 to practice words

例句：我们学习了一些词语。We learned some words.

电子邮件是新词语。"E-mail" is a new term.

60　从来 cónglái　(adv.)　never, always, all along

例句：我从来没有见过这个人。I have never seen this person before.

她从来都不做家务。She has never done any housework.

实战练习（五）

一、听对话，选择正确答案

1. A. 自己想用词典　　B. 李红在找材料　　C. 现在没有时间　　D. 李红可能知道
2. A. 男的　　　　　　B. 女的　　　　　　C. 李刚　　　　　　D. 王东

二、选词填空

A 吃惊　B 重新　C 抽烟　D 出差　E 出发　F 出生

1. 刚到公司就听到这个消息，她觉得非常（　　）。
2. 王东下星期要去北京（　　）。
3. 你还记得他的（　　）年月吗？
4. 从明天起，我们要（　　）开始好好儿生活。
5. A：你还在公司吗？
   B：我已经（　　）了，你也快些出门吧。
6. A：你什么时候开始不（　　）的？
   B：从孩子出生以后，老婆就不让抽了。

A 传真　B 窗户　C 出现　D 从来　E 厨房　F 词语

7. 我（　　）都没有乘坐过飞机。
8. 晚饭后，我常去（　　）帮妈妈洗碗。
9. 退休后，老王再没在公司里（　　）过。
10. 不会的（　　）就去查词典。
11. A：昨天让你给王东发（　　），你发了没有？
    B：早就发过了。
12. A：这个房间里没有（　　），太暗了。
    B：是啊，白天都得开灯。

三、排列顺序

1. A. 他觉得非常吃惊　　B. 自己是哪年出生的
   C. 因为自己从来没有告诉过李丽

2. A. 他父母却从来也不管他
   B. 就已经学会了抽烟
   C. 这个孩子今年不过十四岁

四、完成句子

1. 没有 老师 表扬过 从来都 他 _____
2. 李明 出发 明天 我猜 可能是 _____
3. 打开 早上起来 李丽喜欢 就把 窗户 _____
4. 抽烟 生气的时候 特别 王东 爱 _____
5. 满意 这个 让他 答案 并不能 _____

五、看图，用词造句

1. 吃惊

2. 出差

Unit 06

粗心　　　　打印
存　　　　　打招呼
错误　　　　打折
答案　　　　打针
打扮　　　　大概
打扰　　　　大使馆

Unit 06

61 粗心 cūxīn (adj.) careless, thoughtless
搭配：非常粗心 be very careless；粗心大意 carelessness
例句：小王最大的问题就是工作粗心。Xiao Wang's biggest problem is his carelessness in work.
我家孩子总是粗心大意怎么办？ How should I deal with my child's carelessness?

62 存 cún (v.) deposit, store, keep, reserve
搭配：存钱 to save money；存包 to deposit one's bag；存行李 to deposit luggage
例句：你下午去银行把钱存起来吧，放在家里不安全。Deposit your money in the bank this afternoon and it's not safe at home.
先把行李存在这儿，等一会儿再来拿。Deposit our luggage here first and take it later.

63 错误 cuòwù (adj./n.) mistaken, wrong; mistake, fault, error, blunder
搭配：错误的思想 wrong idea；错误的决定 wrong decision；犯错误 to do sth wrong；改正错误 to correct one's mistakes
例句：他没考虑清楚，做了错误的决定。He didn't think it through and made a wrong decision.
如果你能改正错误的话，还是个好孩子。You are still a good kid if you correct your mistakes.

64 答案 dá'àn (n.) answer, key, solution
搭配：标准答案 a correct answer；得到答案 to get an answer
例句：李红手里拿着的才是标准答案。Li Hong has the correct answer.
我一直没有找到能让我满意的答案。I haven't found the satisfactory answer yet.

65 打扮 dǎban (v./n.) make/dress up; style/way of dressing
搭配：打扮自己 to make / dress oneself up；学生打扮 dressed as students
例句：你今天打扮得这么漂亮，要去哪儿啊？ You look so beautiful today. Where are you going?
没想到这么小的孩子也知道爱美，开始打扮自己了。I didn't expect that such a young child would know what beauty is and begins to dress herself up so early.

66 打扰 dǎrǎo (v.) disturb
搭配：打扰大家 to disturb everyone；不要再来打扰我 don't disturb me again
例句：他现在工作很忙，我不想打扰他。He is working busily now, I don't want to disturb him.
对不起，先生，打扰您一下，请问去故宫怎么走？ Excuse me, sir. How can I get to the Forbidden City?

67 打印 dǎyìn 动 (v.) print

搭配：打印机 a printer ；打印材料 to print some material

例句：这些材料都需要打印出来吗？ Do I need to print all these materials?

这是刚打印出来的会议活动安排表，您看一下。This Conference Activity Schedule is newly printed. Please have a look.

68 打招呼 dǎ zhāohu greet sb, say hello to sb

搭配：没打招呼 without a greeting ；打了一个招呼 to greet sb with a nod; to say hello

例句：刚才看到王东，你怎么都没和他打招呼？ Why don't you greet Wang Dong when you see him just now?

在回家的路上我给王先生打了个招呼。I greeted Mr. Wang on my way home.

69 打折 dǎzhé 动 (v.) sale at a discount, give a discount

搭配：打折卡 discount card ；打五折 at 50% discount ；打折品 discounts merchandise

例句：现在的机票都在打折，坐飞机比火车还便宜。The air tickets are on sale now, so traveling by airplane is cheaper than by train.

这件衣服打折以后还要一千多呢。This dress is still more than one thousand RMB with the discount.

70 打针 dǎzhēn 动 (v.) give/ get an injection

搭配：打针吃药 to take injections and medicines ；去医院打针 to get an injection at hospital

例句：这两天我都要去医院打针。I have to get injections at hospital these two days.

他非常害怕打针。He is afraid of taking an injection.

71 大概 dàgài 名/形/副 (n./adj./adv.) general idea; rough; briefly

搭配：大概情况 a general situation ；大概的想法 a vague idea

例句：他嘴上没说，心里却明白了大概。He said nothing, but had a general idea in his mind.

从这儿到学校，大概需要三十分钟。It takes roughly 30 minutes to get to school from here.

72 大使馆 dàshǐguǎn 名 (n.) embassy

搭配：中国大使馆 the Chinese Embassy ；驻华大使馆 Embassy to the People's Republic of China

例句：王东的爸爸在大使馆工作。Wang Dong's father works at the embassy.

他下午准备去大使馆办签证。He is going to the embassy to receive his visa in the afternoon.

实战练习（六）

一、听对话，选择正确答案

1. A. 公司　　　　　B. 医院　　　　　C. 超市　　　　　D. 材料室
2. A. 帽子不好看　　B. 女儿更喜欢黑色　C. 女儿不愿戴帽子　D. 女儿喜欢便宜的

二、选词填空

　　　　　　A 打扮　B 打扰　C 打印　D 打折　E 打针　F 大概

1. 雨并没有下多大，（　　）半夜就不下了。
2. 真没有想到，她（　　）一下会这么漂亮。
3. 很抱歉，我们商店的这次（　　）活动已经结束了。
4. 妈妈，我能不能只吃药，不去（　　）啊？
5. A：（　　）了您这么长时间，真是不好意思。
　　B：别这么客气，如果还有什么问题随时都可以来找我。
6. A：小王，经理问上午让你（　　）的材料好了没有。
　　B：马上就好。

　　　　　　A 大使馆　B 存　C 打招呼　D 粗心　E 答案　F 错误

7. 我去银行（　　）钱。
8. 如果你不（　　），就一定能考到一百分。
9. 我现在也不知道，这两个（　　）哪一个才是对的。
10. 我觉得你还是先给（　　）打个电话，如果签证下来了，你再去。
11. A：你刚刚跟谁（　　）呢？
　　B：我们经理。
12. A：你对小李还有信心吗？
　　B：年轻人，犯（　　）很正常。

三、排列顺序

1. A. 让你先跟王总打声招呼　　B. 王东刚才打电话来　　C. 说参观还没结束
2. A. 我想下班以后去看看　　　B. 东西都非常便宜　　　C. 李红昨天说商场现在在打折

四、完成句子

1. 打扮过　从来　这样　她　都没有　_____
2. 想法　错误　你的　是　的_____
3. 打印出来　安排我　经理　把　这些材料_____
4. 去　办了　大使馆　他　签订_____
5. 打针　孩子　不愿意　一直　去_____

五、看图，用词造句

1. 打针

2. 打扮

Unit 07

大约	导游
大夫	到处
戴	到底
当	倒
当时	道歉
刀	得意

73 大约 dàyuē (adv./adj.) about, around; approximate

搭配：大约一个小时 about an hour；大约的数量 an approximate number of

例句：他这次去上海出差，大约要一个星期才能回来。He went on a business trip to Shanghai and would be back in about one week.

李刚大约四点钟的时候去了公司。Li Gang went to the company around four o'clock.

74 大夫 dàifu (n.) doctor

搭配：王大夫 Doctor Wang；大夫和护士 doctors and nurses；医院的大夫 a hospital doctor

例句：我和王大夫是邻居。Doctor Wang lives next to me.

李大夫，32床的病人不舒服，您快去看看吧。Doctor Li, bed No.32 felt uncomfortable. Please have a look as soon as possible.

75 戴 dài (v.) put on, wear

搭配：戴帽子 to wear a cap/ hat；戴眼镜 to put on glasses

例句：因为平时没保护好眼睛，他不得不戴上了眼镜。Not having taken care of his eyes, he has to put on a pair of glasses.

外面太冷了，你还是戴上帽子和手套再出去吧。It is too cold outside. You'd better wear a hat and gloves.

76 当 dāng (v./prep.) work as, bear; when, while

搭配：当代表 to be a representative；当领导 to become a leader；当面 be face to face；当场 on the spot

例句：大家都同意选王东当这个代表。All of us agreed to choose Wang Dong as our representative.

这件事你应该当面和李红说。You should talk this matter to Li Hong face to face.

当我回来的时候，爸爸妈妈已经睡了。When I came back, dad and mum had gone to sleep.

77 当时 dāngshí (n.) that time, then

例句：我当时非常生气，不过现在已经不生气了。I was angry at that time, but now I am ok.

当时大家都认为他不过是随便说说，谁都没有认真。Everybody thought he was merely talking wildly at that time and nobody took him seriously.

她当时就被气哭了。She cried with anger right at that time.

78 刀 dāo (n.) knife

搭配：一把刀 a knife；水果刀 a fruit knife

例句：你帮我把桌子上的水果刀拿过来，好吗？Please bring that fruit knife on the table for me, ok?

妈妈今天去超市重新买了一把菜刀。My mother bought one more knife from the supermarket today.

Unit 07

79 导游 dǎoyóu （名）(n.) conduct a sightseeing tour, tour guide, tourist guide

搭配：导游人员 a tour guide；导游资格考试 a tourist guide qualification exam

例句：小王想去参加这次的导游资格考试。Xiao Wang wants to attend the tourist guide qualification exam this time.

导游工作其实是非常辛苦的。In fact, being a tourist guide is very tiring.

80 到处 dàochù （副）(adv.) in every place, at all places, everywhere

搭配：到处看看 to look around；到处参观 to visit around

例句：你怎么在这儿坐着？王东在到处找你呢。Why did you sit here? Wang Dong is looking for you everywhere.

小李是第一次来北京，我当然得带着他到处走一走了。Xiao Li came to Beijing for the first time. I do have to show him around.

81 到底 dàodǐ （副）(adv.) at last, finally, on earth

例句：你说这话到底是什么意思？ What on earth does that mean?

他有些生气地说："你到底去还是不去？"He said angrily: "Do you want to go or not?"

到底有多少人知道这件事情？ How many people on earth know this thing?

火星上到底有没有生命？ Are there really any lives on the Mar?

82 倒 dào （动/副）(v./adv.) back, pour; but, on the contrary, after all, instead

搭配：倒车 to back a car；倒茶 to pour a cup of tea；倒垃圾 to litter

例句：你帮我倒杯茶送到经理室，好吗？ Please bring a cup of tea to the manager's room for me.

她这个当姐姐的，倒没有弟弟懂事。As an elder sister, she is not so sensible as her brother though.

你说得倒容易，可做起来并不容易。Easy said than done.

83 道歉 dàoqiàn （动）(v.) apologize

搭配：道歉信 a letter of apology；表示道歉 to express an apology

例句：他决定明天向王红说明事情的经过，并且向她道歉。He decides to tell the whole thing to Wang Hong and apologize to her.

我为今天的事向你道歉。I apologize for what happened today.

84 得意 déyì （形）(adj.) be pride of oneself, be complacent about, glow with pride

搭配：得意地笑 to smile proudly；得意地说 to speak proudly；非常得意 be very proud; complacent

例句：看你得意的样子，我猜今天的事情一定是成功了。Your proud looking told me that the thing went successfully today.

得到领导的表扬也不要太得意。There is no need to gloat over your teacher's commend.

33

实战练习（七）

一、听对话，选择正确答案

1. A. 女朋友生气了 　　　　　 B. 再也不去海南了
   C. 想去买一些礼物 　　　　 D. 不满意导游的服务
2. A. 王东不该得到表扬 　　　 B. 到月底能超过王东组
   C. 今天可以早些下班 　　　 D. 经理会安排更多工作

二、选词填空

A 当　B 大约　C 当时　D 刀　E 导游　F 到处

1. 这辆旅游车上除了老师和学生之外，还有两个司机和一位（　　）。
2. 他（　　）非常生气，站起来就出去了。
3. 李红希望一直在学校里（　　）老师。
4. 这次旅游（　　）花了一万块钱。
5. 我（　　）找我的手机都没找到，原来忘在你这儿了。
6. 你怎么买了这么大一把（　　）？

A 到底　B 道歉　C 得意　D 戴　E 大夫　F 倒

7. A：听说今天新经理要来？
   B：已经来了，你看，前面那个（　　）眼镜的人就是。
8. A：李（　　），我女儿现在怎么样？
   B：你放心，已经给她打了针，烧退下来了。
9. 她都已经向你（　　）了，你就别再生气了。
10. 你和他们（　　）有什么关系？
11. 他去（　　）垃圾了。
12. 老师的表扬让我（　　）了好长一段时间。

三、排列顺序

1. A. 我想问一下　　　　 B. 大约得多少钱　　　　 C. 像这样一台传真机
2. A. 所以当时就没想明白　 B. 王东到底还是年轻　　 C. 经理这话代表的意思

四、完成句子

1. 房间里　衣服　到处　都是 _____
2. 到底　多长时间　你　还要我　等 _____
3. 很不错　王红　当　觉得　一名导游 _____
4. 这件　小李当时　事情　并不知道 _____
5. 你应该　不觉得　道歉吗　你　向她 _____

五、看图，用词造句

1. 道歉

2. 刀

Unit 08

得	地球
登机牌	地址
等	调查
低	掉
底	丢
地点	动作

Unit

85 得 děi (v.) need, have to, certainly will

例句：这个得多少钱？ How much is it?

这一次你考这么好，回家你爸爸妈妈一定得表扬你。Your parents certainly will praise you for your excellent performance in the exam.

你快一点儿，要不我们今天就得迟到了。If you don't hurry up, we will certainly be late today.

要取得好成绩，就得努力学习。We have to work hard to earn good marks.

86 登机牌 dēngjīpái (n.) boarding pass, embarkation card

搭配：一张登机牌 a boarding pass；换登机牌 to get one's boarding pass

例句：先生，这是您的登机牌，请从二号门登机。Sir, this is your boarding pass. Please board at gate 2.

对不起，小姐，我可以看一下您的登机牌吗？Excuse me, madam, your boarding pass please.

87 等 děng (part.) etc, and so on (and so forth)

搭配：等等 etc.；等地 and somewhere else

例句：长江、黄河等河流在中国非常有名。Rivers such as Yangtze River, Yellow River and so on are very famous in China.

北京、上海等大城市人非常多。Big cities such as Beijing, Shanghai and so on have a large population.

88 低 dī (adj.) low, below general standard

搭配：楼层低 a lower floor/ storey；水平低 a low standard；低空 at a low altitude

例句：他家住二层，楼层很低。He lives on the second floor, a lower floor.

他这个人做事总是眼高手低。He always thinks himself above his business.

89 底 dǐ (n.) bottom

搭配：海底下 sea bed, bottom of the sea；底层 ground floor / bottom (of the society)；年底 the end of the year；月底 the end of the month

例句：你再等两天吧，到这个月底，我一定重新给你买一个。I will buy a new one for you at the end of this month. Please just wait for several days.

你仔细看看，树底下的那个人是不是王东？Look carefully over there. The man under the tree is Wang Dong, right?

90 地点 dìdiǎn (n.) place, site, location

例句：北京是这部小说的背景地点。Beijing is the setting of the novel.

开会地点在宾馆会议室。The place for the meeting is in the meeting room of the hotel.

91 地球 dìqiú (n.) earth

搭配：地球仪 a terrestrial globe；世界地球日 World Earth Day；保护地球 to protect the earth

例句：人类在地球上生活了几百万年。Human beings have been living on earth for millions of years.

每年的四月二十二日，我们都要举办"世界地球日"活动。Every year on April 22, we hold a theme activity for the World Earth Day.

92 地址 dìzhǐ (n.) address

搭配：家庭地址 home address；电子邮件地址 E-mail address

例句：你把地址给我，我把书给你寄过去。Give me your address. I will send the book to you.

这上面有王东的地址、电话，你可以和他联系一下。Here is Wang Dong's address and phone number. You can contact him first.

93 调查 diàochá (v.) investigate, survey

搭配：市场调查 a market survey；调查结果 findings；调查真相 to find out/ investigate into the truth

例句：他下决心一定要把这件事情调查清楚。He is determined to make a full investigation.

王东打算明天去做一下市场调查。Wang Dong plans to make a market survey tomorrow.

94 掉 diào (v.) drop, lose, fall

搭配：掉眼泪 be in tears；掉头发 to lose hair；吃掉 to eat out

例句：桌子上的饼干被谁吃掉了？Who ate the biscuits on the desk?

李红发现自己最近总是掉头发。Li Hong found herself losing some hair recently.

你的钱包掉地上了。Your wallet dropped on the floor.

95 丢 diū (v.) lose, throw away

搭配：丢掉 to throw away；丢脸 to lose face；丢东西 to lose sth；丢三落四 be forgetful and always leaving things behind

例句：你真是太粗心，这么重要的东西怎么会丢了呢？Why are you so careless to lose such an important thing?

你不觉得这样做很丢脸吗？Don't you think your behavior is so shameful?

他常常丢三落四。He is a man who always forgets things.

96 动作 dòngzuò (n.) action, act

搭配：动作电影 an action movie；标准动作 a standard action；小动作 a small action

例句：你这个动作做得不太标准。Your action is not right.

这两天没见王东有任何动作。Wang Dong has no actions in these days.

实战练习（八）

一、听对话，选择正确答案

1. A. 王东知道地址　　　　B. 男的想找张明
   C. 王东身体不舒服　　　D. 女的要去看李红
2. A. 生气　　B. 高兴　　C. 害怕　　D. 吃惊

二、选词填空

A 地球　B 地址　C 掉　D 调查　E 丢　F 动作

1. 事情还没（　　）清楚，你先别生气。
2. （　　）是我们共同的家，我们要保护它。
3. 你的东西（　　）在地上了。
4. 上课时要认真听，不能做小（　　）。
5. A：收信人的（　　）写谁的？
   B：写李红的吧，寄到她那儿就行了。
6. A：小王的电话怎么老是打不通？
   B：他的手机前两天就（　　）了，正打算去买个新的呢。

A 得　B 登机牌　C 等　D 低　E 底　F 地点

7. 出国旅游（　　）先办好护照和签证。
8. 这本词典原来掉到桌子（　　）下了。
9. 没有（　　）是上不了飞机的。
10. 虽然是小城市，这儿的生活成本却不（　　）。
11. 这次的会议（　　）是在办公楼818，时间还没定。
12. 抽烟、喝酒（　　）不良习惯都对健康不利。

三、排列顺序

1. A. 得先热一下　　　B. 你别给孩子吃这么凉的东西　　C. 现在天气太冷
2. A. 小王真是粗心　　B. 就把手机丢了　　C. 到对面超市去了一趟

四、完成句子

1. 政府　这起事故　正在对　进行　调查 _____
2. 母亲　是　人类　地球　的 _____
3. 把　钱包　了　丢　他 _____
4. 都　这几个　你　错了　动作　做 _____
5. 王东　我把　地址　给了　李红家的 _____

五、看图，用词造句

1. 掉

2. 动作

Unit 09

堵车	儿童
肚子	而
短信	发生
对话	发展
对面	法律
对于	翻译

97 堵车 dǔchē (v.) be in traffic jam

搭配：堵车现象 the phenomenon of traffic jam；遇到堵车 be in traffic jam

例句：真抱歉，来的路上堵车，所以迟到了。I'm sorry to be late. I was in a traffic jam on the way here.

今年三月份以来，这条路堵车现象很严重。There is often a traffic jam on this road from March this year.

98 肚子 dùzi (n.) belly, abdomen

搭配：肚子疼 stomachache；吃饱肚子 be full

例句：她因为肚子疼去医院了。She went to the hospital because of stomachache.

还没下班呢，王东就觉得肚子饿了。Wang Dong became hungry before going off work.

99 短信 duǎnxìn (n.) short message, text message

搭配：手机短信 short message；短信祝福 short note bless

例句：生日这天，他收到了许多朋友发来的短信祝福。He received many short messages from his friends to bless his birthday.

他的手机每天都会收到许多垃圾短信。He received lots of junk messages on the cellphone each day.

100 对话 duìhuà (v.) dialogue; hold a dialogue

搭配：中外对话 a Sino-foreign dialogue；一段对话 to have a dialogue；用汉语对话 converse in Chinese

例句：这段对话让他非常吃惊。He was shocked by the conversation.

现在双方已经恢复对话。The two sides have resumed dialogue now.

101 对面 duìmiàn (n.) on the opposite side of

搭配：对面的商店 the store opposite the (street, school...)；学校对面 on the opposite side of the school

例句：我姐姐就住在我家对面。My sister lives opposite to my house.

王东喜欢去公司对面的咖啡馆喝咖啡。Wang Dong likes to go to the cafe on the opposite side of his company.

102 对于 duìyú (prep.) to, for, about, with regard to, of

例句：对于孩子的上学问题，我们还没有找到解决办法。We haven't solved the schooling problem of our kids.

大家对于这个问题的看法是一致的。Their views on this problem are identical.

Unit 09

103 儿童 értóng (名) (n.) children
搭配：儿童节 Children's Day；儿童节目 a children's program；儿童歌曲 nursery rhymes
例句：越来越多的儿童喜欢上了电子游戏。More and more children start playing electronic games.
我送了一个儿童手机给儿子。I gave a children's mobile phone to my son.

104 而 ér (连) (conj.) also, but, nevertheless
搭配：大而不贵 big but not expensive；一而再，再而三 again and again
例句：这种手机成本很低，而价格却非常高。The cost of this mobile phone is very low, but its price is very high.
我们要为了理想而努力工作。We should work hard for our ideals.

105 发生 fāshēng (动) (v.) happen, occur
搭配：发生地震 to have an earthquake；发生矛盾 to have a conflict；发生事故 to have an accident
例句：眼前发生的这一切，让他大吃一惊。He is shocked by what just happened in front of him.
我一直担心的事情终于发生了。The thing I worried most finally happened.

106 发展 fāzhǎn (动) (v.) develop
搭配：发展目标 development goals；发展工业 industrial expansion；发展农业 agricultural development；发展方向 a development direction
例句：王东觉得一直没找到自己的发展方向。Wang Dong hasn't found his orientation yet.
事情发展到现在，我不得不承认，是我错了。I have to admit that I was wrong with the development of the situation.

107 法律 fǎlǜ (名) (n.) law, legislation
搭配：法律知识 legal knowledge；普通法律 general law；学习法律 to study law
例句：法律面前人人平等。All are equal before the law.
他终于拿起了法律武器来保护自己。He finally resorted to law to protect himself.
李红在大学里学的是法律。Li Hong was majored in law in university.

108 翻译 fānyì (名/动) (n./v.) translation; translate, interpret
搭配：同声翻译 simultaneous interpretation；翻译工作 translation；翻译家 translator
例句：我们公司现在需要一个英语翻译。Our company needs an English translator.
你把这个句子再重新翻译一遍。Please retranslate this sentence.

实战练习（九）

一、听对话，选择正确答案

1. A. 男的有女朋友　　B. 女的英文不错　　C. 男的是英语翻译　　D. 女的在翻译材料
2. A. 也要去动物园　　　　　B. 没有好看的电影
   C. 可以换工作时间　　　　D. 想在家里好好儿休息

二、选词填空

A 堵车　B 肚子　C 短信　D 对于　E 对话　F 对面

1. （　　）这件事情，你有什么看法？
2. 银行在火车站的（　　）。
3. 他听到了老师和妈妈的（　　）。
4. 开会的时候别给我打电话，发（　　）就行。
5. A：妈，什么时候可以吃饭？我（　　）饿了。
   B：再等十分钟，你爸回来就吃。
6. A：你动作快一点儿吧，今天星期一，路上一定会（　　）的。
   B：知道了，这就出发。

A 发展　B 法律　C 而　D 儿童　E 翻译　F 发生

7. 她是一个年轻（　　）漂亮的女孩。
8. 过去的30年中，中国经济得到了很大的（　　）。
9. 他学的是（　　）专业，以后想当律师。
10. 他不会说外语，所以出国时得带着（　　）。
11. A：我走这些天，公司里没（　　）什么事情吧？
    B：没有，一切都很正常。
12. A：经理要请大家吃饭，晚上六点，在东方饭店，你别迟到了。
    B：不好意思，我不能去了，今天是（　　）节，我得回家陪儿子。

三、排列顺序

1. A. 公司又发生了这么多的事情　　B. 在她离开以后　　C. 这是她没有想到的
2. A. 对于我的决定　　　　　　　　B. 把我批评了一顿　　C. 爸爸很不满意

四、完成句子

1. 那个公司 不会有 他在 大的发展 什么 _____
2. 都可以 以后 法律上的问题 来找我 再遇到 _____
3. 公司 发生了 我 什么事 要去 看看 _____
4. 肚子 厉害 疼得 觉得 王东 _____
5. 马路 站在 他看到 对面 李红 _____

五、看图，用词造句

1. 翻译

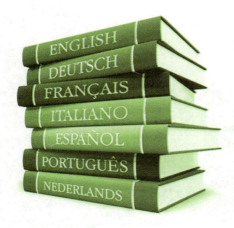

2. 堵车

Unit 10

烦恼	放弃
反对	放暑假
方法	放松
方面	份
方向	丰富
房东	否则

Unit 10

109 烦恼 fánnǎo (形) (adj.) annoyed, worried

搭配：自找烦恼 invite trouble；很多烦恼 a lot of troubles

例句：她也说不清楚自己为什么烦恼。She can't explain her own troubles clearly.
她最近为孩子上学的事情而烦恼。She has been worried about her child's schooling these days.

110 反对 fǎnduì (动) (v.) oppose, resist, act against

搭配：反对意见 an objection；反对的声音 voices of disapproval

例句：全世界人民都反对战争，希望和平。The people all over the world long for peace and stand firm against the war.
女儿反对我的这个决定。My daughter objected my decision.

111 方法 fāngfǎ (名) (n.) way, method, means

搭配：学习方法 a learning method；科学方法 a scientific method

例句：我觉得你的学习方法有问题。I think you have some problems with your learning methods.
大家认为李红的这个方法怎么样？What do you think about Li Hong's method?

112 方面 fāngmiàn (名) (n.) aspect, side, perspective

搭配：三个方面 three aspects；家庭方面 in aspect of family；生活方面 in aspect of life

例句：这件事不能只从这一个方面去考虑。This problem cannot be considered from only one perspective.
这孩子在学习方面是不用人担心的。We needn't worry about this child's study.

113 方向 fāngxiàng (名) (n.) direction

搭配：失去方向 to lose one's direction；发展方向 the direction of development; direction trend

例句：成功不仅需要努力，还需要一个正确的方向。We need both diligence and a correct direction to gain success.
有没有人知道，王东刚才是往哪个方向走的？Anyone know in which direction did Wang Dong go?

114 房东 fángdōng (名) (n.) landlord

搭配：找房东 to go to see the landlord；当房东 to be a landlord

例句：他把房子租给别人住了，他现在是房东。He is the landlord now since he has rented his house out.
我想当房东，想把房子租出去。I want to be the landlord and rent my house out.

115　放弃 fàngqì （动）(v.) abandon, give up

搭配： 放弃爱情 to give up one's love；放弃工作 to abandon one's job

例句： 他放弃了这次去北京总公司参观的机会。He gave up the chance to visit the head office in Beijing.

要成为一个成功的画家太难，所以他放弃了。It is too hard to become a successful painter. So he had to give up this dream.

116　放暑假 fàng shǔjià have a summer vacation

例句： 妈妈说今年放暑假的时候带我去北京。My mother said she would go to Beijing with me this summer vacation.

现在的孩子太累了，放暑假也没有时间玩。Nowadays, the children are too much burdened to have playing time even in the summer vacation.

117　放松 fàngsōng （动）(v.) relax

搭配： 放松身体 to relax one's body；放松肌肉 to loosen one's muscles；放松心情 to get relaxed

例句： 你的肌肉太紧张了，应该放松放松。Loosen your muscles. They're too rigid.

要是放松学习，你的成绩就会下降。You can't afford to relax yourself, otherwise your grades will go down.

118　份 fèn （量）(m.w.) part, portion, piece

搭配： 一份工作 a job；两份材料 two copies of materials；三份报纸 three pieces of newspapers

例句： 王东把我的那份材料拿走了。Wang Dong took away my materials.

那份今天的早报放哪儿去了？ Where is today's morning paper?

119　丰富 fēngfù （形/动）(adj./v.) plentiful; rich/ abundant (in)

搭配： 丰富多样 be rich and varied；资源丰富 be abundant in resources；丰富知识 to enrich one's knowledge

例句： 这本书的内容很丰富。This book is rich in content.

超市里商品非常丰富。The goods in this supermarket are rich and varied.

多读书可以丰富词汇。Extensive reading can enlarge my vocabulary.

120　否则 fǒuzé （连）(conj.) otherwise, or

例句： 今天很冷，你要多穿一些衣服，否则会感冒的。Today is very cold. You'd better put on more clothes otherwise you'll catch a cold.

我们得在八点之前出发，否则会迟到的。We have to set out before eight, or we'll be late.

你得把你的签证材料准备好，否则你很可能拿不到签证。You must get your documents for visa well-prepared. Otherwise you'll fail to get the visa.

实战练习（十）

一、听对话，选择正确答案

1. A. 男的　　B. 王东　　C. 老师　　D. 父母
2. A. 公司　　B. 桂林　　C. 北京　　D. 上海

二、选词填空

A 烦恼　B 方法　C 方面　D 方向　E 反对　F 放弃

1. 你要从多个（　　）来看这个问题。
2. 这么好的机会，你怎么能（　　）呢？
3. 风是从西北（　　）过来的。
4. 这件事应该还有更好的解决（　　）。
5. A：你觉得小王这人怎么样？
   B：他很不诚实，（　　）他的人很多。
6. A：你怎么了？有什么（　　）吗？
   B：想家了。

A 放暑假　B 房东　C 份　D 丰富　E 放松　F 否则

7. 我打算（　　）的时候去上海的小姨家。
8. 你快点儿把衣服穿上，（　　）会感冒的。
9. 每月8号是我给（　　）交房租的日子。
10. 阿姨，给我拿（　　）今天的报纸。
11. A：暑假你有什么计划？
    B：旅游，我要（　　）一下。
12. A：今天的饭菜这么（　　），是什么节日吗？
    B：哪是什么节日，只是觉得这段时间你太累了，想让你好好儿吃一顿。

三、排列顺序

1. A. 特别是经济方面的报道特别多　B. 这份报纸还不错　C. 内容很丰富
2. A. 他连出国访问的机会都放弃了　B. 为了这个会议　C. 可见这次会议有多重要

四、完成句子

1. 三分之二的　都反对　超过　同学　这个决定 _____
2. 他　放弃了　这次　机会　出国的 _____
3. 哪个方向　火车站的　不知道　我　是去 _____
4. 单方面的　他　不过是　这　想法 _____
5. 放暑假的　他　不想　时候　回家 _____

五、看图，用词造句

1. 丰富

2. 烦恼

Unit 11

符合	富
父亲	改变
付款	干杯
负责	赶
复印	敢
复杂	感动

121 符合 fúhé (v.) accord with, comfort to

搭配： 符合标准 to meet the standard；符合要求 to be up to the criteria；符合条件 to quality for sth

例句： 他的说法和事实并不符合。His statement doesn't accord with the fact.
王红的条件完全符合公司的要求。Wang Hong is totally qualified with the company's requirement.

122 父亲 fùqīn (n.) father

搭配： 父亲节 Father's Day；我的父亲母亲 my father and mother

例句： 父亲对孩子的成长有很重要的影响。A father has a very important influence on a child's growth.
我很少得到父亲的表扬。I seldom receive my father' praise.

123 付款 fù kuǎn pay

搭配： 分期付款 divided payments; hire purchase；付款方式 payment terms；信用卡付款 to pay with a credit card；当场付款 to pay on the nail

例句： 有的人买东西的时候喜欢用信用卡付款，不喜欢用现金付款。Some like paying for the bill by credit card instead of paying cash.
他买了一台电脑，是分期付款的，每月还1000元。He bought a computer on hire purchases, paying 1000 RMB each month.

124 负责 fùzé (adj./v.) responsible; be responsible for, be in charge of

搭配： 负责人 person in charge；认真负责 be responsible；对……负责 be responsible for...

例句： 经理让我负责这儿的工作。The manager asks me to be in charge of the work here.
王东对工作非常负责。Wang Dong is a very responsible person at work.

125 复印 fùyìn (v.) copy, duplicate, photocopy

搭配： 复印机 a photocopier；复印材料 to duplicate a document

例句： 王东在办公室里复印材料。Wang Dong is making a copy of the material at the office.
李红不会用复印机。Li Hong can't use the photocopier.

126 复杂 fùzá (adj.) complex, complicated

搭配： 情况复杂 a complicated situation；复杂的问题 a complicated problem

例句： 这份工作看起来简单，其实非常复杂。This work is more complicated than it looks.
我们面对的是一个很复杂的问题。We're facing a complicated problem.

Unit 11

127 富 fù (adj.) rich, wealthy
- 搭配：富人 a rich person；富有 be rich in...；富贵 be rich and powerful
- 例句：他富起来以后，帮助了很多人。He helps a lot of people after becoming rich.
  只有国家富起来，人们的生活才能好起来。Our citizen can have a better life only after our country becomes rich and strong.

128 改变 gǎibiàn (v.) change, transform
- 搭配：改变自己 to change oneself；改变世界 to change the world；发生改变 to undergo a change
- 例句：王东这次的表现，改变了经理对他的看法。Wang Dong's action changed the manager's opinion.
  他的生活发生了很大的改变。His life has changed a lot.

129 干杯 gānbēi (v.) drink a toast
- 搭配：干一杯 cheers; bottoms up；为……干杯 to propose a toast for
- 例句：他站起来说："来！大家一起为明天的幸福生活干杯！" He stood up and said: "Cheers! Let's drink to tomorrow's happy life!"
  我先干了这一杯。I will drink this glass of wine up first.

130 赶 gǎn (v.) catch up with, overtake
- 搭配：赶路 to press ahead；赶上 to catch up with sth；赶时间 be in a hurry
- 例句：你最好现在就走，要不就赶不上火车了。You'd better go now, otherwise you'll miss the train.
  最近公司很忙，我得天天加班赶活儿。Recently our company is very busy, and I have to do extra work every day.

131 敢 gǎn (v.) dare, have the courage to do sth
- 搭配：敢说 to dare to speak；敢想 to dare to think
- 例句：经理很生气，大家都不敢说话。The manager is very angry, so no one dare to speak a word.
  我的汉语不好，不敢跟中国人说话。I don't have the courage to speak to any Chinese people, because my Chinese is not good enough.

132 感动 gǎndòng (adj./v.) be moved, be touched; move, impress
- 搭配：深受感动 be moved by；感动世界 to move the whole world
- 例句：他感动得说不出话来。He was moved beyond words.
  我被李红的话感动了。I was moved by Li Hong's words.

实战练习（十一）

一、听对话，选择正确答案

1. A. 同事　　　　B. 邻居　　　　C. 朋友　　　　D. 夫妻
2. A. 不想看材料　B. 现在就回家　C. 得继续工作　D. 感觉不舒服

二、选词填空

A 符合　B 富　C 父亲　D 复印　E 复杂　F 负责

1. 王东的（　　）在大使馆工作。
2. 找一下你们这儿的（　　）人。
3. 你来检查一下，我做的是不是（　　）要求？
4. 现在事情变得越来越（　　）了，别想得那么简单。
5. A：你看到小王了吗？
   B：他刚刚到三楼（　　）材料去了。
6. A：李红戴的眼镜不便宜，我在网上看过，得两三千呢。
   B：她家里（　　）得很，两三千的眼镜算不了什么。

A 改变　B 干杯　C 付款　D 感动　E 赶　F 敢

7. 他只记得自己不断地和别人（　　），怎么回家的都记不清楚了。
8. 经理的做法让我（　　）极了。
9. 她试着（　　）了一下方法，果然把问题解决了。
10. 早点睡，明天还要（　　）路呢！
11. A：在网上买东西怎么（　　）啊？
    B：可以用信用卡。
12. A：我怕黑，不（　　）一个人睡。
    B：开着灯不就行了。

三、排列顺序

1. A. 人也很热情　　　　B. 这个公司的环境不错　　　　C. 否则我早放弃了
2. A. 李红的感情很丰富　B. 也能感动得哭上半天　　　　C. 即使是一场电影

四、完成句子

1. 改变吗 你 他的 感觉不到 _____
2. 得 来 父亲 说不出话 感动 _____
3. 人 是个 丰富的 李红 感情 _____
4. 材料 我负责 这部分 打印出来 把 _____
5. 复杂性 已经 事情的 王东 知道了 _____

五、看图，用词造句

1. 复印

2. 干杯

Unit 12

感觉	胳膊
感情	各
感谢	工资
干	公里
刚	功夫
高速公路	共同

Unit 12

133 感觉 gǎnjué （名/动）(n./v.) sense, feeling; feel
搭配：复杂的感觉 complex feelings；感觉发热 to feel a little hot
例句：我有种非常难过的感觉。I have a very upset feeling.
　　　他感觉外面非常冷。He feels very cold outside.

134 感情 gǎnqíng （名）(n.) emotion, affection, love
搭配：感情生活 a life attachment；产生感情 to form an attachment to；动感情 be emotional
例句：我们之间有十多年的感情了。Our attachment lasts more than ten years.
　　　最近，李红的感情生活出了些问题。Lately, Li Hong has hard feelings in her life.

135 感谢 gǎnxiè （动）(v.) thank, be grateful, appreciate
搭配：感谢信 a letter of appreciation；感谢父母/老师 to be thankful to parents / teacher
例句：她很感谢我们给她的帮助。She is very thankful to our help.
　　　王东帮我解决了这件事，我还没感谢他呢。Wang Dong helped me to solve this problem, but I haven't expressed my thanks to him yet.

136 干 gàn （动）(v.) do, work, engage (in)
搭配：干活儿 to (go) work；说干就干 to act without delay；干好事 to do good deeds；干坏事 to do evil deeds
例句：他想认真地干好这份工作。He wants to do this job carefully.
　　　这个工作不错，好好儿干！This is a good job. Do your best!
　　　要干就干好。If you do it, do it well.

137 刚 gāng （副）(adv.) just, just about
例句：这件衣服不大也不小，刚合适。The dress fits perfectly.
　　　小王刚去公司了。Xiao Wang has just gone to the company.
　　　我们刚说到你，你就来了。Barely had we talk about you when you came.
　　　刚过"五一"，天气就热了起来。It's getting hot shortly after May Day.

138 高速公路 gāosù gōnglù expressway, highway, freeway
搭配：关闭高速公路 to shut / close the highway；开通高速公路 to open highway；上高速公路 to go onto the highway；走高速公路 to go on the freeway
例句：修建了高速公路以后，开车从北京到上海快多了。It's much quicker to get to Shanghai from Beijing since the highway is open.
　　　因为下大雪，高速公路关闭了。The expressway was closed due to the heavy snow.

139 胳膊 gēbo (n.) arm
搭配：伸胳膊 to push one's arm through；胳膊断了 broken arm
例句：运动以前，你应该伸伸胳膊和腿。Before exercises, spread yourself.
打完网球以后，我的胳膊酸疼，拿不了重东西。After tennis, I got my arm hurt and can't lift the weight.

140 各 gè (pron./adv.) every; each
搭配：各地 everywhere；各位 everyone；各方面 in all aspect；各种各样 of various kinds
例句：这个年轻人各方面的条件都不错。This young man is very good in all aspects.
我非常感谢各位老师在这段时间对我的帮助。I'm thankful to every teacher's help during this time.
双方各进一球。Each side scored a goal.

141 工资 gōngzī (n.) salary, wage
搭配：工资表 a payroll/ pay sheet；工资标准 wage standard
例句：他现在的工资还是按照五年前的标准发的。His wage still maintains in the five-year level.
小王刚参加工作，工资并不高。Xiao Wang, who just attended work, has a low pay.

142 公里 gōnglǐ (m.w.) kilometer
搭配：一公里 one kilometer；平方公里 square kilometer
例句：我家离公司有十几公里。My house is more than ten kilometers away from the company.
这辆车才刚跑了两万公里。The automobile has just covered 20,000 kilometers.

143 功夫 gōngfu (n.) time, workmanship, skill, art, ability, martial arts
搭配：写作的功夫 writing skills；中国功夫 Chinese Kungfu；功夫明星 action movie star；下功夫 to work hard
例句：他泡茶的功夫很好。He is skillful in making tea.
李小龙是有名的功夫明星。Bruce Lee was a famous action movie star.
为了这次表演，他花了很多时间准备，下了很大功夫。The performance costs him lots of time and work.

144 共同 gòngtóng (adj./adv.) common, mutual; together
搭配：共同参加 to participate in concert；共同负责 to jointly take charge of；共同努力 joint effort
例句："五一"劳动节是全世界劳动人民共同的节日。May Day, the International Labor Day, is a common festival around the world.
大家的共同努力，让我们按时完成了工作。Thanks to our joint efforts, we finished the work on time.

实战练习（十二）

一、听对话，选择正确答案

1. A. 东西便宜　　B. 感觉安全　　C. 服务热情　　D. 不想逛街
2. A. 接客人　　　B. 去公司　　　C. 看朋友　　　D. 找李明

二、选词填空

A 感谢　B 干　C 刚　D 高速公路　E 各　F 胳膊

1. 你在这儿（　　）什么呢？
2. 他喜欢健身，（　　）很粗。
3. 我非常（　　）你对我的关心。
4. 我刚学车，不敢上（　　）。
5. A：你感觉李明和张强，谁更合适当这个班长？
   B：他们两个（　　）有优点和缺点，我也说不好。
6. A：我给你打了好几个电话，你怎么一直不接啊？
   B：我（　　）在干活儿呢，没听到手机响。

A 公里　B 功夫　C 工资　D 共同　E 感觉　F 感情

7. 公司在广告上下了很大（　　），吸引了很多顾客。
8. 他们从小就在一起，（　　）非常好。
9. 从这儿到北京有多少（　　）啊？
10. 你仔细看一下，它们之间有什么（　　）特点？
11. 她生病了，（　　）不舒服。
12. A：你们这个月的（　　）怎么到现在还没发啊？
    B：谁知道呢，小王说可能得到二十号以后。

三、排列顺序

1. A. 工资只有一千二百元　　B. 他刚到公司的时候　　C. 还不够他自己生活的
2. A. 王东是我的好朋友　　　B. 那就是中国功夫　　　C. 我们有着共同的爱好

四、完成句子

1. 回来　刚　从　他　图书馆　_____
2. 对我的　各位老师　这些年来　感谢　帮助　_____
3. 让李红　满意　他　都不能　各方面的条件　_____
4. 身上的钱　这一顿饭　王东　够　刚刚　吃　_____
5. 工资　她用　一件衣服　一个月的　买了　_____

五、看图，用词造句

1. 功夫

2. 感觉

Unit 13

购物	挂
够	关键
估计	观众
鼓励	管理
故意	光
顾客	广播

145 购物 gòu wù (v.) go shopping
搭配：上街购物 to go shopping；旅游购物 tourist shopping；网上购物 online shopping
例句：他现在很喜欢在网上购物。He likes going shopping on the Internet.
李红打算下午和朋友一起去购物。Li Hong plans to go shopping with her friends in the afternoon.

146 够 gòu (v./adv.) reach enough; be sufficient
例句：饼干放得太高了，我够不着。The biscuit is out of my reach.
男朋友一直说李红还不够成熟。Li Hong's boyfriend always says that she is not mature enough.
我总是觉得时间不够用。My time is often barely adequate.

147 估计 gūjì (v.) estimate
搭配：估计人数 an estimated number of people；据估计 by estimate
例句：估计公司今年的情况可能不会太好。It is estimated that the company's situation will not be better in this year.
我估计，有人把这件事告诉了李红。In my estimate, someone told this matter to Li Hong.

148 鼓励 gǔlì (v.) encourage, inspire
搭配：鼓励自己 to encourage oneself；鼓励大家 to encourage everyone；鼓励的话 incentive words
例句：我非常感谢他给了我许多鼓励。I'm thankful to his encouragement.
李红一直在鼓励自己，一定可以完成这些工作。Li Hong encouraged herself that she can surely finish these works.

149 故意 gùyì (adv.) intentionally, on purpose
搭配：故意生气 be deliberately angry；不是故意的 have no intention to do sth
例句：他不是故意不理你。He didn't mean to ignore you.
她故意把声音提高，希望能被人注意。She raised her voice on purpose to draw others' attention.

150 顾客 gùkè (n.) customer, client
搭配：一位顾客 a customer；外国顾客 a foreign customer
例句：现在店里有很多顾客，李红非常忙。The shop has a large number of customers, so Li Hong is very busy.
顾客对她的服务很满意。Customers are satisfied with her service.

Unit 13

151 挂 guà (v.) hang (up)
搭配：挂衣服 to hang up clothes；挂上去 to hang up；挂电话 to ring off
例句：她把洗好的衣服挂了起来。She hung the washed clothes up.
李红挂了电话后才发现王东正坐在自己对面。Li Hong didn't notice Wang Dong, who was sitting opposite to her until she rang off.

152 关键 guānjiàn (adj./n.) crucial; key
搭配：关键问题 a crucial problem；关键时刻 at the critical moment；关键点 a critical point
例句：在关键时刻，是李红给了我鼓励，我才没有放弃。I didn't give up thanks to Li Hong's encouragement at the critical moment.
在这次谈判中小王是关键。Xiao Wang played a key role during this negotiation.

153 观众 guānzhòng (n.) audience
搭配：现场观众 live audience；当地的观众 local audience
例句：观众朋友，欢迎收看本期节目。Dear audience, thank you for watching this program.
当地的观众非常热情。Local audiences are very warm.

154 管理 guǎnlǐ (v.) manage, administrate, run
搭配：公司管理 to run a company；严格管理 be strictly managed；管理办法 an administrative method
例句：要管理这么大的公司是很不容易的。It is not easy to run such a big company.
很多老师都认为，这个班不好管理。According to many teachers, this class is hard to manage.

155 光 guāng (n./adj.) light
搭配：阳光 sunlight；月光 moonlight；灯光 lighting；眼光 the way of looking at things；风光 scenery
例句：房间里的灯光这么暗，怎么能看书呢？How can you read books in such a dark room?
他很害怕别人看他时那奇怪的眼光。He is afraid of others' strange look on him.
弟弟吃光了盘子里的饭菜。The younger brother eats up all the food in the dish.

156 广播 guǎngbō (v./n.) broadcast
搭配：听广播 to listen to broadcast；广播电视 radio and television；广播找人 to find a person through broadcast
例句：小王习惯早上起来的时候边听广播边做饭。Xiao Wang has a habit of listening to the radio while cooking his breakfast.
他在新闻广播里听到了王东的名字。He heard Wang Dong's name in the news broadcast.

实战练习（十三）

一、听对话，选择正确答案

1. A. 车站　　B. 超市　　C. 饭店　　D. 银行
2. A. 女的是一位老师　　B. 男的在学校工作
   C. 女的在鼓励男的　　D. 男的在打扫卫生

二、选词填空

A 购物　　B 估计　　C 鼓励　　D 够　　E 顾客　　F 故意

1. 我（　　）这件衣服不会太便宜。
2. 米饭不（　　）的话可以再加。
3. 他是我们店的老（　　）了，几乎每个星期都会来。
4. 她的爱好是去商场（　　）。
5. A：李明最近的表现比以前好多了，你是用了什么方法啊？
   B：很简单，经常（　　）他，表扬他，让他相信自己。
6. A：我估计李红是真的生气了，给她打电话都不接。
   B：那你就去找她解释啊，告诉她你不是（　　）的。

A 挂　　B 关键　　C 观众　　D 管理　　E 光　　F 广播

7. 发现问题很重要，解决问题是（　　）。
8. 我把饼干都吃（　　）了，还是感觉肚子很饿。
9. 看到（　　）这么热情，大家都特别感动。
10. 他有早上起来就听（　　）的习惯。
11. A：你在干什么？
    B：我想把这张地图（　　）在这儿。
12. A：现在看来，选王东当经理还是对的。
    B：是啊，这两年他把公司（　　）得很不错。

三、排列顺序

1. A. 关键是你的学习态度　　B. 在哪儿学不重要
   C. 跟谁学也不重要

2. A. 我和姐姐已经说好了
   B. 否则他会感觉孤单
   C. 每个星期天都要回家看父亲

四、完成句子

1. 掉光了　自己的头发　他　快要　感觉　_____
2. 不是　我刚刚　这样　故意　说的_____
3. 挂　谁把　在　衣服　这儿_____
4. 明天　很有可能　我估计　会　下雨_____
5. 说了　对我　很多　他　鼓励的话_____

五、看图，用词造句

1. 购物

2. 挂

Unit 14

广告	过程
逛	海洋
规定	害羞
国籍	寒假
国际	汗
果汁	航班

157 广告 guǎnggào （名）(n.) advertisement

搭配：电视广告 TV advertising；广告公司 an advertising company；广告设计 advertising design

例句：这个产品的广告做得非常有意思。The advertisement of this product is very interesting.
这个手机没有广告说得那么好。This mobile phone is not as good as advertised.

158 逛 guàng （动）(v.) ramble, roam, walk around

搭配：逛街 to stroll through streets；逛商店 to go shopping；逛一逛 to walk around

例句：李红准备带孩子去公园逛一逛。Li Hong is planning to stroll around the park with her child.
逛了这么长时间，她觉得又累又饿。Strolling around for such a long time, she felt tired and hungry.

159 规定 guīdìng （动/名）(v./n.) prescribe; regulation, rules

搭配：关于……的规定 by the rule of ...；规定时间 the given time；规定动作 set exercise；学校规定 school rules

例句：学校规定考试时不准带手机。By the rule of school, we can't carry mobile phones to examinations.
关于休年假的问题，公司有最新的规定。The company has a new rule about the annual leave.

160 国籍 guójí （名）(n.) nationality

搭配：申请国籍 to apply for naturalization；获得国籍 to obtain nationality；加入某国国籍 be naturalized；双重国籍 dual nationality

例句：他的国籍是中国，也没打算改变国籍。His nationality is Chinese and he doesn't intend to change it.
他们突然发现一架不明国籍的飞机。All of a sudden they found an unidentified plane.

161 国际 guójì （形/名）(adj./n.) international

搭配：国际会议 an international conference；国际标准 an international standard；国际友人 a foreign friend

例句：他最近要去北京参加一个国际会议。He will go to Beijing to attend an international conference recently.
李红最喜欢看国际新闻。Li Hong is interested in watching international news.

162 果汁 guǒzhī (n.) fruit juice

搭配：喝果汁 to drink fruit juice；买果汁 to buy some fruit juice；新鲜果汁 a glass of fruit juice

例句：我渴了，想喝瓶果汁。I'm thirsty and would like to drink some fruit juice.
服务员，我要一杯果汁。Waiter, give me a glass of juice please.

163 过程 guòchéng (n.) process, course

搭配：调查过程 a process of inspection；认识过程 a process of cognition

例句：事情的大概过程就是这样。The main process is just like this.
他想知道整个调查过程。He wants to know the whole process of inspection.

164 海洋 hǎiyáng (n.) sea, ocean

搭配：海洋公园 ocean park；海洋面积 ocean area；海洋学家 an oceanographer

例句：在几万年前，这些地方大多是海洋。More than tens of thousands years ago, these places were mainly covered by ocean.
我希望爸爸星期天带我去海洋公园。I hope my father can take me to the ocean park this Sunday.

165 害羞 hàixiū (adj.) shy

例句：她是一个害羞的女孩。She is shy.
得到了老师的表扬，她害羞地笑了。She smiled shyly when the teacher praised her.
他第一次在这么多观众面前讲话，有些害羞。He was a little shy when speaking in public for the first time.

166 寒假 hánjià (n.) winter vacation

搭配：放寒假 to have a winter vacation；寒假作业 an assignment for winter vacation

例句：他的寒假作业已经写完了。He had finished the assignment for winter vacation.
放寒假的时候，我去了北京旅游。During the winter vacation, I traveled to Beijing.

167 汗 hàn (n.) sweat

搭配：汗水 sweat；出汗 to sweat；擦汗 to wipe sweat；冷汗 cold sweat；汗珠 sweat

例句：今天很热，坐那儿不动都会出一身的汗。It's too hot today. I cannot stop sweating even if I stay still.
王东的衣服都被汗弄湿了。Wang Dong's clothes are soaked with sweat.

168 航班 hángbān (n.) flight

搭配：国际航班 an international flight；航班中断 to interrupt a flight

例句：今天有几个航班飞往北京？How many flights are heading to Beijing today?
乘坐这次航班的人不多。There are few passengers on this flight.

Unit 14

实战练习（十四）

一、听对话，选择正确答案

1. A. 李红想去逛街　　B. 自己没有时间
   C. 最近感觉很累　　D. 明天要见经理
2. A. 小王现在在机场　　B. 男的正在打电话
   C. 女的在安排工作　　D. 李经理下了飞机

二、选词填空

　　　　A 广告　　B 逛　　C 规定　　D 国际　　E 国籍　　F 果汁

1. （　　）了这么长时间，你不感觉累吗？
2. 这是他第一次参加（　　）比赛。
3. 儿子要吃昨天在电视（　　）里看到的那种饼干。
4. 他这样做不符合公司的（　　）。
5. A：想喝点什么？
   B：来杯（　　）吧！
6. A：请问您是哪国人？
   B：我的（　　）是法国，但我是在上海出生的。

　　　　A 过程　　B 海洋　　C 害羞　　D 寒假　　E 汗　　F 航班

7. 他第一次当着大家表演的时候，一点儿也不（　　）。
8. （　　）中生活着很多鱼类。
9. 请问，今天还有从北京去桂林的（　　）吗？
10. 听王东这么一说，我出了一身冷（　　）。
11. A：事情的（　　）就是这样，大家都认为李红没有做错。
    B：我知道了，我会把大家的看法告诉经理的。
12. A：你们学校什么时候放（　　）？
    B：要等到这周六考完试。

三、排列顺序

1. A. 她擦了一下脸上的汗水　　B. 感觉好极了　　C. 看着干净的房间

2. A. 我要的不是事情的过程　　　B. 你告诉王东　　　C. 而是结果

四、完成句子

1. 从　进来　外面　他满头大汗地　跑 _____
2. 不太　逛　李红　商场　喜欢 _____
3. 已经　她的　做完了　寒假作业 _____
4. 我们上班　不准　规定　经理　玩游戏 _____
5. 一个人　妈妈　过马路　不让我 _____

五、看图，用词造句

1. 逛

2. 害羞

Unit 15

好处	后悔
好像	厚
号码	互联网
合格	互相
合适	护士
盒子	怀疑

169 好处 hǎochù (名) (n.) advantage, benefit

搭配：没有好处 to have no good to ；得到好处 to benefit

例句：王东给我讲了很多喝茶的好处。Wang Dong told me a lot about the advantages of drinking tea.

她相信这样做对公司有一定的好处。She believed that the company will benefit a lot from doing so.

170 好像 hǎoxiàng (动/副) (v./adv.) seem; be like

例句：他们一见面就好像是多年的老朋友一样。They met each other for the first time. But it seems like they're old friends for many years.

这道题的答案好像不对。It seems like this answer is wrong.

妹妹坐在窗户边不说话，好像在想什么事。The younger sister is sitting silently by the window. She seems to be thinking of something.

171 号码 hàomǎ (名) (n.) number

搭配：电话号码 phone number ；房间号码 room number

例句：这个电话号码很不好记。This phone number is hard to remember.

李红把自己的手机号码换了。Li Hong changed her phone number.

172 合格 hégé (形) (adj.) qualified, up to standard

搭配：合格产品 qualified products ；考试合格 to pass the exam ；质量合格 be qualified ；合格标准 the standard of qualification

例句：这次的考试，他和王明都不合格。He and Wang Ming both failed this exam.

李红是一位合格的老师。Li Hong is a qualified teacher.

173 合适 héshì (形) (adj.) suitable, proper

搭配：合适的词语 suitable words ；合适的工作 a suitable job

例句：毕业已经一年了，他还没有找到合适的工作。Having graduated for more than a year, he still couldn't find a suitable job.

那双鞋虽然很漂亮，但是对我来说不合适。This pair of shoes is beautiful but not suitable to me.

174 盒子 hézi (名) (n.) box, case

搭配：饼干盒子 a biscuit box ；纸盒子 a paper box ；鞋盒子 shoebox

例句：他把那个饼干盒子拿走了。He took that biscuit box away.

她把信放在一个非常漂亮的小盒子里。She put the letter in a small and beautiful box.

Unit 15

175 后悔 hòuhuǐ (动) (v.) regret
搭配：后悔药 an undo key；后悔自己的做法 to be regrettable for what one has done
例句：不管今后会遇到什么困难，我都不会后悔现在的选择。Whatever difficulties I will encounter in the future, I would not regret my current choice.
他很后悔把这件事告诉了李红。He is regrettable for telling Li Hong about this.

176 厚 hòu (形) (adj.) thick
搭配：厚衣服 thick clothes；又厚又重 thick and heavy
例句：今天天冷，你出门可得穿厚一点儿。Today's very cold. You'd better go out with thick clothes.
这本词典太厚了，没办法放在书包里。This dictionary is too thick to put into the bag.

177 互联网 hùliánwǎng (名) (n.) internet
例句：他想开一家国际互联网公司。He wants to start an Internet business.
互联网正吸引着越来越多的用户。The Internet attracts more and more users.

178 互相 hùxiāng (副) (adv.) mutually, each other
搭配：互相帮助 mutual help；互相关心 mutual care
例句：李红和王东互相看了一眼，都笑了起来。Li Hong and Wang Dong gave each other a look, and burst into laughter.
朋友之间就应该要互相帮助，互相关心。Friends should help each other and care for each other.

179 护士 hùshi (名) (n.) nurse
搭配：护士节 Nurses' Day；护士学校 nurses' school
例句：王东的女朋友是一位护士。Wang Dong's girlfriend is a nurse.
她干了二十多年的护士工作。She has been working as a nurse for twenty years.

180 怀疑 huáiyí (动) (v.) doubt, suspect
搭配：产生怀疑 a doubt come to one's mind；非常怀疑 to strengthen one's doubt；怀疑一切 to have doubts about everything；怀疑别人 to have a doubt about others
例句：我怀疑他今天来不了了。I doubt he will not come today.
他怀疑自己得了重病。He doubts himself of having a serious illness.

实战练习（十五）

一、听对话，选择正确答案

1. A. 男的现在想找李红　　　B. 男的给李红打了电话
   C. 女的没有李红的号码　　D. 女的在给朋友打电话
2. A. 带男的喂猴子　　　　　B. 给男的讲故事
   C. 在书店里买书　　　　　D. 陪男的看电视

二、选词填空

　　　　A 好处　　B 好像　　C 号码　　D 合格　　E 合适　　F 盒子

1. 我不知道小王的手机（　　）。
2. 他发现（　　）上写着王东家的地址。
3. 你这样做对孩子一点儿（　　）也没有。
4. 小明不敢告诉爸爸自己这次考试不（　　）。
5. A：我明天穿这件衣服怎么样？
   B：穿这样的衣服去面试不太（　　）吧。
6. A：王东没在办公室吗？
   B：刚刚出去了，（　　）是去银行了。

　　　　A 互联网　　B 厚　　C 后悔　　D 互相　　E 怀疑　　F 护士

7. 他现在特别（　　）自己以前没有好好儿学习。
8. 这个产品质量一直很好，我（　　）是安装的问题。
9. 现在流行在（　　）上购物，便宜又方便。
10. 同学之间应该（　　）帮助。
11. A：妈妈，我不打针行不行？
    B：不打针病怎么能好呢？你听话，让（　　）阿姨轻轻地给你打。
12. A：外面下雪了，你得穿（　　）点儿才行。
    B：等出去的时候再穿。

三、排列顺序

1. A. 我去了上海以后　　B. 后来慢慢就没有了联系　　C. 刚开始还经常和李红打电话

2. A. 你得问问她　　　　B. 等会儿护士来了　　　C. 这药应该什么时候吃

四、完成句子

1. 好像　来　李红　上班　没 _____
2. 衣服　别忘了　你　多带些　厚 _____
3. 把　那个盒子　想　我　拿下来 _____
4. 对你　这样做　什么　有　好处 _____
5. 才　算　这次考试　合格　通过 _____

五、看图，用词造句

1. 厚

2. 护士

Unit 16

回忆	积累
活动	基础
活泼	激动
火	及时
获得	即使
积极	寄

Unit 16

181 回忆 huíyì (v.) recall
- 搭配：回忆过去 a past memory；回忆往事 to recall the past；痛苦的回忆 a painful memory
- 例句：我经常回忆和王东在一起工作的日子。I often recall the time I worked with Wang Dong.
  李红不愿意回忆童年生活。Li Hong is not willing to recall the past.

182 活动 huódòng (v./n.) exercise; activity
- 搭配：活动活动 to have an exercise；活动结束 to finish an exercise
- 例句：你坐了这么长时间，也得站起来活动活动。You've been sitting for too long. You need to stand up and move about a little bit.
  对不起，我们今天的活动已经结束了。Sorry, our activity is over today.

183 活泼 huópō (adj.) lively
- 搭配：非常活泼 be very lively；活泼可爱 be lively and cute
- 例句：这个孩子非常活泼。This kid is very cute.
  我觉得这个表演还可以再活泼一些。In my opinion, this performance can be livelier.

184 火 huǒ (n.) fire
- 搭配：着火 to be under fire；失火 to catch fire；大火 a big fire；火光 glare; flame
- 例句：这次的失火原因到现在还没有调查清楚。The reason for the fire remains unclear.
  这场大火一直烧了两天两夜。The fire has been burning for two days and two nights.

185 获得 huòdé (v.) gain, get
- 搭配：获得成功 to achieve success；获得自由 to gain freedom；获得机会 to get a chance
- 例句：我觉得你获得这份工作的机会非常小。I think you have a slim chance to getting this job.
  他终于获得了成功。He finally hit the mark.

186 积极 jījí (adj.) positive, active
- 搭配：积极作用 positive / active role；积极参加 active participation；特别积极 be very active
- 例句：王东对社会工作一直都很积极。Wang Dong is always positive in doing social works.
  我们应该积极参加课外活动。We should actively participate in field activity.

187 积累 jīlěi (v.) accumulate
- 搭配：积累经验 to accumulate experience；积累材料 to accumulate materials；多年的积累 years of accumulation
- 例句：这些年他积累了丰富的工作经验。He has accumulated a wealth of working experience during these years.
  他在阅读中积累了丰富的词语。He accumulated a big vocabulary by reading.

188 基础 jīchǔ (名) (n.) base, foundation

搭配： 基础知识 basic knowledge ； 基础科学 basic science ； 基础课 basic courses ； 基础教育 basic education

例句： 我把这些材料在原来的基础上又改了一遍。I modified these materials on its former base.
他的英语基础没有打好。He did not lay a good foundation for English learning.

189 激动 jīdòng (形)/(动) (adj./v.) excited; get excited

搭配： 非常激动 be very excited ； 激动极了 be extremely excited ； 心情激动 be heated with passion ； 激动人心 exciting

例句： 你别这么激动，先听王东把话说完。Don't be so excited. Listen to Wang Dong first.
他激动得一夜都没睡着觉。He was too excited to fall asleep last night.

190 及时 jíshí (形)/(副) (adj./adv.) in time; timely, without delay

搭配： 及时解决 to solve a problem in time ； 及时安排 to arrange sth in time

例句： 工作中遇到问题必须及时解决。We need to solve problems at work in time.
他说如果有合适的工作，一定会及时通知我。He said he would inform me without delay if there is a suitable job.
这场雪下得很及时。This snow has come at the right time.

191 即使 jíshǐ (连) (conj.) even, though

搭配： 即使……也…… even if ； 即使这样 for all that

例句： 即使明天下雨，我们也会按时出发。Even if it rains tomorrow, we will set out on time.
只要我努力了，即使不成功也没关系。As long as I try my best, I won't regret it.

192 寄 jì (动) (v.) send

搭配： 寄信 to send a letter ； 寄钱 to send money ； 寄衣服 to send clothes

例句： 爸爸妈妈在外地工作，每个月都给她寄钱。Her parents are far away from home, and send money to her each month.
你下午帮我把信寄出去。Help me to send this letter in the afternoon.

实战练习（十六）

一、听对话，选择正确答案

1. A. 要他晚上早点回家　　　　B. 让他晚点来接自己
   C. 请他参加公司的活动　　　D. 告诉他自己晚上有事
2. A. 这次的会议非常重要　　　B. 小王不应该去北京开会
   C. 李明不满意经理的决定　　D. 李明的身体一直不太好

二、选词填空

　　　　A 及时　　B 即使　　C 回忆　　D 活动　　E 活泼　　F 火

1.（　　）你不告诉我，我也会知道的。
2. 有话好好儿说，你发什么（　　）啊。
3. 王东这么一提醒，他也慢慢（　　）起来了。
4. 刚学过的生词要（　　）复习。
5. A：你都坐在这儿半天了，也不起来（　　）一下。
   B：我看完这份材料就出去走走。
6. A：新来的小王怎么样？
   B：很（　　），很快就跟大家成了朋友。

　　　　A 获得　　B 基础　　C 激动　　D 积极　　E 积累　　F 寄

7. 事情的成功，都是从小到大逐渐（　　）的。
8. 普通话以北方话为（　　）。
9. 你的信已经帮你（　　）出去了。
10. 这是王东第一次（　　）老师的表扬。
11. 小王工作（　　），常常受到表扬。
12. A：第一次当父亲，感觉怎么样？
    B：我现在很（　　），不知道说什么好。

三、排列顺序

1. A. 但态度非常积极　　　B. 麦克的基础很差　　　C. 因此获得了巨大的进步
2. A. 回忆起当时的情况　　B. 我仍然非常激动　　　C. 那次活动特别火

四、完成句子

1. 不　怀疑　我们　应该　互相 _____
2. 你让他　再　一下　好好儿　回忆 _____
3. 得　积极　表现　李红　非常 _____
4. 大多数人的　了　王东　获得　支持 _____
5. 这次　报名　她　活动　参加了 _____

五、看图，用词造句

1. 获得

2. 激动

Unit 17

记者	加油站
计划	家具
技术	假
既然	价格
继续	坚持
加班	减肥

193 记者 jìzhě (n.) journalist, reporter, correspondent

搭配：记者节 Reporters' Day；记者调查 a reporter's review；广播记者 a broadcast reporter；电视记者 a TV reporter

例句：我希望以后能成为一名记者。I wish to become a journalist.

他不希望记者来打扰自己的生活。He doesn't want to be bothered by journalists.

194 计划 jìhuà (n./v.) plan

搭配：学习计划 a study plan；工作计划 a working plan

例句：我有一个重要计划要告诉你。I want to tell you an important plan.

我得先知道她的决定，才能开始计划第二步。Only to know her decision first, I could plan the second.

195 技术 jìshù (n.) technology

搭配：技术员 a technician；学习技术 to learn a skill；科学技术 scientific technology

例句：小王的开车技术非常好。Xiao Wang drives skillfully.

我的这些技术都是跟王东学的。I learned these skills from Wang Dong.

196 既然 jìrán (conj.) since

搭配：既然……就…… since；既然……还…… as；既然……也…… now that

例句：既然他的病好得差不多了，就应该回学校上课。Since he has almost recovered, he should return to the class.

既然大家都同意，那就这么办吧。Since we have reached an agreement, let's do it.

既然你已经做了决定，我也不会不同意的。Since you've made a decision, I have no objection.

197 继续 jìxù (v.) continue

搭配：继续学习 to continue one's education；继续开会 to go on a meeting；继续购物 to continue shopping

例句：王东希望我能继续留在公司。Wang Dong hopes I could stay in the company.

李红刚告诉我，下午还要继续开会。Li Hong told me the meeting will go on this afternoon.

198 加班 jiābān (v.) work overtime

搭配：经常加班 to work overtime regularly；继续加班 to continue working overtime；加班工资 overtime pay

例句：最近这段时间，我们经常要加班。It is quite common for us to work overtime lately.

我们这个星期可能还要继续加班。Maybe we will work overtime this week.

Unit 17

199 加油站 jiāyóuzhàn (n.) gas/gasoline station

搭配：汽车加油站 a gasoline station；手机加油站 a charger for mobile phone

例句：我不知道前面还有没有加油站。I'm not sure if there is a gas station on the way ahead.
请不要在加油站里使用手机。Please don't use a mobile phone in a gas station.

200 家具 jiājù (n.) furniture

搭配：中式家具 Chinese furniture；西式家具 western furniture；高级家具 a costly furniture；简单家具 simple furniture

例句：因为王东工作忙，这些家具都是我一个人去买的。Wang Dong is busy with working, so I bought the furniture myself.
这些家具漂亮是漂亮，就是太贵了。This furniture is beautiful but costly.

201 假 jiǎ (adj.) false, fake

搭配：假话 a lie；假山 a rockery；假发 a wig；假牙 artificial teeth; toupee

例句：他去年病得很严重，掉了很多头发，所以需要戴假发。He was seriously ill last year and grew bald, so he bought a toupee.
老师告诉我们，好孩子不应该说假话。The teacher told us that a good kid shouldn't tell a lie.

202 价格 jiàgé (n.) price

搭配：价格低 a low price；价格便宜 cheap

例句：这家商场的家具不仅价格便宜，还可以送货上门。In this mall, the furniture is not only very cheap, but also can be delivered to your door.
李红的那个笔记本电脑比我这个电脑的价格贵多了。Li Hong's laptop is far more expensive than my computer.

203 坚持 jiānchí (v.) insist, persist

搭配：坚持学习 to insist on learning；坚持工作 to persist in working；坚持下去 to stick it out；坚持不了 cannot persist in (doing) sth

例句：他觉得自己真的再也坚持不下去了。He felt that he really can't hold on any more.
李红坚持每天早上都去公园跑步。Li Hong keeps outdoor jogging every morning.

204 减肥 jiǎnféi (v.) lose weight

搭配：减肥计划 a banting；坚持减肥 to insist on dieting；减肥方法 a method of weight-reducing

例句：我觉得你并不需要减肥。I don't think that you need to lose your weight.
医生告诉她，运动是最好的减肥方法。The doctor told her that doing exercises is the best way to lose weight.

实战练习（十七）

一、听对话，选择正确答案

1. A. 开会　　B. 加班　　　C. 去上海　　D. 看朋友
2. A. 八点　　B. 八点三十　C. 九点　　　D. 九点三十

二、选词填空

　　　　　　A 假　　B 价格　　C 坚持　　D 减肥　　E 记者　　F 计划

1. 我觉得这双鞋的（　　）太高了。
2. 这么多年来，他一直（　　）给那个孩子寄学费。
3. （　　）真的很不容易，天天得在外边跑。
4. 他说的都是（　　）话，你不要相信他。
5. A：明天就放假了，你有什么（　　）？
   B：我只想在家好好儿休息。
6. A：你最近在（　　）吗？瘦了很多。
   B：没有，最近工作太累，经常加班，没休息好。

　　　　　　A 既然　　B 技术　　C 继续　　D 家具　　E 加班　　F 加油站

7. 她打算明年（　　）送女儿来学跳舞。
8. 王东想把这些旧（　　）都换掉。
9. 我希望能够继续跟你学（　　）。
10. 李红今天要（　　），不能来了。
11. A：我明天可能要出差，不能和你去看电影了。
    B：（　　）你不能去，那我也不去了，等有时间再看吧。
12. A：还没到（　　）吗？
    B：就快到了，不用担心，车里还有点儿油呢。

三、排列顺序

1. A. 既然你不想继续在这儿工作
   B. 到别的地方再找一份自己喜欢的
   C. 那就离开吧

2. A. 那就应该发加班工资
   B. 否则没人会愿意干的
   C. 如果你要求大家加班

四、完成句子

1. 休息一下　到　再走吧　我们　加油站 _____
2. 把　寄给　我想　李红　这本工具书 _____
3. 记者　加班　当　经常　要 _____
4. 李红　集合　不知道　我估计　时间 _____
5. 明年　计划　王东　家具店　开一家 _____

五、看图，用词造句

1. 家具

2. 加班

Unit 18

减少	交
建议	交流
将来	交通
奖金	郊区
降低	骄傲
降落	饺子

Unit 18

205 减少 jiǎnshǎo 动 (v.) reduce, decrease

- 搭配：减少数量 to hold down the number of；减少收入 the reduction of income；减少人员 to reduce the staff；不断减少 a continuing reduction
- 例句：坚持运动会减少你生病的可能性。Doing exercises can help reduce chances of illnesses.
  大家希望能减少一点儿工作量。We wish to have less workload.

206 建议 jiànyì 动/名 (v./n.) propose, suggest, advise; proposal, suggestion, advice

- 搭配：提建议 to make a suggestion；合理的建议 a reasonable proposal
- 例句：我能给你提一个建议吗？Can I make a suggestion to you?
  他想买房，我建议他明年再买。He wants to buy a house, but I suggest him to buy it next year.

207 将来 jiānglái 名 (n.) future

- 搭配：过去、现在和将来 the past, present and the future；为将来做准备 to get ready for the future
- 例句：我也不知道将来会怎么样。I don't know what will happen in the future.
  如果将来有机会，我一定会回来看你。If possible, I will come back to see you in future.

208 奖金 jiǎngjīn 名 (n.) bonus, prize money

- 搭配：发奖金 to award bonuses；获得奖金 to gain bonuses；诺贝尔奖金 the Nobel Prize bonuses
- 例句：这个月的工资奖金加在一起，他拿了八千多块钱。He received a total of more than eight thousand RMB, putting this month's salaries and bonuses together.
  我们公司几乎不发奖金。We hardly receive any bonus from our company.

209 降低 jiàngdī 动 (v.) reduce, lower

- 搭配：降低标准 to lower the standard；降低要求 to lower one's expectation；降低条件 to moderate one's condition
- 例句：你的要求太高了，得降低点标准。The standard of recruitment is too high, and need to be lowered.
  这次考试的难度降低了，大多数孩子都考了九十分以上。The difficulty of this exam was lowered down, so most of the kids got more than ninety points.

210 降落 jiàngluò 动 (v.) land, touch down

- 搭配：降落伞 parachute；飞机降落 to land the plane；安全降落 a perfect landing; to land safely
- 例句：往下跳之前再检查一遍你的降落伞。Check your parachute again before your bailing out.
  飞机马上就要降落了，请大家系好安全带。The plane will land soon. Please fasten your safety belt.

211 交 jiāo (v.) make, meet

搭配: 交朋友 to make friends；交作业 to hand in homework；交税 to pay tax；交钱 to hand in the money

例句: 把这些工作交给我们，您就放心吧。 Please rest assured to leave these work to us.
王红今年都二十六岁了，还没有交男朋友。Wang Hong is twenty-six years old this year and hasn't have a boyfriend yet.

212 交流 jiāoliú (v.) exchange, communicate

搭配: 文化交流 cultural exchange；交流感情 to share feelings；交流经验 experience exchange

例句: 李红不太喜欢和别人交流。Li Hong doesn't like communicating with others.
我和他很少交流，但都知道对方的想法。We know each other's thoughts, although we had a little communication.

213 交通 jiāotōng (n.) transportation, traffic

搭配: 交通发达 to have a well-developed transportation system；交通大学 university of communications；交通事故 a traffic accident

例句: 这个地方经常发生交通事故。This is an accident-prone area.
这边的交通很方便，到公司最多十分钟。This area has traffic facilities. It takes no more than ten minutes to get to the company.

214 郊区 jiāoqū (n.) suburbs, outskirts

搭配: 城市郊区 suburbs of the city；郊区生活 suburban life

例句: 虽然我家住在郊区，但是交通很方便。Though my family is in the suburbs, the traffic is readily available.
郊区的房价不高，而且环境也很好。House prices in the suburbs are not high and the envionment is excellent.

215 骄傲 jiāo'ào (adj./n.) be proud of, proud; pride

搭配: 非常骄傲 be very proud；感到骄傲 to feel proud of, take pride in

例句: 即使你考了好成绩也不要骄傲。Even if you get a good performance in the exam, don't be arrogant.
他是父母的快乐和骄傲。He is the pride and joy of his parents.

216 饺子 jiǎozi (n.) jiaozi (Chinese dumpling)

搭配: 包饺子 to make dumplings；吃饺子 to eat dumplings

例句: 妈妈说今天晚上包饺子吃。Mom said we'll make some dumplings tonight.
中国人在过年的时候都会吃饺子。Chinese people usually eat dumplings during the Chinese New Year.

实战练习（十八）

一、听对话，选择正确答案

1. A. 女的不想买家具　　B. 男的最近经常加班
   C. 现在家具在打折　　D. 女的现在要去医院
2. A. 工资少　B. 非常累　C. 责任大　D. 没意思

二、选词填空

　　　　A 建议　B 降落　C 郊区　D 饺子　E 减少　F 将来

1. 飞机已经在首都机场（　　）了。
2. 今天的观众比昨天（　　）了百分之十。
3. （　　）的空气好，房价也比市区便宜。
4. 中国北方过年时喜欢吃（　　）。
5. A：你（　　）想做什么工作？
   B：我最想当一个导游，可以全国各地到处去玩。
6. A：对于这次活动，你有什么好的（　　）吗？
   B：减少广告。

　　　　A 奖金　B 降低　C 交　D 交流　E 交通　F 骄傲

7. 因为太骄傲，所以他没（　　）到几个朋友。
8. 今天温度忽然（　　）了。
9. 她的男朋友是一个（　　）警察。
10. 李红不知道该怎样和别人（　　）。
11. A：你这个月发了多少（　　）？
    B：还没发呢，经理说等到过年的时候和年终奖一起发。
12. A：这次考了好成绩也不要（　　），还得继续努力才行。
    B：爸，你怎么和我们老师说的一样。

三、排列顺序

1. A. 等发了奖金再买吧　　B. 就是价格有点儿高　　C. 这个手机看起来还行
2. A. 这个月的工作量不但没有减少　　B. 看来我们要更忙了　　C. 反而变得更多了

四、完成句子

1. 坚持　一件　不是　减肥　简单的事 _____
2. 只有　获得　坚持到底　成功　才能 _____
3. 一直　和我　坚持　他　交流　用汉语 _____
4. 妻子　全都　王东把　交给了　奖金 _____
5. 里　减少了　人　超市　的 _____

五、看图，用词造句

1. 交通

2. 交流

Unit 19

教授	结果
教育	解释
接受	尽管
接着	紧张
节	进行
节约	禁止

217 教授 jiàoshòu 名 (n.) professor
搭配：老教授 a senior professor；大学教授 a university professor
例句：张教授让王东下午去办公室找他。Professor Zhang asked Wang Dong to go to his office in the afternoon.
他爸爸是一位大学教授。His father is a university professor.

218 教育 jiàoyù 名/动 (n./v.) education; educate
搭配：发展教育 the development of education；教育工作 schooling；继续教育 further education
例句：家庭教育对孩子的成长影响非常大。Family education has a deep influence on children.
事实教育了我。Facts have taught me a lesson.

219 接受 jiēshòu 动 (v.) accept
搭配：接受帮助 to accept a help；接受批评 to accept criticisms；接受表扬 to accept / acknowledge praise；接受任务 to accept a task
例句：大家都不能接受我的意见。Nobody accepts my advice.
我觉得我们应该接受他们的道歉。I think we should accept their apology.

220 接着 jiēzhe 动/副 (v./adv.) follow, carry on, go on with, proceed
例句：我们接着刚才的话题继续聊。We pick up the topic again.
这本书，你看完了我接着看。I'll read the book after you.
他吃了很多饺子，接着又吃了一大包零食。After a lot of dumplings, he had a large package of snacks.

221 节 jié 名/量 (n./m.w.) festival, holiday; section, length
搭配：国庆节 National Day；节日 festival；一节课 a class；两节火车 two carriages
例句：每年春节我们一家四口都要回老家过年。Each Spring Festival we four go home to spend our holiday together.
这节火车上的人特别多。It's very crowded in this carriage.

222 节约 jiéyuē 动 (v.) save; economize
搭配：节约用电 to save on electricity；节约用水 to save on water；节约时间 to save time
例句：为了节约时间，我和王东只吃了几口饭就继续开始工作了。In order to save time, Wang Dong and I only got a bite and continued our work.
我们应该从小就养成节约的好习惯。We should develop a good habit of economization from childhood.

Unit 19

223 结果 jiéguǒ 名/连 (n./conj.) result; findings; outcome

搭配：调查结果 findings；比赛结果 the outcome of a game

例句：你知不知道这次的比赛结果？ Do you know the outcome of this game?
他上学的时候不努力，结果没考上大学。 He didn't work hard at school, so he failed the college entrance examination.

224 解释 jiěshì 动 (v.) explain

搭配：解释词语 to explain a word；科学的解释 scientific explanation；解释误会 to explain/clear away a misunderstanding

例句：我给王东解释了半天他才明白过来。 After all my explanations, Wang Dong finally understood it.
你必须给我一个解释。 You must give me an explanation.

225 尽管 jǐnguǎn 副/连 (adv./conj.) despite

搭配：尽管这样 in spite of；尽管……还是…… even though；尽管……但是…… despite of

例句：你尽管按照自己的想法去做吧。 Feel free to do it by following your own thoughts.
大家想吃就尽管吃，今天我请客。 It's my treat today. Help yourself to whatever you like.
你有什么困难尽管说，我们一定帮助你解决。 Feel free to tell us your problems and we'll try our best to help you.

226 紧张 jǐnzhāng 形 (adj.) nervous, tense

搭配：特别紧张 be very nervous；学习紧张 a tough studying；紧张的工作 a rush work

例句：我们的学习非常紧张。 Our academic task is tough and tense.
第一次在这么多人面前表演，他有些紧张。 He felt a little bit nervous for performing before so many people for the first time.

227 进行 jìnxíng 动 (v.) proceed, be in progress

搭配：进行工作 to carry on a work；进行活动 to engage in activities；进行讨论 to hold a discussion

例句：会议已经进行了两个多小时。 The meeting has been lasting for more than two hours.
老师说我们下个星期就要开始进行训练。 Our teacher said the training will begin next week.

228 禁止 jìnzhǐ 动 (v.) prohibit, forbid

搭配：禁止抽烟 no smoking；禁止检查 no checking

例句：经理说禁止任何人去打扰他。 The manager said he shouldn't be bothered in any circumstances.
对不起，先生，这儿禁止抽烟。 Sorry, sir, no smoking here.

实战练习（十九）

一、听对话，选择正确答案

1. A. 自己迟到的原因　　　　B. 自己不会包饺子
   C. 李强和自己的关系　　　D. 自己不去王教授家
2. A. 男的认为女的胖　　　　B. 女的身体不舒服
   C. 女的正计划减肥　　　　D. 他们在同一家公司

二、选词填空

A 接着　B 教授　C 教育　D 接受　E 结果　F 节约

1. 虽然现在富起来了，但他仍然很注意（　　　）。
2. 这本书你先看，看完了我再（　　　）看。
3. 我父亲从事（　　　）工作快四十年了。
4. 这件事情弄到现在也没有个（　　　）。
5. A：王东现在怎么样？
   B：事情来得太突然了，他到现在还是（　　　）不了。
6. A：李红，张（　　　）叫你现在去三楼的会议室。
   B：知道了，我这就去。

A 解释　B 尽管　C 紧张　D 进行　E 禁止　F 节

7. 有什么事你（　　　）说，能帮忙的我一定帮。
8. 李红（　　　）别人动她桌子上的东西。
9. 听了王东的（　　　），我才明白是怎么回事。
10. 她感觉特别（　　　），手都出汗了。
11. A：活动（　　　）到哪儿了？
    B：你快点儿去吧，马上就要结束了。
12. A：今天是什么日子？街上这么多人。
    B：今天是中国的春（　　　）。

三、排列顺序

1. A. 真让人无法接受　　B. 换来的却是这样一个结果　　C. 大家努力了那么长时间
2. A. 大家还是都来集合了　　B. 尽管天气很冷　　C. 而且没有一个人迟到

四、完成句子

1. 想不到　谁也　会是　事情的结果　这样 _____
2. 这个事　解释　把　你得　清楚　给我 _____
3. 观众　让他　很紧张　这么多的 _____
4. 六月一日　孩子们的　是　节日 _____
5. 计划　怕是　不下去了　这个　进行 _____

五、看图，用词造句

1. 禁止

2. 解释

Unit 20

京剧	警察
经济	竞争
经历	竟然
经验	镜子
精彩	究竟
景色	举

Unit 20

229 京剧 jīngjù (名) (n.) Peking opera
- 搭配：京剧团 a Peking opera troupe ；京剧表演 a performance of Peking opera
- 例句：他非常喜欢京剧。He likes Peking opera very much.
  爷爷每天早上起来都会唱上一段京剧。After getting up, grandpa sings a Peking opera every morning.

230 经济 jīngjì (名/形) (n./adj.) economy; economic
- 搭配：发展经济 economic development ；经济条件 economic condition
- 例句：他家里的经济条件不太好。His family's economic condition is not very good.
  公司在经济方面出了一点儿问题。The company has some financial problems.

231 经历 jīnglì (名/动) (n./v.) experience
- 搭配：工作经历 working experiences ；感情经历 romance; love story
- 例句：王东从来没有经历过这样的事情。Wang Dong had never experienced anything like this.
  他不愿意向别人提起这段经历。He is not willing to mention this experience.

232 经验 jīngyàn (名/动) (n./v.) experience
- 搭配：工作经验 working experiences ；学习经验 learning experiences
- 例句：王东有丰富的工作经验。Wang Dong is rich in working experiences.
  他把自己的经验都告诉了我。He told me all of his experiences.

233 精彩 jīngcǎi (形) (adj.) wonderful
- 搭配：精彩生活 colorful / rich life ；精彩世界 colorful world
- 例句：在大会上，许多代表都做了精彩的发言。At the meeting, many representatives delivered wonderful speeches.
  他给大家带来了精彩的表演。He gave us a wonderful performance.

234 景色 jǐngsè (名) (n.) scenery, view, scene, landscape
- 搭配：景色迷人 charming scenery ；美丽的景色 a nice view ；海边的景色 scene of the seaside
- 例句：日出时，海边的景色非常迷人。The scene is magnificent at the seashore in the sunshine.
  这里景色优美，交通便利，是一个居住的好地方。It's an agreeable place to live with the beautiful scenery and convenient traffic.

235 警察 jǐngchá (名) (n.) policeman
- 搭配：交通警察 a traffic policeman ；人民警察 people's policeman
- 例句：他当警察已经八年了。He has been working as a policeman for eight years.
  有了警察的保护，学校安全多了。The school is safer under the police's protection.

236 竞争 jìngzhēng (v.) compete

搭配: 公平竞争 to compete on an equal footing; 互相竞争 mutual competition

例句: 王红是我最大的竞争对手。Wang Hong is my biggest rival.

我们之间不存在竞争。There's no competition between us.

237 竟然 jìngrán (adv.) unexpectedly

例句: 这么大的事情,你竟然都不知道? Why don't you know such a big matter?

她竟然只用一天时间就完成了这些工作。Unexpectedly, she finished this work only in one day.

真没想到他竟然敢当面说假话。What a surprise! He dare to lie to our face.

238 镜子 jìngzi (n.) mirror

搭配: 照镜子 to look into the mirror; 对着镜子 to face to the mirror

例句: 她正站在镜子前面打扮自己。She is standing in front of a mirror to dress herself up.

这镜子是谁的? Whose mirror is this?

239 究竟 jiūjìng (n./adv.) truth, outcome; actually

例句: 大家都想知道个究竟。We all want to know what actually happened.

究竟发生了什么事? What's the matter?

我不明白你这究竟是怎么了? I wonder what exactly happened to you.

240 举 jǔ (v.) lift, raise, hold up, cite, choose, start, elect

搭配: 举起来 to lift; 举手 to raise one's hand; 举重 weight lift; 举例子 to set an example

例句: 请你举一个例子来证明你的观点。Justify yourself with an example.

会上,一名记者举手要求提问题。A journalist raised his hand to ask a question in the conference.

在这次运动会,他获得了举重比赛的第一名。In the sports games, he won the first prize in the weightlifting competition.

实战练习（二十）

一、听对话，选择正确答案

1. A. 男的现在非常生气　　　　　　　　B. 女的不想被人打扰
   C. 女的觉得肚子饿了　　　　　　　　D. 男的想找个人说话
2. A. 饭店　　B. 超市　　C. 商场　　D. 家具店

二、选词填空

A 精彩　B 经济　C 经历　D 经验　E 京剧　F 警察

1. （　　）过那样的事以后，他变得不爱说话了。
2. 中国（　　）发展得很快。
3. 她不希望男朋友当（　　）。
4. 现在的年轻人很少有喜欢唱（　　）的。
5. A：昨天的表演怎么样？
   B：特别（　　），你没来看真是太可惜了。
6. A：我从来没干过这个，我怕做不好。
   B：放心，王东会帮助你，他在这方面很有（　　）。

A 竟然　B 竞争　C 镜子　D 究竟　E 景色　F 举

7. 结果（　　）会怎么样，明天大家就知道了。
8. 李红对着（　　）仔细打扮自己。
9. 北京郊区的（　　）真是太美了。
10. 他一直认为，没有（　　）就没有发展。
11. A：真没想到，这事（　　）是他干的。
    B：是啊，我知道后也很吃惊。
12. A：这是什么比赛？
    B：举重，那个人再（　　）一次就能得第一了。

三、排列顺序

1. A. 商场现在正举办特卖活动　　B. 下班后我们去看看吧　　C. 家具竟然打到五折
2. A. 如果我请她来我们学校表演　　B. 她的京剧唱得这么好　　C. 她不会拒绝吧

四、完成句子

1. 镜子　这么　竟然　这一面　贵 _____
2. 拒绝　为什么　参加　他究竟　这次会议 _____
3. 王东的　了　警察　要求　拒绝 _____
4. 有留学经历的　是一个　竞争对手　博士生　我的 _____
5. 他一说到　来了　精神　就　京剧 _____

五、看图，用词造句

1. 警察

2. 镜子

Unit 21

举办	开心
举行	看法
拒绝	考虑
距离	烤鸭
聚会	科学
开玩笑	棵

241 举办 jǔbàn (v.) hold

搭配：举办地 host；举办活动 to hold an activity；举办训练班 to run a training session

例句：下周六我们学校将会举办一场运动会。Our school will hold a sports competition next Saturday.

在学校举办的数学比赛中，他获得了第一名。He got the first prize on a mathematic contest held by our school.

242 举行 jǔxíng (v.) hold

搭配：举行会议 to hold a meeting；举行比赛 to hold a match；举行考试 to have an exam

例句：我们学校举行了足球比赛。Our school held a football match.

考试下个星期一举行。There'll be an exam next Monday.

243 拒绝 jùjué (v.) refuse

搭配：拒绝加班 to refuse to work overtime；拒绝接受 to refuse to accept；拒绝道歉 to refuse to apologize

例句：为了交通安全，我们要拒绝酒后开车。We should refuse drunken driving for the sake of safety.

王东想请她去喝咖啡，但是她拒绝了。Wang Dong wanted to invite her to drink some coffee, but she refused.

244 距离 jùlí (v./n.) away from; distance

例句：天津距离北京大约有一百二十公里。Tianjin is about 120km away from Beijing.

这里距离公司很远，你还是坐车去好了。The company is far away from here. You'd better take a bus.

我们的心和心之间没有任何距离。There's no distance between our hearts.

245 聚会 jùhuì (n./v.) gathering, meeting, party; get together, meet

搭配：生日聚会 birthday party；家庭聚会 family gatherings；同学聚会 class party

例句：今年，三叔因为出差没有参加家庭聚会。This year my younger uncle didn't attend our family gathering because he was on business.

每年我都会和很多大学同学聚会。Each year I'll have a party with many of my college classmates.

246 开玩笑 kāi wánxiào make a joke

例句：小红特别爱开玩笑。Xiao Hong is fond of making jokes.

她真生气了，你不要再开玩笑了。Don't make any more jokes on her. She is really angry.

Unit 21

247 开心 kāixīn (v./adj.) feel happy, rejoice; happy, joyful, amused
搭配：开开心心 very happy ；开心果 a great delight
例句：弟弟考上北京大学，我们全家人都很开心。We're all delighted for my younger brother admitted to Peking University.
你今天看起来很高兴，一定有什么开心的事吧？ You're so happy today. Any good news?

248 看法 kànfǎ (n.) opinion
搭配：个人看法 a personal opinion ；几点看法 some opinions ；有看法 to have an opinion
例句：能谈谈你对这件事的看法吗？ Could you tell us about your opinion on this matter?
对于这个问题，人们有着不同的看法。People hold different opinions on this problem.

249 考虑 kǎolǜ (v.) consider
搭配：考虑清楚 to consider throughly ；考虑问题 to take a consideration (of)
例句：做任何事情之前都要考虑清楚。We should have a careful consideration before doing anything.
考虑到妈妈的健康问题，我决定回家找份工作。Considering of my mother's state of health, I decided to find a job in hometown.

250 烤鸭 kǎoyā (n.) roast duck
搭配：烤鸭店 roast duck restaurant ；北京烤鸭 roast Beijing duck ；一只烤鸭 a roast duck
例句：北京烤鸭非常有名，味道好极了。Roast Beijing duck is well-known and delicious.
每一只烤鸭都是店里的师傅用心烤出来的。Each roast duck is cooked by the cook in the restaurant with great care.

251 科学 kēxué (n./adj.) science; scientific
搭配：科学家 a scientist ；科学减肥 to lose weight scientifically
例句：李静从小就想成为一名科学家。Li Jing has been dreaming of being a scientist from her childhood.
女孩子们减肥一定要科学。Girls should lose weight scientifically.

252 棵 kē (m.w.) (used for plants)
搭配：一棵树 a tree ；一棵草 a grass
例句：这颗小树将来一定会长成大树的。This small tree will grow into a tall one.
雨中的这棵小草没有低下头。The grass didn't lower its head in the rain.

实战练习（二十一）

一、听对话，选择正确答案

1. A. 走路　　B. 坐火车　　C. 坐出租车　　D. 坐公交车
2. A. 医生　　B. 作家　　C. 科学家　　D. 导演

二、选词填空

A 距离　B 烤鸭　C 举办　D 开玩笑　E 棵　F 看法

1. 我爱吃北京（　　）。
2. 我觉得你的（　　）是错的，这样对他很不公平。
3. 2008年，中国北京成功（　　）了奥运会。
4. 天津（　　）北京很近。
5. A：我怎么没听过这件事，假的吧？
   B：我是认真的，不是在（　　）。
6. A：这（　　）树上的花儿真美！
   B：春天是最美的季节！

A 举行　B 拒绝　C 考虑　D 科学　E 聚会　F 开心

7. 这是我们毕业后的第一次（　　）。
8. 张教授经常对我们说一定要相信（　　）。
9. 这次比赛将在上海（　　）。
10. 得到了老师的鼓励，我非常（　　）。
11. 因为太忙，我（　　）了她一起逛街的建议。
12. A：你回去吧，我不能帮你。
    B：您再（　　）一下吧，我真的是没有办法了才来找您的。

三、排列顺序

1. A. 小王爱跟别人开玩笑
   B. 跟他在一块儿很开心
   C. 所以大家都很喜欢他

2. A. 可是最近的科学研究证明
   B. 花草离不开泥土
   C. 有些植物离开了它也可以活下去

四、完成句子

1. 科学问题　他在　考虑　一个　认真地 _____
2. 烤鸭　很　受欢迎　北京 _____
3. 举办　世华公司　这次活动　拒绝 _____
4. 您　说出来　请把　看法　对他的 _____
5. 爱开玩笑的人　和　我喜欢　在一起 _____

五、看图，用词造句

1. 开心

2. 考虑

Unit 22

咳嗽	空
可怜	空气
可是	恐怕
可惜	苦
客厅	矿泉水
肯定	困

253 咳嗽 késou (动) (v.) cough

搭配：咳嗽得厉害 to cough badly；咳嗽了半天 to cough for a long time

例句：爷爷夜里咳嗽醒了，喝了点儿水又睡了。The grandpa coughed to wake up at night. He had to drink some water and went to bed again.

怎么咳嗽得这么厉害呀？下午去医院看看吧。Why did you cough so badly? Let's go to hospital this afternoon.

254 可怜 kělián (形/动) (adj./v.) poor; pity

搭配：可怜的人 a poor man；哭得很可怜 to cry pathetically；可怜虫 a poor wretch

例句：这个小女孩特别可怜，我们帮帮她吧。Let's help this poor little girl.

小丽哭得这么可怜，肯定是发生什么事情了吧。There must be something. Xiaoli is crying loudly.

对这种总是做坏事的人，我们不能可怜他。We shall not have mercy on such a regular wrongdoer.

255 可是 kěshì (连/副) (conj./adv.) but; used for emphasis

例句：天都黑了，可是妈妈还没有回来。It goes dark, but my mother hasn't come back yet.

虽然我不想去，可是他都开车来接我了，我只能去了。Although I didn't want to go, he drove to pick me up. I had to go anyway.

虽然学汉语不容易，可是我们都坚持下来了。It's hard to learn Chinese, but we keep it up.

这钢笔可是很贵的。This pen is really expensive.

256 可惜 kěxī (形) (adj.) regrettable

例句：机会难得，错过了就太可惜了。To miss this rare chance will be a real pity.

他真是难得的人才，可惜被经理开除了。It is a pity that he, a rare talent, was fired by the manager.

很可惜你没来参加同学聚会。You did not show up in our class gathering. It's really a pity.

257 客厅 kètīng (名) (n.) saloon, parlor, drawing room

搭配：布置客厅 to lay the parlor；大客厅 a large drawing-room

例句：明天有同事要到我们家做客，下午你把客厅布置一下。Tomorrow we'll treat my colleagues. Please furnish our parlor.

他们经常在这个大客厅里举办家庭聚会。They often hold family parties in this big drawing-room.

258 肯定 kěndìng (v./adj.) affirm; sure

例句： 经理肯定了我的努力和成绩。The manager affirmed my efforts and achievements.
请给我一个肯定的回答。Please give me a definite answer.
我明天肯定会去的，你放心吧。I assure you that I will come tomorrow, take it easy.
我问他去还是不去，他的回答是肯定的。He gave the positive answer when I asked whether he would go.

259 空 kōng (adj.) empty

搭配： 空盒子 empty box；空想 day dream；空话 empty talk
例句： 这个瓶子是空的。This bottle is empty.
他把空盒子扔进了垃圾箱。He threw the empty envelope in the bin.
他总是喜欢说空话。He is liable to make empty talk.

260 空气 kōngqì (n.) air

搭配： 新鲜空气 fresh air；空气质量 air quality；呼吸空气 to breathe
例句： 这儿的空气质量很好。The air quality here is very good.
森林里的空气很新鲜。The air is very fresh in the forest.

261 恐怕 kǒngpà (v./adv.) for fear of; be afraid of

搭配： 恐怕有困难 may have difficulties；恐怕不行 may not
例句： 六点了，银行恐怕已经下班了。It's six o'clock now. I'm afraid that the bank is closed.
天突然黑了，恐怕要下雨了。It goes dark. I'm afraid that it will rain.

262 苦 kǔ (adj.) bitter

搭配： 味道苦 a bitter taste；苦药 bitter pills；苦日子 hard life；苦笑 a bitter smile
例句： 生活再苦，她也没有放弃希望。She has never given up hope, despite life is hard.
中药太难喝了，特别苦。The traditional Chinese medicine is too bitter to swallow.

263 矿泉水 kuàngquánshuǐ (n.) mineral water

搭配： 一瓶矿泉水 a bottle of mineral water；一箱矿泉水 a case of mineral water
例句： 我渴了，想去超市买瓶矿泉水喝。I am thirsty and want to buy a bottle of mineral water in the supermarket.
买矿泉水之前，一定要看清生产日期。Make sure of the date of production before you buy the mineral water.

264 困 kùn (adj./v.) be stranded; feel sleepy

搭配： 困极了 be very sleepy；困在屋里 to be stranded in the room
例句： 我现在很困，只想睡觉。I feel sleepy and yearn to sleep.
我现在被困在电梯里，你快找人来救我。Hurry to find someone to help me. I'm stranded in the elevator.

实战练习（二十二）

一、听对话，选择正确答案

1. A. 睡不着　　B. 生病了　　C. 电视坏了　　D. 睡得太晚
2. A. 没钱看病　B. 没有子女　C. 没有工作　　D. 身体不舒服

二、选词填空

A 苦　B 恐怕　C 可是　D 可怜　E 咳嗽　F 可惜

1. 天气这么闷热，（　　）要下雨了。
2. 很多事情都是先（　　）后甜，只有坚持到最后的人，才能尝到成功的甜味。
3. 我刚走到门口就听到了妈妈的（　　）声。
4. 红红三岁就没了妈妈，太（　　）了。
5. 今天早上一直在下大雨，（　　）大家上班都没有迟到。
6. A：最后一本书刚刚被人买走了。
   B：真是太（　　）了，我要是早来几分钟就好了。

A 困　B 矿泉水　C 空　D 客厅　E 空气　F 肯定

7. （　　）更有营养，所以价格要贵一些。
8. 那个房间是（　　）的，里面什么都没有。
9. 这件事（　　）不是小红做的，她是一个诚实的孩子。
10. 客人们快到了，你把果汁拿到（　　）去。
11. （　　）对人就像水对鱼一样重要。
12. A：都十一点了，我快（　　）死了。
    B：你先睡吧，我明天不上班。

三、排列顺序

1. A. 这个可怜的小女孩儿虽然吃过了感冒药
   B. 可是还在一直咳嗽
   C. 我们很心疼她
2. A. 肯定是过期了　　　B. 这瓶矿泉水是苦的　　　C. 你再去客厅拿一瓶

四、完成句子

1. 这里的 肯定 空气 很新鲜 _____
2. 一直 孩子 可怜的 在咳嗽 _____
3. 我 困得 现在 不得了 _____
4. 太 了 真是 可惜 _____
5. 客厅 近 距离 厨房 非常 _____

五、看图，用词造句

1. 咳嗽

2. 空气

Unit 23

困难	来自
拉	懒
垃圾桶	浪费
辣	浪漫
来不及	老虎
来得及	冷静

265 困难 kùnnan (形/名) (adj./n.) difficult; difficulty

搭配：解决困难 to solve difficulties；生活困难 be badly off；克服困难 to overcome difficulties

例句：这些困难的学生，肯定拿不出这么多钱。Those students who have difficulties can't take out such an amount of money.

有什么困难你说出来，大家一起帮你解决。Tell us about your difficulties. We'll help you.

266 拉 lā (动) (v.) pull, draw

搭配：拉近 to get close；拉小提琴 to play the violin；拉开距离 to pull away

例句：这个人学拉手风琴很长时间了，所以拉得特别好。This man learns accordion for a long time and plays it very well.

他的话拉近了我们之间的距离。His words draw us closer.

267 垃圾桶 lājītǒng (名) (n.) dustbin

例句：请把垃圾扔进垃圾桶里。Please throw the garbage into the dustbin.

垃圾桶都满了，不要再往里扔东西了。The dustbin is full of garbage. Don't throw any more things into it.

268 辣 là (形/动) (adj./v.) hot, spicy; burn

搭配：辣眼睛 to burn acutely；火辣辣的 stinging

例句：这个菜特别辣，你还是不要吃了。This dish is too hot. You'd better give it up.

夏天中午的太阳火辣辣的，街上的行人都变少了。The sun is scorching in the afternoon. There are fewer people outside.

269 来不及 láibují (动) (v.) not have enough time to do sth

例句：还有一个小时火车就要开了，来不及去看他了。The train will leave in one hour and we have not enough time to see him.

今天起晚了，来不及吃早饭我就上班了。I got up late this morning. There is no time to have a breakfast so I went to work directly.

时间来不及了，我就不送你去机场了。I don't have enough time to see you off at the airport.

270 来得及 láidejí (动) (v.) have enough time to do

例句：时间还早，我们还来得及去喝杯咖啡。It's still early. We have enough time to have a cup of coffee.

他下个月才出国呢，我们还来得及见见他。He'll go abroad next month. We still have time to see him.

电影七点才开始，现在刚六点半，你马上去还来得及。The film will begin at 7. It's 6:30 and you can catch it in a hurry.

Unit 23

271 来自 láizì (动) (v.) come from, be from
搭配：来自远方 from a far；来自南方 be from the south；来自农村 to come from the countryside
例句：他来自农村，想在城里找一份工作。He comes from the countryside and wants to find a job in the city.
虽然同学们来自不同的省市，但大家相处得很好。Though all the students come from different provinces, they get along well with each other.

272 懒 lǎn (形) (adj.) lazy
搭配：偷懒 to be lazy；懒虫 lazybones；好吃懒做 to eat one's head off
例句：张红是一个好吃懒做的人，大家都不喜欢她。Zhang Hong is too lazy, no one likes her.
我都懒得和你说话，你快回去吧。I'm in no mood for talking to you. Please go home now.

273 浪费 làngfèi (动) (v.) waste
搭配：浪费时间 to waste time；浪费水电 to waste water and electricity
例句：我们要节约用水，千万不能浪费。We must save water and not waste it.
不要在吃喝上浪费时间。Don't waste time on eating and drinking.

274 浪漫 làngmàn (形) (adj.) romantic
搭配：浪漫的爱情 a romantic love；浪漫的故事 be very romantic
例句：去年夏天我们一起过了一个非常浪漫的假期。We have a very romantic vacation last summer.
这个爱情故事非常浪漫。This love story is very romantic.

275 老虎 lǎohǔ (名) (n.) tiger
搭配：纸老虎 a paper tiger；可怕的老虎 a dreadful tiger
例句：老虎是森林之王。Tiger is the king of forest.
老虎是一种危险的动物。Tiger is a dangerous animal.

276 冷静 lěngjìng (形) (adj.) calm, cool
搭配：非常冷静 be very calm；头脑冷静 be cool headed；保持冷静 to keep cool
例句：等你头脑冷静了再来和我谈。You can talk to me after calming down.
事情都已经发生了，你冷静点，不会有事的。The thing had happened. You should calm down. It will be fine.

实战练习（二十三）

一、听对话，选择正确答案

1. A. 不甜　　B. 很酸　　C. 太辣　　D. 盐多了
2. A. 六点半　B. 六点四十　C. 七点　　D. 七点五分

二、选词填空

A 困难　B 浪费　C 垃圾桶　D 来不及　E 来得及　F 浪漫

1. 王东是个（　　）的人，常带给女朋友惊奇和感动。
2. 这个城市很干净，每隔一段距离就有一个（　　）。
3. 不用的东西就别买，（　　）钱。
4. 离登机时间不多了，我们（　　）回去看妈妈了。
5. A：现在才九月二十号，我们还（　　）为张红准备结婚礼物。
   B：那我们明天去超市里看看吧。
6. A：你是不是遇到什么（　　）了？或许我可以帮你。
   B：没有，就是最近睡觉总是做梦。

A 老虎　B 辣　C 冷静　D 懒　E 来自　F 拉

7. 这件事（　　）近了我们之间的距离。
8. 他是四川人，从小就喜欢吃（　　）的饭菜。
9. 先别生气了，（　　）一下。
10. 我的同学（　　）五湖四海。
11. A：周末你有什么计划吗？
    B：我想带孩子去动物园看（　　）。
12. A：你男朋友怎么样？
    B：除了有点儿（　　），其他还挺好的。

三、排列顺序

1. A. 它需要朋友们拉起手来
   B. 生活中的酸甜苦辣不能像垃圾一样扔进垃圾桶
   C. 一起面对

2. A. 恐怕下午不能陪你去逛街了
   B. 现在实在是太困了
   C. 我昨晚加班到很晚

四、完成句子

1. 办法　再大的　都有　困难　解决的　_____
2. 浪漫　浪费　常常　带来　会　_____
3. 我　说话　还没　他就走了　来得及　_____
4. 这个　恐怕　垃圾桶　不能用了　_____
5. 修　请把　这条路　宽一点儿　_____

五、看图，用词造句

1. 困难

2. 垃圾桶

Unit 24

礼拜天　　厉害
礼貌　　　例如
理发　　　俩
理解　　　连
理想　　　联系
力气　　　凉快

Unit 24

277 礼拜天 lǐbàitiān （名）(n.) Sunday (colloq.)

搭配：每个礼拜天 every Sunday；这个礼拜天 this Sunday

例句：上个礼拜天，我陪小红逛了一天街。Last Sunday I roamed about the streets with Xiaohong a whole day.

大家礼拜六和礼拜天都不用去上班。We need not go to work on weekends.

278 礼貌 lǐmào （名/形）(n./adj.) manners; courtesy

搭配：有/没礼貌 to have (no) manners；懂礼貌 to be polite；礼貌用语 polite languages

例句：小明是一个懂礼貌的好孩子。Xiaoming is a polite boy.

"谢谢"、"对不起"等都是礼貌用语。"Thank you", "sorry" are polite expressions.

279 理发 lǐfà （动）(v.) give/ get a haircut

搭配：理发店 a barber's shop；理发师 hair dresser；理理发 to have one's hair cut

例句：十号理发师正在给张红理发。Barber No.10 is giving Zhang Hong a haircut.

路口新开了一家理发店。A new barber's shop is opened at the crossing.

280 理解 lǐjiě （动）(v.) understand

搭配：互相理解 mutual understanding；理解能力 understanding ability；理解别人 to understand other people

例句：作为孩子，我们要理解父母的一片苦心。As children, we should understand our parents' true hearts.

朋友之间要相互理解。As friends, we need mutual understanding.

281 理想 lǐxiǎng （名/形）(n./adj.) goal; ideal

搭配：理想生活 an ideal life；人生理想 a life ideal

例句：儿子这次考试的成绩很不理想。My son got a poor grade in this exam.

她的理想是当一名记者。To become a reporter is her goal.

282 力气 lìqi （名）(n.) physical strength, effort

搭配：有力气 to have physical strength；力气活儿 a manual/ heavy work；花力气 to take effort

例句：公司应该花大力气来招聘人才。Companies should take great efforts in recruiting talents.

这是一个力气活儿，一般人还真干不了。Common people cannot do this heavy work.

283 厉害 lìhai （形）(adj.) stern, violent

搭配：厉害对手 a gut fighter; a tough opponent；病得厉害 be badly ill

例句：他真厉害，很快就把这本很厚的书看完了。He finished reading the book in a short time. How smart!

天热得厉害，没空调真不行。It is terribly hot. To live without an air conditioner is impossible.

284 例如 lìrú (v.) take sth for an example

例句：体育运动有很多，例如跑步、打篮球、游泳等。There're many sports, such as running, playing basketball and swimming, etc.

中国有很多个省，例如江苏省、广东省、福建省等。China has many provinces, such as Jiangsu Province, Guangdong Province and Fujian Province, etc.

285 俩 liǎ (num.) two (colloq., numeral)

搭配：咱俩 we two；他们俩 they two

例句：这俩大西瓜是妈妈从市场买回来的。My mother bought this two watermelons from the market.

你俩快点出去看看，好像是李阿姨来了。Both of you, go out and have a look quickly. It seems that Aunt Li has arrived.

286 连 lián (v./prep.) link, in succession; besides

搭配：心连心 heart on heart；连……也（都）…… even

例句：请把这把这几个词连成一句话。Please put these words into a sentence.

刚来北京时，她连"你好"都不会说。When she just came to Beijing, she even couldn't say "hello".

287 联系 liánxì (v.) contact

搭配：联系方法 a method of contact；联系人 contacts；电话联系 a telephone contact；联系实际 to combine sth with practice

例句：他们虽然不常见面，但总是用手机联系。Although they can't meet each other very often, they keep contact through mobile phones.

我不知道他的电话号码，也联系不上他。I don't know his phone number and can't contact him.

288 凉快 liángkuai (adj./ v.) cool; cool off

搭配：非常凉快 be very cool；天气凉快 a cool weather

例句：这几天很热，什么时候才能凉快一点儿呢？ It's too hot these days. When will it cool off？

承德的夏天很凉快，你可以在这儿多住几天。Chengde is very cool in summer. You can stay here for some more days.

实战练习（二十四）

一、听对话，选择正确答案

1. A. 想理发　　B. 要回家　　C. 想去超市　　D. 没有时间
2. A. 医院　　　B. 公司　　　C. 小华家　　　D. 男的家

二、选词填空

A 礼拜天　B 礼貌　C 力气　D 理解　E 厉害　F 俩

1. 你现在怎么还有（　　　）跳舞呀，我都快累死了。
2. 这个小孩子的（　　　）能力很好，才四岁就读过很多书了。
3. 他们（　　　）昨天去理发店看了看，可是没有理发。
4. 这个老师很（　　　），学生们都怕他。
5. A：今天是周六吗？
   B：不是，今天是（　　　）。
6. A：老李的孙女真有（　　　），每次见到我都喊"奶奶好"。
   B：是啊，我也很喜欢她。

A 理想　B 连　C 理发　D 例如　E 联系　F 凉快

7. 你平时都是找几号（　　　）师啊？
8. 他太忙了，（　　　）周日都不休息。
9. 工作后太忙了，我已经很少跟同学（　　　）了。
10. 家里很（　　　），不用开电扇。
11. A：你平时都喜欢做什么呀？
    B：很多啊，（　　　）听音乐、上网、逛街等。
12. A：你将来打算做什么？
    B：我的（　　　）是成为一名医生。

三、排列顺序

1. A. 我觉得李明理解能力很强
   B. 将来一定可以成为一名厉害的律师
   C. 平时又很冷静

2. A. 是个旅游的好地方
　　B. 昆明是一个美丽浪漫的城市
　　C. 那里四季如春

四、完成句子

1. 王东　很有　对人　礼貌 _____
2. 连　她　自己的妈妈　不关心　都 _____
3. 是一种　老虎　动物　很厉害的 _____
4. 纸上　请把　写在　你的理想 _____
5. 这样做　我不能　为什么　理解他　会 _____

五、看图，用词造句

1. 联系

2. 理发

Unit 25

零钱	旅行
另外	律师
留	麻烦
流利	马虎
流行	满
乱	毛

289 零钱 língqián 〈名〉 (n.) change, pocket money

搭配: 换零钱 to change some pocket money; 找零钱 to give sb the change

例句: 大家出去玩的时候要准备好坐公交车的零钱。When going out, always bring change with you.

今天上午我去银行换了很多零钱。This morning I went to bank for having lots of change.

290 另外 lìngwài 〈代〉/〈连〉/〈副〉 (pron./conj./adv.) other; another

例句: 他今天找我，还有另外的事。He has other things to discuss with me today.

有车的骑车先走，另外的人走过去。Those who have bikes go first while others walk there.

别忘了出去买菜，另外再带点水果回来。Don't forget to buy vegetables and bring back some fruits.

他另外又提了几点意见。He gave some more advice.

291 留 liú 〈动〉 (v.) stay

搭配: 留校 to become a teacher after graduation; 留学 to study abroad; 留心 to be aware of; 留客人 to entertain guest

例句: 你今天晚上留下来吃晚饭吧。Would you like to stay here for dinner tonight?

公司想把这些人才留住，所以给他们涨了工资。The company would like to keep these talents and raised their salaries.

292 流利 liúlì 〈形〉 (adj.) smooth, fluent

例句: 你汉语说得真流利，来中国多长时间了？Your Chinese is very fluent. How long have you been in China?

他不仅话说得流利，办事的速度还很快。He not only speaks fluently but also works fast.

293 流行 liúxíng 〈动〉 (v.) prevail, be popular

搭配: 流行病 an epidemic; 流行色 a popular color; 流行音乐 a pop music

例句: 今年春天很流行绿色，要不你也买一件绿色的吧。Green is the popular color in this spring. You should buy a green one.

现在的中学生就爱听流行歌曲。Middle school students like listening to pop music nowadays.

294 乱 luàn 〈形〉/〈副〉 (adj./adv.) messy; random

搭配: 乱说 to speak carelessly; 乱写 to scribble; to doodle; 乱批评人 to make thoughtless remarks

例句: 房间真是太乱了，你快点收拾一下。This room is too messy. You should clean it up soon.

他是乱说的，根本没有发生过这件事情。He talked nonsense. It never happened at all.

Unit 25

295 旅行 lǚxíng (动) (v.) travel, journey, tour

例句：现在外出旅行的人比过去多了。Nowadays people travel much more than before.

我们班要去海边旅行。Our class will make an excursion to the seaside.

296 律师 lǜshī (名) (n.) lawyer, counsel

搭配：原告 / 被告律师 a prosecution counsel/ a counsel for the defense；律师信 a lawyer's letter；请律师 to employ a lawyer

例句：张律师在这里工作了很长时间。Lawyer Zhang has been working here for a long time.

把律师信拿给她看看。Show this lawyer's letter to her.

297 麻烦 máfan (名/形) (n./adj.) trouble; troublesome, inconvenient

搭配：自找麻烦 to bring troubles on oneself；解决麻烦 to tackle with troubles；麻烦的事 a problem

例句：他是一个聪明人，从来不自找麻烦。He is a smart man and never brings troubles on himself.

这真是一件麻烦的工作，他不想做了。It's a real trouble and he doesn't want to do it.

298 马虎 mǎhu (形) (adj.) careless, sloppy

例句：王小明太马虎，这事还是让李刚做吧。Wang Xiaoming is a careless fellow and let Li Gang do it.

王小丽可真够马虎的，这次考试名字都没写。Wang Xiaoli is always so careless that she even forgot to write her name on the exam paper this time.

299 满 mǎn (形/动) (adj./v.) full; fill

例句：教室里坐满了人。The classroom was packed with people.

再过半个月，他就满二十岁了。He will be twenty years old half month later.

别倒酒了，杯子已经满了。Don't pour anymore wine. The glass is full.

300 毛 máo (名/量) (n./m.w.) hair, wool, feather, fur; mao(a fractional unit of money in China, colloq.)

搭配：毛毛虫 a caterpillar；毛衣 sweater；鸡毛 chicken feather；一毛钱 one *mao*

例句：这件毛衣是用羊毛做的，非常暖和。The sweater is made of wool and it's very warm.

苹果三块四毛钱一斤！ The apple is 3 *yuan* and 4 *mao* per *jin*.

实战练习（二十五）

一、听对话，选择正确答案

1. A. 家里　　B. 公司　　C. 超市　　D. 服装店
2. A. 上班　　B. 吃饭　　C. 打电话　　D. 过生日

二、选词填空

A 零钱　B 麻烦　C 旅行　D 乱　E 另外　F 流行

1. 你把桌子上的东西都放到厨房，（　　）再把地扫扫。
2. 你的房间怎么这么（　　）啊？快起来，我帮你收拾收拾。
3. 我钱包里只有一张一百的，没有（　　）了。
4. 我希望有机会到各地去（　　）。
5. A：我来吧。
   B：老是（　　）你，真不好意思。
6. A：今年这本书很（　　），很多人都读过。
   B：那我也买一本吧。

A 毛　B 满　C 马虎　D 律师　E 流利　F 留

7. 别倒了，瓶子里的水已经（　　）了。
8. 这只小狗的（　　）很长。
9. 他能用（　　）的汉语与朋友交流。
10. 李红做事不认真，非常（　　）。
11. A：妈妈，把这些旧衣服都扔了吧。
    B：等一下，把这件（　　）着，还能穿呢！
12. A：（　　）这个工作怎么样？
    B：虽然收入高，但是非常忙。

三、排列顺序

1. A. 否则会很麻烦
   B. 出门旅行的时候
   C. 身上要多带些零钱

2. A. 他学的专业是法律
   B. 所以没当成律师
   C. 但是因为工作太马虎

四、完成句子

1. 找　零钱　这是　您的　_____
2. 换　麻烦　房子　非常　_____
3. 流行　今年　这种　特别　毛衣　_____
4. 你另外　一点儿　准备　得　零钱　_____
5. 怎样　汉语　说一口　才能　流利的　_____

五、看图，用词造句

1. 旅行

2. 满

Unit 26

毛巾	秒
美丽	民族
梦	母亲
迷路	目的
密码	耐心
免费	难道

Unit 26

301 毛巾 máojīn (名) (n.) towel
搭配：一条毛巾 a towel；洗脸毛巾 a hand towel；干/湿毛巾 a dry/ wet towel；毛巾被 a toweling coverlet
例句：明天去超市买条新毛巾吧。Go to supermarket and buy a new towel tomorrow!
这条毛巾是小王的，你用那条干毛巾吧。This towel belongs to Xiao Wang and you can use the dry towel.

302 美丽 měilì (形) (adj.) beautiful
搭配：美丽而聪明 be beautiful and clever；美丽的地方/春天 a beautiful place/ spring
例句：上海是一个既干净又美丽的地方。Shanghai is a clean and beautiful place.
我妈妈年轻时非常美丽。My mother is very beautiful when she was young.

303 梦 mèng (名/动) (n./v.) dream
搭配：在梦里 in the dream；做梦 dream；白日梦 fantasy；梦见 to dream about
例句：昨晚我做了一个很快乐的梦。I had a happy dream last night.
我做梦也没有想到他都快七十岁了。I never dreamed that he is nearly seventy years old.

304 迷路 mílù (动) (v.) lose one's way
例句：这个小孩好像迷路了，找不到回家的路了。The kid seems to lose his way home.
别走得太远，你会迷路的。Don't go too far or you'll get lost.

305 密码 mìmǎ (名) (n.) secret code
搭配：银行卡密码 the code of a credit card；手机密码 the code number of a mobile phone；密码箱 suitcase card
例句：你的密码是多少？ What's your secret code?
一定要记住你的银行卡密码。You must remember the secret code of your bank card.

306 免费 miǎnfèi (动) (v.) free
搭配：免费品尝 a free taste；免费试用 a free trial；免费午餐/门票 a free lunch/ ticket
例句：先生，这些巧克力是免费品尝的，您要不要试试？ Sir, would you like to have a taste of these free sample chocolates?
学生可以拿学生证免费参观北大校史馆。Students can use student ID to have a free visit of Peking University Museum.

307 秒 miǎo 量 (m.w.) second
搭配：一分一秒 every moment；秒表 stopwatch
例句：距离飞机起飞的时间还有五十秒。50 seconds are left before the plane's taking off.
篮球比赛中，即使只剩最后一秒，也不能放弃。In the basketball game, you shall never give up till the last second.

308 民族 mínzú 名 (n.) nationality
搭配：少数民族 national minority；民族精神 national spirit；民族音乐 national music
例句：中国有 56 个民族。There're 56 nationalities in China.
民族精神对于一个民族来讲非常重要。National spirits are very crucial to a nation.

309 母亲 mǔqīn 名 (n.) mother
搭配：我的母亲 my mother；父亲母亲 father and mother
例句：昨天王林的母亲来北京看他了。Wang Lin's mother arrived in Beijing to see him yesterday.
母亲对孩子的爱是不能用语言来表达的。A mother's love for her child is beyond expression.

310 目的 mùdì 名 (n.) goal
搭配：目的地 destination；教学目的 the pedagogical goal；达到目的 to accomplish one's objective；活动目的 purpose of the activity
例句：目的地还没到，车又坏了。The automobile broke before reaching the destination.
你这么做到底有什么目的？What's your purpose in doing so?

311 耐心 nàixīn 形/名 (adj./n.) be patient; patience
例句：教育子女要有耐心，不能着急。To educate a child, we need patience and endurance.
等了一天了，我没有耐心再等了。I had waited all day long. I don't have any more patience.
只要耐心地学，没有什么东西学不会。Nothing is impossible as long as you're patient enough.

312 难道 nándào 副 (adv.) (use to reinforce a rhetorical question)
例句：都晚上 12 点了，难道你还不困吗？It's twelve o'clock already. Don't you feel sleepy?
门口有个行李箱，难道是爸爸回来了？There's a luggage in front of the door. Could it be that father came back?
他能学会跳舞，难道我就学不会吗？He can dance. Could it be impossible for me to learn it?
太阳难道会从西边出来吗？How can the pig fly!

实战练习（二十六）

一、听对话，选择正确答案

1. A. 很贵　　B. 该洗了　　C. 很漂亮　　D. 不是买的
2. A. 换工作　B. 改掉坏习惯　C. 不要麻烦他　D. 多做事少说话

二、选词填空

A 迷路　B 秒　C 毛巾　D 目的　E 密码　F 梦

1. 这条（　　）质量很好，用起来非常舒服。
2. 我做（　　）也没有想到，你竟然是他姐姐。
3. 他跑完 100 米只用了 11（　　）。
4. 妈妈这么做的（　　）是让小明养成早睡早起的好习惯。
5. A：你怎么还没到啊？
   B：我好像（　　）了。
6. A：你的银行卡（　　）是 789493 吗？
   B：不是，我前天改了。

A 母亲　B 免费　C 难道　D 民族　E 耐心　F 美丽

7. 在我心中，母亲是世界上最（　　）的女人。
8. 每一个（　　）都有它特有的生活习惯。
9. 我已经失去（　　）了，不等了。
10. 这么简单的事情（　　）你都做不好吗？
11. A：你好，请问这瓶洗发水怎么卖？
    B：这是我们公司的新产品，正在做（　　）试用活动。
12. A：（　　）是世界上对我们最好的人。
    B：所以我们长大后要好好儿爱她。

三、排列顺序

1. A. 擦掉母亲脸上的泪水
   B. 在我心中有一个美丽的梦
   C. 希望我可以变成一条毛巾

2. A. 就要改掉马虎这种坏习惯
   B. 想要养成这种好习惯
   C. 优秀是一种习惯

四、完成句子

1. 是 国家 教育 的 这个 免费的 _____
2. 马虎的 笔记本电脑的 小红 密码 忘记了 _____
3. 昨晚我 地方 梦到了 美丽的 一个 _____
4. 他的 把 洗干净 毛巾 目的是 _____
5. 吗 是 迷路了 难道 _____

五、看图，用词造句

1. 美丽

2. 密码

Unit 27

难受	暖和
内	偶尔
内容	排队
能力	排列
年龄	判断
弄	陪

313 难受 nánshòu (adj.) uncomfortable, sad

搭配： 非常难受 be very uncomfortable；心里难受 to feel sad

例句： 看见她流泪，我心里也很难受。I also felt sad when I saw her tears.
听到这句话，我难受极了。I felt very bad when I heard these words.
他病了，全身疼得难受。He was ill and ached here and there.

314 内 nèi (n.) inside

搭配： 内部 the internal part；内心 inner heart；市内 downtown；十年内 in ten years；国内 at home；内衣 underwear

例句： 请不要在办公室内抽烟。Please don't smoke in the office.
请你在三个月内把这些书看完。Please read these books over in three months.

315 内容 nèiróng (n.) content

搭配： 主要内容 the main content；全部内容 all contents；内容丰富 be abundant in content

例句： 你能说说这本书的主要内容吗？Can you say something about the main content of this book?
这些是今天上午开会的全部内容，请您看看。Here are all the contents of today's morning meeting. Please have a look.

316 能力 nénglì (n.) ability

搭配： 个人能力 personal ability；读写能力 literacy；学习能力 learning ability；工作能力很强 be very competent

例句： 这份工作主要看你的个人能力，其他的都不重要。This work mainly depends on your personal ability, and anything else is secondary.
你的表达能力很好，这次演讲就你参加吧。You are very fluently in expressing yourself, so this time you are going to attend the speech contest.

317 年龄 niánlíng (n.) age

搭配： 年龄大/小 older/younger；心理年龄 psychological age；结婚年龄 marriageable age

例句： 这个人年龄不大，但看上去很老。This person is young but looks older than his age.
他今年6岁了，已经到了入学年龄。He is six years old and is old enough for school.

318 弄 nòng (v.) play, manage

搭配： 弄坏 to ruin；弄丢 to lose；弄错 to misunderstand/ to make a mistake；弄清楚 to make clear

例句： 小明把家里的钥匙弄丢了。Xiaoming lost the key to his home.
那把椅子是我弄坏的。I broke that chair.
小孩儿爱弄沙土。Little kids are fond of playing with sands.
请帮我弄点儿水来。Please fetch me some water.

Unit 27

319 暖和 nuǎnhuo (adj.) warm
例句：这几天天气很暖和。It is very warm these days.
快到屋里来暖和暖和。Come in and warm yourself.

320 偶尔 ǒu'ěr (adv./adj.) occasionally; once in a while
例句：农村的晚上很安静，偶尔能听到一两声狗叫声。It is very quiet in rural area at night, and one can occasionally hear a few dog barks.
我平时自己做饭，偶尔也出去吃。I usually cook by myself and occasionally eat out.
我们偶尔见面。We saw each other once in a while.

321 排队 páiduì (v.) line up, queue up
搭配：排队参观 to line up for a visit；排队买票 to line up to buy tickets；排队上车 to get on the bus by turn
例句：请大家排队上车，我送大家回宾馆休息。Please line up to get into the bus, and follow me to the hotel and have a rest.
很多人在排队买火车票。A crowd is queuing up to buy railway tickets.

322 排列 páiliè (v.) rank, put in order, arrange
搭配：排列顺序 to put in order；排列大小 to arrange according to size
例句：十几名学生排列在学校门口两旁，欢迎外国朋友的到来。A dozen of pupils were lining up at both sides of the school gate, welcoming our foreign friends.
飞机整齐地排列在飞机场上。Airplanes are orderly arranged on the parking apron.

323 判断 pànduàn (n./v.) judgment; judge
搭配：判断题 true or false telling；判断错误 to identify the error；判断好坏 to judge right from wrong；正确的判断 a right judgment
例句：请大家自己做出判断。Please judge by your own opinion.
不能根据外表判断一个人的能力。We can't judge a person's ability by his appearance.

324 陪 péi (v.) accompany
搭配：陪伴 to keep sb accompany；陪客人 to take care of the guest / accompany the guests
例句：我今天下午要陪他去医院看医生。I'll accompany him to see a doctor in hospital.
张丽这几十年都陪在他身边。Zhang Li has been accompanying him for several decades.

实战练习（二十七）

一、听对话，选择正确答案

1. A. 夫妻　　B. 母子　　C. 同事　　D. 师生
2. A. 老师　　B. 医生　　C. 律师　　D. 司机

二、选词填空

A 排队　B 内容　C 偶尔　D 能力　E 弄　F 判断

1. 请大家把这节课的主要（　　）记在笔记本上。
2. 这道（　　）题是对是错啊？
3. 他汉语的听说（　　）很好，应该能在比赛中得奖。
4. 买车票的人很多，都在（　　）呢！
5. A：你不是骑自行车出去的吗？怎么走着回来了？
   B：我不小心把自行车（　　）丢了。
6. A：你经常带孩子去动物园玩吗？
   B：不是，我只是（　　）带他去看看。

A 陪　B 排列　C 内　D 暖和　E 难受　F 年龄

7. 我上午感觉很难受，班长（　　）我去医院了。
8. 包括我在（　　），这里一共有九个人。
9. 等过段时间天气（　　）了，我再带你去看奶奶。
10. 这些人（　　）都比较大，你要有礼貌。
11. A：请你（　　）出这几句话的正确顺序。
    B：好的，没有问题。
12. A：小红，你怎么了？
    B：我肚子（　　），一定是早上吃错东西了。

三、排列顺序

1. A. 想要做对这道排列顺序题
   B. 否则是找不出正确答案的
   C. 就必须要有耐心

2. A. 好像很难受的样子
   B. 他们走得都非常快
   C. 偶尔有几个人从这个化工厂经过

四、完成句子

1. 请你　看完　这些内容　把　耐心地 _____
2. 肯定　以你的　翻译好　能力　这篇文章　没有问题 _____
3. 他们　难道　谈话的　你不知道　内容 _____
4. 弄丢了　特别难受　手机　我心里　妈妈送的 _____
5. 我　中国朋友　陪着　去　办签证 _____

五、看图，用词造句

1. 难受

2. 陪

Unit 28

批评	平时
皮肤	破
脾气	葡萄
篇	普遍
骗	普通话
乒乓球	其次

Unit 28

325 批评 pīpíng (v.) criticize
- 搭配：自我批评 self-criticism；表扬与批评 commend and criticism；受到批评 to accept criticism；批评教育 criticism and education
- 例句：你不要批评小丽了，她不小心才把钥匙弄丢的。Don't criticize Xiaoli anymore. She lost the key unintentionally.
  懂得自我批评的人更容易打开成功的大门。Those who understand self-criticism are easy to gain access to success.

326 皮肤 pífū (n.) skin
- 搭配：皮肤好 to have a good skin；皮肤黑 to have a dark skin；保护皮肤 to protect the skin；皮肤病 skin diseases
- 例句：你女儿的皮肤真白，好看极了。Your daughter is very good-looking with her fair skin.
  我的皮肤不好，缺少水分。My skin condition is not good enough for the lack of water.

327 脾气 píqi (n.) temper
- 搭配：脾气好/坏 to have a good/bad temper；发脾气 to go into a temper；脾气大 be bad-tempered；牛脾气 stubbornness
- 例句：一个人脾气的好坏与他的家人和朋友有很大的关系。A person's temper closely relates to his family and friends.
  这个孩子老对父母发脾气。The child is always bad-tempered to his parents.

328 篇 piān (m.w.) piece of writing
- 搭配：一篇文章 an essay；一篇小说 a novel
- 例句：这篇文章写得很精彩。This article is very wonderful.
  我认识这篇文章的作者。I know the author of this article.

329 骗 piàn (v.) cheat, deceive
- 搭配：骗人 to cheat sb；骗子 a cheater；受骗 to rise to the bait；骗钱 to trick sb out of his money
- 例句：他在骗你呢，你真容易被骗。He is cheating you. You're easy to rise to the bait.
  你就是一个骗子，我再也不相信你了。You're a liar. I don't believe you anymore.

330 乒乓球 pīngpāngqiú (n.) table tennis, ping-pong
- 搭配：打乒乓球 to play ping-pong；乒乓球比赛 a match of ping-pong；一只乒乓球 a table tennis；乒乓球桌/拍 a table tennis table/bat
- 例句：他过去是一位乒乓球运动员。He was a ping-pong player once.
  昨晚的那场乒乓球比赛很精彩，你看了吗？Did you watch the exciting game of table tennis last night?

331 平时 píngshí (n.) normal times, the usual time

例句：张静平时喜欢上网，还经常在网上买东西。Zhang Jing likes surfing and net shopping.
在平时的工作中，他的表现一直都很优秀。He always does well in daily work.

332 破 pò (v./adj.) break; broken

搭配：破坏 to destroy；破开 to break off；破旧 be worn out；打破 to break down；破东西 a broken thing

例句：破坏东西是小孩子的天性。To break things is children's nature.
这个桌子又破又旧，怎么会这么贵呢？Why is this old and shabby table so expensive?
我的衣服破了一个洞。There's a hole in my clothes.

333 葡萄 pútao (n.) grape

搭配：葡萄干 raisins；葡萄酒 wine；葡萄糖 glucose

例句：这种葡萄汁很好喝。This kind of grape juice tastes very good.
我喜欢吃黑葡萄。I like black grape.

334 普遍 pǔbiàn (adj.) universal

搭配：普遍现象 common phenomenon；普遍意义 universal meanings；普遍问题 issue of universal

例句：迟到问题在员工当中很普遍。Being late is a common problem among staff.
大家普遍认为这个小区的环境很差。People generally hold that the environment of this community is not good enough.

335 普通话 pǔtōnghuà (n.) Mandarin, Putonghua

例句：我会说普通话，也会说方言。I can speak both in Putonghua and in dialect.
他普通话说得很标准。He speaks standard Putonghua.

336 其次 qícì (pron.) next, secondary

搭配：首先……，其次……，再其次……，最后…… first..., secondly..., third...., at last...

例句：俄罗斯是全世界面积最大的国家，其次是加拿大。Russia, followed by Canada, is the largest country in the world.
首先确定出差人员，其次再考虑出发时间。First, we need to determine the business staff, and then to think about the departure time.

实战练习(二十八)

一、听对话,选择正确答案

1. A. 做题　　　　B. 穿袜子　　　　C. 买东西　　　　D. 洗衣服
2. A. 经常迟到　　B. 弄破了衣服　　C. 经常发脾气　　D. 不会打乒乓球

二、选词填空

A 其次　B 篇　C 批评　D 破　E 乒乓球　F 脾气

1. 你不要动不动就（　　）孩子,他会没信心的。
2. 爱发（　　）的人非常容易变老。
3. 请你把桌子上的那（　　）文章翻译成汉语。
4. 我把（　　）的地方补好了,你看还能穿吗?
5. A:什么对您最重要?
   B:首先是家庭,（　　）是健康。
6. A:你平时都喜欢做什么运动?
   B:打打（　　）,游游泳。你呢?

A 骗　B 葡萄　C 普遍　D 平时　E 普通话　F 皮肤

7. 这种现象很（　　）,你不要担心,这不会影响商品的使用。
8. 我只喝（　　）酒,不喝白酒。
9. 我（　　）不会一个人去树林里散步,除非心情非常不好的时候。
10. （　　）人是一种非常不好的行为。
11. A:你怎么不说广东话啊?
    B:来中国当然得学（　　）啊。
12. A:你的（　　）怎么这么红啊?
    B:刚才喝了点儿酒,吹吹风就好了。

三、排列顺序

1. A. 如果这周六你没事的话
   B. 或者去超市买点葡萄什么的
   C. 陪我到万事达广场去看画展吧

2. A. 今天早上怎么会破了呢
   B. 一定是家里的猫弄的
   C. 昨天晚上这个瓶子还好好儿的

四、完成句子

1. 骗子　是坏人　不会说　永远　自己 _____
2. 有很多　那个　瓶子里　漂亮的　彩色的乒乓球 _____
3. 一篇　这是　批评　的　文章　乒乓球运动员 _____
4. 发脾气　他　在这么多人　从来不　面前 _____
5. 小红陪我　都是　乒乓球比赛的　去看　平时 _____

五、看图，用词造句

1. 乒乓球

2. 批评

Unit 29

其中	巧克力
气候	亲戚
千万	轻
签证	轻松
敲	情况
桥	穷

337 其中 qízhōng (名) (n.) within, among/ of them
搭配：其中的原因 the reason for；其中的一段 one of the chapters
例句：收到我寄给你的书了吗？其中有一章是写你的。Have you received the book I sent to you? One of the articles is about you.
我们班有十个人，其中一半是男的。There're ten students in our class. Half of them are boys.

338 气候 qìhòu (名) (n.) climate
搭配：气候干燥/湿润 a damp/ humid/dry/arid climate；气候寒冷/温暖 a frigid/warm climate；全球气候变暖 Global Warming；政治气候 a political climate
例句：这里的气候很湿润，适合植物生长。The climate here is humid and suitable for plants' growth.
南极气候非常寒冷。The climate in Antarctic is frigid.

339 千万 qiānwàn (副) (adv.) be sure to
例句：电梯出问题的时候千万别着急。Don't be anxious when the elevator is malfunctioning.
千万别忘了明天的考试。Don't ever forget the exam tomorrow.
过马路的时候千万要小心。Be careful when you cross the street.

340 签证 qiānzhèng (动) (v.) visa
搭配：办签证 to grant a visa；拿签证 to get a visa；等候签证 to wait for visa；签证材料 documents for visa application
例句：我的签证还没办下来，不能按计划出国了。My visa was not granted. I can't go abroad as planned.
我下午去大使馆办签证。 I will go to the embassy to get the visa in the afternoon.

341 敲 qiāo (动) (v.) knock
搭配：敲门 to knock on the door；敲桌子 to tap at the desk
例句：小李，进门前请你先敲门。Xiao Li, please knock on the door before coming in.
听了小张的话后，王经理敲了敲桌子，这说明经理现在非常生气。After listening to Xiao Zhang, Manager Wang expressed his anger by tapping the desk a few times.

342 桥 qiáo (名) (n.) bridge
搭配：木桥 wooden bridge；立交桥 flyover；长江大桥 the Yangtze River Bridge；过街天桥 overpass
例句：河水在桥下安静地流着。The river glides through the bridge silently.
立交桥上又堵车了。There's again a traffic jam on the flyover.

Unit 29

343 巧克力 qiǎokèlì (n.) chocolate

搭配：黑巧克力 black chocolates；白巧克力 pure chocolates；巧克力蛋糕 a chocolate cake；一颗巧克力 a piece of chocolate；巧克力冰激凌 chocolate icecream

例句：我不喜欢吃巧克力。I don't like eating chocolates.
情人节那天，很多人送巧克力做礼物。Chocolates are frequently given as a gift on Valentine's Day.

344 亲戚 qīnqi (n.) relative, relation

搭配：亲戚朋友 relatives and friends；走亲戚 to visit relatives；一门亲戚 a set of relatives；亲戚关系 the relationship between relatives

例句：李红不在家，走亲戚去了。Li Hong is visiting a relative and not at home.
他在北京的亲戚不多，只有一个叔叔。He has no other relatives in Beijing but an uncle.

345 轻 qīng (adj.) light

搭配：轻轻地 lightly；轻拿轻放 to handle gently；轻音乐 a light music；病得不轻 badly ill；年纪轻 young

例句：他走路很轻，进来的时候我都没有发现。He walked lightly, even I didn't notice him entering the room.
你还年纪轻，不用着急找女朋友。You are young and there's no hurry for a girlfriend.

346 轻松 qīngsōng (adj.) light, relaxed

搭配：轻松的工作 a piece of cake；轻松轻松 to have a relaxation；放轻松 be at ease

例句：你不要紧张，放轻松，不会有事的。Don't be so nervous. Relax and it will be fine.
他轻轻松松就把这道题做出来了。He breezed through this question.

347 情况 qíngkuàng (n.) situation, condition

搭配：紧急情况 an emergency；在……情况下 under the situation of...；交通情况 the traffic；新情况 new situation；情况复杂 a complex situation

例句：遇到紧急情况就打110。Calling 110 when encountering an emergency.
在那种危险情况下，我只想赶快跑回家。I only wanted to run home quickly under that dangerous situation.

348 穷 qióng (adj.) poor

搭配：穷人 the poor；穷苦 poverty-stricken；穷开心 be happy without ground

例句：穷人有穷人的活法，你们这些富人是不能理解的。The rich cannot understand the life of the poor.
虽然生活很穷苦，但她从来没有放弃希望。She never gives up hopes, even if life is hard.

实战练习（二十九）

一、听对话，选择正确答案

1. A. 父女　　　　B. 夫妻　　　　C. 同事　　　　D. 师生
2. A. 在洗水果　　B. 要过生日　　C. 来参加晚会　　D. 喜欢吃蛋糕

二、选词填空

A 轻　B 签证　C 亲戚　D 轻松　E 情况　F 气候

1. 你的（　　）什么时候下来，我等你一起出国。
2. 他平时学习认真，所以考试很（　　）。
3. （　　）点儿放，别摔坏了。
4. 这里的（　　）非常好，我想在这儿买套房子。
5. A：吃巧克力的那个人是谁啊？
   B：她是我的一个（　　），来上海出差的。
6. A：现在公司的（　　）怎么样？
   B：还不错。

A 巧克力　B 穷　C 敲　D 其中　E 桥　F 千万

7. 这座（　　）已经有很多年的历史了。
8. 你（　　）不要把这件事告诉别人。
9. 进我办公室请先（　　）门。
10. 天太热了，（　　）都快化了。
11. A：这个小孩儿家里很（　　），父母没有钱让他继续上学。
    B：真可怜。要不我们帮帮他吧。
12. A：你觉得这套房子怎么样？
    B：很好，我非常喜欢（　　）那间向阳的卧室。

三、排列顺序

1. A. 其次再想解决的办法
   B. 面对困难
   C. 首先要保持冷静

2. A. 等我穿好衣服打开门
   B. 发现你已经走了
   C. 你敲门的时候我还没有起来

四、完成句子

1. 签证　千万不要　把　家里　丢在 _____
2. 看上去　一座小桥　这种巧克力　很像 _____
3. 气候　我的亲戚　这里的　不喜欢 _____
4. 请在　把手机　飞机起飞前　关上 _____
5. 墙上的　妈妈　那些相片　都是　照的 _____

五、看图，用词造句

1. 巧克力

2. 敲

Unit 30

区别　　　　确实
取　　　　　然而
全部　　　　热闹
缺点　　　　任何
缺少　　　　任务
却　　　　　扔

Unit 30

349 区别 qūbié （名/动）(n./v.) difference; distinguish
搭配：有区别 to have a difference；区别好坏 to distinguish right from wrong
例句：这两台电脑区别不大，都不错。There's no big differences between the two computers and they are both good.
这两个词有什么区别？What's the difference between the two words?

350 取 qǔ （动）(v.) take, obtain, withdraw
搭配：取钱 / 信 / 行李 to take money/ letter/luggage；取出来 to take out
例句：我在银行取钱呢，你过来找我吧。I'm withdrawing some money at the bank. Come here to find me.
我们最后取得了比赛第一名。We finally gained a first prize in the game.

351 全部 quánbù （名）(n.) all
搭配：全部内容 all contents；全部想法 entire thoughts；全部的收入 entire income
例句：这次考试我们全部不及格。All of us failed the exam.
问题已经全部解决了。All the problems have been solved.

352 缺点 quēdiǎn （名）(n.) defect, disadvantage, shortcoming
搭配：优点与缺点 merits and defects；改正缺点 to correct one's shortcoming；克服缺点 to overcome one's defects
例句：有缺点就要及时改正。Disadvantages should be correct promptly.
人无完人，谁都会有缺点。No one is perfect and without shortcomings.
他的缺点就是太骄傲。Pride swell his heart and that's his shortcoming.

353 缺少 quēshǎo （动）(v.) lack
搭配：缺少耐心 be lack of patience；缺少雨水 be lack of rain；缺少经验 be lack of experience
例句：因为缺少技术方面的人才，经理计划开场招聘会。For lacking of technical personnel, the manager planned to hold a new round of recruitment.
他失败的主要原因是缺少经验。His main reason of failure is the lack of experiences.

354 却 què （副）(adv.) but, yet
搭配：虽然……却……despite...
例句：他虽然年纪很大了，身体却十分健康。He was old but healthy.
谁都没想到事情最后却变成了这个样子。No one expected that things would eventually end like this.

355 确实 quèshí （副）(adv.) truely, in deed
例句：事实确实如此，他没有骗你。This is the truth and he didn't lie to you.

花瓶确实不是我打破的，你可以问爸爸。Actually I didn't break the vase. You can ask father about it.

这件事确实不是他干的。It's really not he who did this.

356 然而 rán'ér (conj.) however

搭配：虽然（尽管）……然而…… however...

例句：我以为事情就这样结束了，然而这只是一个开始。I think the matter is over, however, it's just the beginning.

已经是春天了，然而最近天气比冬天还冷。It's already spring now, but the recent weather is colder than winter.

357 热闹 rènao (adj./v.) lively; full of activity

搭配：热热闹闹 lively；热闹的地方 a noisy place

例句：今天公司门口非常热闹，好像来了一位明星。It is very crowded outside the company entrance. It seems like a star has come here.

春节到了，亲戚朋友喜欢在一起热闹热闹。The Spring Festival is coming. Relatives and friends like to have a lively party.

358 任何 rènhé (pron.) any

搭配：任何时候 anytime；任何人 / 地方 / 问题 any person/ place/ problem；任何情况下 in any situation

例句：任何情况下，我们都不能忘记关心父母。In any case, we shouldn't forget to show concern and love to our parents.

任何时候我们都不能丢掉自己内心的理想。At any time, we can't lose our own ideals.

359 任务 rènwu (n.) task, assignment

搭配：安排任务 to allot an assignment；完成任务 to finish/complete a task；接受任务 to accept a task

例句：王经理还没有给我们安排任务，不要着急。Don't hurry. Manager Wang hasn't allotted us any assignments yet.

这项任务你必须在这个月底之前完成。You must finish this task by the end of this month.

360 扔 rēng (v.) throw, litter

搭配：扔垃圾 to litter；扔掉 to throw away；乱扔 to leave about

例句：手上的纸别扔掉，上面有重要的号码。Don't throw that piece of paper away. There's an important number on it.

请不要把垃圾扔到地上，这会影响公园的环境。No littering, otherwise it will ruin the park's environment.

实战练习（三十）

一、听对话，选择正确答案

1. A. 男的错了　　B. 任务很难　　C. 李平很优秀　　D. 工作没做完
2. A. 要去上海　　B. 喜欢男的　　C. 没完成任务　　D. 出差回来了

二、选词填空

A 然而　B 全部　C 取　D 却　E 缺少　F 区别

1. 大家觉得王东已经很优秀了，（　　）他自己并不这么认为。
2. 这个学校（　　）老师，有的老师一个人带三四个班。
3. 这是我身上（　　）的钱，都给你！
4. 我想吃完饭再去逛街，她（　　）希望逛完街再吃饭。
5. A：这两件衣服是一样的，只是颜色上有（　　）。
   B：我不喜欢红色，还是买那件绿色的吧。
6. A：你什么时候来办公室（　　）表格？
   B：明天上午十点吧。

A 确实　B 热闹　C 任务　D 任何　E 扔　F 缺点

7. （　　）人都不能让我放弃自己的理想。
8. 我（　　）不认识这个人，你不相信也没有办法。
9. 小兰最大的（　　）就是没有耐心。
10. 请不要随地乱（　　）垃圾。
11. A：你家里真（　　）！
    B：是啊，我家来了很多亲戚，现在大家正在吃饭呢！
12. A：你知道经理会给我们什么（　　）吗？
    B：不知道，但不管他让我们做什么，我相信我们都可以做好。

三、排列顺序

1. A. 李明这个人平时很马虎
   B. 然而关键时刻总能想出好点子
   C. 我看你把这个任务交给他肯定没错

2. A. 获得事业的成功
　　B. 但有的人却能把缺点改掉
　　C. 每个人都有缺点

四、完成句子

1. 很难　确实　这个任务　经理　交给　我们的 _____
2. 热闹的　他　记得　仍然　那个　生日晚会 _____
3. 这群　任何事情　难不住　都　年轻人 _____
4. 耐心　他的　缺少　缺点　是 _____
5. 昨天我　真的　那些人民币　确实是　给你的 _____

五、看图，用词造句

1. 热闹

2. 扔

Unit 31

仍然	伤心
日记	商量
入口	稍微
散步	勺子
森林	社会
沙发	申请

361　仍然 réngrán　(adv.)　still

例句：张丽仍然记得小时候唱过的歌。Zhang Li still remembers the song she sang when she was young.
毕业十年了，王东仍然单身。Wang Dong is still single ten years after graduation.
这些问题仍然没有解决。These problems still remain.

362　日记 rìjì　(n.)　diary

搭配：写/记日记 to keep a diary；日记本 a diary book
例句：你的日记本真好看，在哪里买的呀？Where did you buy this good-looking diary book?
我养成了每天记日记的好习惯。I have a good habit of writing diary everyday.

363　入口 rùkǒu　(n.)　entrance

搭配：超市入口 a supermarket entrance；入口处 entrance
例句：别把车停在入口处。Don't park your car at the entrance.
看到入口的那张广告了吗？Do you see the advertisement at the entrance?

364　散步 sànbù　(v.)　have a walk

搭配：散散步 to take/have a walk；出去散步 to go out for a walk；饭后散步 to take a walk after dinner
例句：天气太冷了，我不想出去散步。I don't want to walk outside. It's too cold.
陪我到公园散散步吧。Would you like to accompany me to have a walk in the park?

365　森林 sēnlín　(n.)　forest

搭配：一片森林 a forest；森林大火 forest fires；保护森林 forest protection
例句：政府应当扩大森林面积，增加森林资源。The government should expand forest coverage and increase forest resources.
森林里禁止使用明火。Open flame is strictly prohibited in the forest.

366　沙发 shāfā　(n.)　sofa

搭配：一对沙发 a pair of armchairs；单人沙发（upholstered）armchair；搬沙发 to move a sofa；沙发床 a sofa bed
例句：这个沙发很好看，是从哪儿买的呀？Where did you buy this good-looking sofa?
你先在沙发上坐会儿，我去给你洗水果。Please feel free to take a seat on the sofa. I'm washing some fruits for you.

Unit 31

367 伤心 shāngxīn (adj.) broken-hearted, sad
- 搭配：伤透了心 to be heart-broken；伤心落泪 to weep in grief；伤心而死 to die of a broken heart
- 例句：考试没考好，李红很伤心。Li Hong is very sad about the bad result of the exam.
  小狗丢了，东东伤心得直掉眼泪。Dongdong, who lost his little dog, wept in grief.

368 商量 shāngliang (v.) discuss
- 搭配：商量商量 to talk over；共同商量 to take counsel together
- 例句：我觉得这件事你可以找爸爸商量一下。I think you could have a discussion with your father about this matter.
  我们在商量事情，你把电视声音关小一点。Please turn down of the TV. We're discussing some issues.

369 稍微 shāowēi (adv.) a little bit
- 搭配：稍微不同 be slightly different；稍微有点儿大 / 小 a little bit big/ small
- 例句：最左边的男孩子，你稍微往右一点。The boy on the left, please move a little bit right.
  这双鞋稍微有点儿小，请帮我换双大点儿的。The size of this pair of shoes is a little bit small. Please change a bigger pair for me.

370 勺子 sháozi (n.) spoon
- 搭配：一把勺子 a spoon；木勺子 wooden spoons；小勺子 a small spoon
- 例句：中国人一般用勺子喝汤。Chinese usually have soup with spoons.
  我吃饭喜欢用勺子，不喜欢用筷子。I like eating with spoon instead of chopsticks.

371 社会 shèhuì (n.) society
- 搭配：社会环境 social environment；社会关系 social relationship；社会新闻 social news
- 例句：他的社会关系很复杂，你少和他来往。His social relation is very complicated. You'd better leave him alone.
  欢迎收看社会新闻。Thank you for watching social news.

372 申请 shēnqǐng (v.) apply for
- 搭配：申请书 / 表 / 信 an application; an application form / letter；申请出国 to apply for studying abroad；申请护照 / 签证 to apply for a passport/visa
- 例句：我想申请加入销售部。I would like to apply to join the sales department.
  来中国留学可以申请奖学金。Overseas students can apply for a scholarship while studying in China.

实战练习（三十一）

一、听对话，选择正确答案

1. A. 结婚　　B. 留学　　C. 工作　　D. 考研究生
2. A. 搬家时间　　B. 哪个房间亮　　C. 今晚谁做饭　　D. 沙发放在哪儿

二、选词填空

A 仍然　B 散步　C 森林　D 申请　E 勺子　F 社会

1. 在（　　）深处有一条小河，小河里有很多鱼游来游去。
2. 喝汤得用（　　）。
3. 人口出生率低在发达国家是个普遍的（　　）问题。
4. 这么多年过去了，他（　　）是那么浪漫。
5. A：你（　　）去总公司的材料通过了吗？
   B：不知道，通知还没有下来。
6. A：昨天陪你在公园（　　）的那个人是谁呀？
   B：是我同事，来找我谈工作上的事。

A 入口　B 伤心　C 稍微　D 日记　E 商量　F 沙发

7. 我每天都记（　　）。
8. 你稍微往那边坐一点，我都快从（　　）上掉下去了。
9. 时间快来不及了，你就不能（　　）快一点儿吗？
10. 奶奶去世了，小丽现在很（　　）。
11. A：老王，你说我到底该不该把这件事告诉小丽？
    B：我也不知道，要不你和张红（　　）一下。
12. A：请问去森林公园怎么走最近？
    B：前边就有一个（　　）。

三、排列顺序

1. A. 每一个生命就像是一棵树
   B. 才能成为森林中美丽的一景
   C. 只有经过风雨

2. A. 因为我还需要和张教授商量商量再做决定
   B. 你先回去等消息吧
   C. 关于你申请出国这件事

四、完成句子

1. 申请书　小红　沙发上　正坐在　写 _____
2. 稍微　会　颜色　更好看　我觉得　深一点儿 _____
3. 养成了　写日记的　李红　习惯 _____
4. 买　哪个沙发　他们　没商量好　最后也 _____
5. 散散步　你陪我　那片　去　森林　吧 _____

五、看图，用词造句

1. 散步

2. 森林

Unit 32

深	剩
甚至	失败
生活	失望
生命	师傅
生意	十分
省	实际

Unit 32

373 深 shēn (adj.) dark

搭配：深颜色 a dark color；感情深 deep feelings / affection；深深的 deep；深信 / 知 be deeply convinced / know very well

例句：这条河很深，小孩子在这里玩非常危险。It is very dangerous for children to play along this deep river.
你最好穿一条深色的裙子。You'd better wear a dark-colored skirt.

374 甚至 shènzhì (conj.) even

搭配：甚至连……也（都）…… so much so that；甚至于 even to the extent that...

例句：她没上过学，甚至连名字都不会写。She has never attended a school and even can't write down her own name.
老龄化是中国甚至世界性的难题。Aging population is not only a national but also a worldwide problem.
他甚至没说再见就走了。He left without even saying goodbye.

375 生活 shēnghuó (n./v.) life; live

搭配：感情生活 emotional life；生活条件 life condition；留学生活 life of studying abroad；生活水平 living level

例句：他们的感情生活出现了一些问题。They have some problem with their emotional life.
和李奶奶在一起生活我感到很快乐。I feel very glad to live with Grandma Li.

376 生命 shēngmìng (n.) life

搭配：热爱生命 to cherish life；保护生命 to protect life；一条生命 a life

例句：这只小狗也是一条生命，我们要好好儿对它。This puppy is also a creature, we should be kind to it.
生命只有一次，要认真过好生命中的每一天。Every person only has one life, so we should treat every day seriously.

377 生意 shēngyi (n.) business, trade

搭配：做生意 be engaged in business；放弃生意 to quit the business；影响生意 to affect one's business

例句：他在这笔生意中赚了 10000 美元。He earned 10, 000 dollars in pocket by the transaction.
他与朋友们合伙做生意。He carried on the business in combination with his friends.

378 省 shěng (n./v.) province; save

搭配：山东 / 湖北 / 江苏省 Shandong/ Hubei/ Jiangsu Province；省会 the capital city of a province；省内 in the province of...；省时间 to save time；省事 to save trouble；省钱 to save money

例句：石家庄是河北省的省会。Shijiazhuang is the capital city of Hebei Province.

不如你坐我的车去吧，这样能省很多时间。How about I drive you there? In this way you can save a lot of time.

379 剩 shèng (动) (v.) leave, remain

搭配：剩下 be left (over)；剩菜 leftovers；剩饭 leftovers

例句：从小爷爷就告诉我即使不喜欢吃也不能剩饭。When I was young, my grandfather always taught me that I should not leave any food uneaten, even if I don't like it.

这是昨天办晚会剩下的钱，你收起来吧。Here's the rest of money after holding yesterday's evening party. You can keep it.

380 失败 shībài (动) (v.) fail, lose

搭配：失败的人 / 事 a loser/ failure；成功与失败 success and failure；失败者 a loser

例句：失败是成功之母。Failure is the mother of success.

比赛虽然失败了，但我们仍然有信心。Although we lost this match, we still have confidence.

381 失望 shīwàng (形/动) (adj./v.) disappointed; disappoint

搭配：表示失望 to express one's disappointment；感到失望 be disappointed at / about

例句：他失望地走下台，消失在了人群中。He went down stage disappointedly and soon disappeared in the crowd.

我对你很失望，你怎么能骗我呢？How can you lie to me? I feel so disappointed about you.

382 师傅 shīfu (名) (n.) master worker

搭配：司机 / 工人师傅 a master of driving/ a master worker；李 / 王 / 张师傅 Master Li/ Wang/ Zhang；修车师傅 a garageman

例句：张师傅，你给看看我这车是怎么回事。Master Zhang, would you please take a look at my car?

师傅，请你开慢一点。Hey Mister, please drive slowly.

383 十分 shífēn (副) (adv.) very

搭配：十分好看 be very good-looking；十分快乐 be very happy

例句：这个手机十分好看，而且价格也很便宜。This mobile phone is very good-looking and cheap.

小丽是一个十分有趣的人，大家都喜欢她。Xiaoli is a very interesting girl and she is popular among us.

384 实际 shíjì (名/形) (n./adj.) reality; practical

搭配：实际上 as a matter of fact；不实际 impractical；注重实际 down-to-earth；实际情况 practical situation；联系实际 to link with reality

例句：实际上，我根本就不认识那个人，他只是在问路。Actually, I don't know that person at all. He just asked me for some directions.

他是一个很注重实际的人，从来不做白日梦。He is a practical man and never daydreams.

实战练习（三十二）

一、听对话，选择正确答案

1. A. 家里　　　　B. 车上　　　　C. 超市　　　　D. 动物园
2. A. 面条　　　　B. 米饭　　　　C. 包子　　　　D. 饼干

二、选词填空

A 十分　B 生命　C 失败　D 深　E 省　F 生活

1. 在我的（　　　）中，父母最重要。
2. 这里水太（　　　），别在这儿游泳。
3. 在哪里（　　　），就要在哪里站起来。
4. 李红今天穿得（　　　）漂亮。
5. A：老人在这里（　　　）得很好，你们不用担心。
   B：谢谢你一直照顾妈妈。
6. A：这些食品是从哪个（　　　）运过来的？
   B：山东。有问题吗？

A 剩　B 实际　C 失望　D 甚至　E 生意　F 师傅

7. 我没想到你会不好好儿学习，实在是太让我（　　　）了。
8. （　　　），请问这个城市都有哪些有名的小吃呀？
9. 你还（　　　）多少钱，够买这箱酸奶吗？
10. （　　　）上我并不知道你是什么时候离开的。
11. 他让所有人都很失望，（　　　）包括他的父母。
12. A：你在北京做什么？
    B：做（　　　）。

三、排列顺序

1. A. 但是我并不后悔
   B. 我相信总有一天成功的大门会为我打开
   C. 这件事虽然失败了

2. A. 生意失败不要紧
   B. 因为这也是生命中的一课
   C. 相信你不会让大家失望的

四、完成句子

1. 一个人　就剩　教室里　我　_____
2. 实际上每个人　都　很失望　张师傅　对　_____
3. 电影　现场直播的　一部　就是　生活　_____
4. 李静的车上　把　都拿到　去吧　剩下的东西　_____
5. 并不是　失败　一件　事情　可怕的　_____

五、看图，用词造句

1. 失败

2. 失望

Unit 33

实在	适应
使	收
使用	收入
世纪	收拾
是否	首都
适合	首先

385 实在 shízài (adj./adv.) real, well-done; really
搭配：说话实在 to talk straight；说实在话 to tell the truth; to be frank
例句：说实在话，我不觉得她漂亮。To tell the truth, I don't think she is as pretty as you said.
这里实在是太美了，我都不想回去了。It is really beautiful here. I even don't want to go back.

386 使 shǐ (v.) have (sb to do sth)
例句：只有这样才能使他明白做任何事都不容易。Only in this way can he learn that nothing is so easy.
这个消息真使人难过。It is really a pity to hear the sad news.
运动使身体更健康。Doing exercises is helpful to one's health.

387 使用 shǐyòng (v.) use
搭配：使用说明 an instruction；使用方法 method of use；使用电脑/手机 to use a computer/mobile phone
例句：先生，请按照说明书使用这个热水器。Sir, please use this water heater under instruction.
我已经把使用方法写在这张纸上了，你回来看看就知道怎么用了。I've written down the instructions on this paper. You just take a look after you come back, then you will understand how to use it.

388 世纪 shìjì (n.) century
搭配：上个世纪 last century；20 世纪 90 年代 the 1990s
例句：一个世纪就是一百年。A century is equal to one hundred years.
20 世纪七八十年代，中国发生了很大的变化。During 1970s to 1980s, China changed greatly.

389 是否 shìfǒu (adv.) whether or not, whether, if
例句：比赛是否举行要看天气而定。Whether the contest will be held depends on the weather.
对于她是否聪明大家看法不同。Whether she's clever or not is a matter of opinion.
我不知道是否应该告诉你。I wonder if I ought to tell you that.

390 适合 shìhé (v.) suit, fit
例句：你个子不够高，不适合打篮球。You're too short to play basketball.
这里的气候很适合种花。The climate here is very suitable for planting flowers.
这些书都适合儿童阅读。Those books are all suitable for children.

391 适应 shìyìng (v.) adjust / adapt to, be suited to

搭配：适应能力 adaptive capacity；适应环境 to adjust to the new environment；适应需要 to suit the needs (of)

例句：我实在不能适应这里的环境。I really cannot adapt to the environment here.
等你适应这里的生活，我就带你到外面去看看。When you get used to the living environment here, I'll accompany you to look around.

392 收 shōu (v.) receive, get, take back

搭配：收到 to get；收房租 to receive house rent；收回 to take back

例句：你必须收回刚才的话，不然我就生气了。You must take back what you just said, or I'll be angry.
什么时候才能收到你送我的巧克力啊？When can I receive your chocolates?

393 收入 shōurù (n.) income

搭配：增加 / 降低收入 to increase/ decrease income；其他收入 other income；收入和支出 income and expenditure；高 / 低收入 high / low income；总收入 total income

例句：他除了工资外，还有其他收入。He has a lot of additional income other than wages.
这个月我们的收入增加了很多。Our income greatly increased this month.

394 收拾 shōushi (v.) tidy up

搭配：收拾收拾 to tidy up；收拾干净 to clear away；收拾房间 / 行李 to tidy up a room/ luggage

例句：快点儿把房间收拾干净，一会儿妈妈就要回来了。Hurry to clean up the room. Mother will be back in no time.
他们收拾好行李出发了。They gathered their belongings together and set off.

395 首都 shǒudū (n.) capital

搭配：首都北京 Beijing, the capital；国家的首都 national capital

例句：北京是中国的首都。Beijing is the capital city of China.
南京、西安曾经是中国古代的首都。Nanjing and Xi'an were once capital cities of ancient China.

396 首先 shǒuxiān (adv./ pron.) first

搭配：首先……然后…… first...then...；首先……其次…… first...next...

例句：想出国首先得把护照签证办好。One must first get his passport and visa before going abroad.
我们招聘员工首先看能力，其次才看学历。We look into one's ability first while recruiting a new staff, then the educational background.

实战练习（三十三）

一、听对话，选择正确答案

1. A. 机场　　　B. 家里　　　C. 服装店　　　D. 出租车上
2. A. 请假　　　B. 加工资　　C. 招新人　　　D. 做市场调查

二、选词填空

A 收　B 实在　C 使　D 适合　E 首都　F 收拾

1. 现在的市场变化（　　）太快，我们必须要努力适应这些新变化。
2. 王东在（　　）工作了好多年了。
3. 这个房间被服务员（　　）得非常干净。
4. 对不起，我们公司没有（　　）你的工作。
5. A：你没有（　　）到我寄给你的东西吗？
   B：没有啊，你是不是把地址写错了？
6. A：这次活动为什么会失败？
   B：场地太小，（　　）很多排队进场的人失去了耐心。

A 收入　B 世纪　C 是否　D 适应　E 首先　F 使用

7. 一个（　　）等于一百年。
8. 这是复印机的（　　）说明书。
9. 如果你不能（　　）这里的工作环境，就只能换一份工作了。
10. 我这个月的（　　）多了三百块钱。
11. A：你说这件事我应该交给谁做？
    B：我觉得你（　　）应该看看他们的工作成绩，然后再决定让谁去做。
12. A：（　　）耐心是好售货员和普通售货员的主要区别。
    B：你说得太对了。

三、排列顺序

1. A. 然后再开车去机场接爸妈
   B. 你首先把家里收拾干净
   C. 回来的路上不要忘了去超市买点红酒

2. A. 在新世纪里
   B. 我们的公司已经不能适应那里的市场环境了
   C. 南方的市场变化很大

四、完成句子

1. 生长　不适合　香蕉　在北方　_____
2. 了吗　世纪公司的　你收到　复试信息　_____
3. 银行卡　把　你这个月的收入　我已经　打到　里了　_____
4. 在一周之内　你必须　这里的　适应　一切　_____
5. 生活　适应　是否　你　首都的　_____

五、看图，用词造句

1. 收入

2. 收拾

Unit 34

受不了	数字
受到	帅
售货员	顺便
输	顺利
熟悉	顺序
数量	说明

Unit 34

397 受不了 shòubuliǎo / be unable to endure, can't stand, can't bear, unable to put up with

搭配：冷 / 热 / 疼得受不了 can't stand the cold / heat / pain

例句：我实在是受不了这群小孩子了。I cannot stand these children anymore.
我受不了的是你竟然会骗我。What I'm really unable to bear is you deceived me.

398 受到 shòudào / be subjected to, receive, get

搭配：受到表扬 / 批评 to receive praise; to come in for criticism；受到伤害 / 照顾 to be wounded; be tended；受到欢迎 / 重视 / 影响 to receive welcome; to draw attention; to be affected

例句：他受到了张经理的重视，估计很快就要升职了。He has received Manager Zhang's attention and is about to be promoted in no time.
受到表扬时不要骄傲，受到批评时也不要放弃。Don't get overly proud when being praised, and don't give up easily when being criticized either.

399 售货员 shòuhuòyuán / 名 (n.) / seller, shop-assistant

搭配：超市售货员 a supermarket seller；招聘售货员 to advertise for shop-assistant

例句：这个售货员捡到了客人的钱包。The seller picked up a customer's wallet.
请左一区的售货员到前台来一下。The seller at the Left One area please go to the front office.

400 输 shū / 动 (v.) / lose

搭配：输球 to concede a goal；输赢 lose or win；输不起 cannot afford to lose

例句：中国队输了，大家都很难过。Chinese team lost the game and we felt very sorry about it.
爸爸输给了我。Dad lost to me.

401 熟悉 shúxī / 动 (v.) / be familiar with

搭配：熟悉环境 to get familiar with the environment；熟悉情况 to get familiar with the conditions

例句：请带我熟悉一下公司的环境。Please show me around the company.
我是第一次来这儿，对这里很不熟悉。It is the first time I've been here and everything is new to me.

402 数量 shùliàng / 名 (n.) / quantity

搭配：统计数量 a statistical magnitude；人口数量 size of population；数量小 / 大 a small/ large amount of；减少数量 to reduce the amount of...

例句：数量太大了，我要回去问一下李经理。The total amount is too large and I should ask Manager Li about it.
你回去把数量统计一下，下午开会前送到我办公室。Please go back and make a statistic report, and then bring it to my office before the meeting in the afternoon.

403 数字 shùzì (名) (n.) number
搭配：数字游戏 a numbers game；排列数字 to array；小写 / 大写数字 lowercase/ capitalize

例句：小孩子总是喜欢玩这些简单的数字游戏。Children always like playing these simple number games.

看见这么多数字我真是头疼。It's a headache to see so many numbers.

404 帅 shuài (形) (adj.) handsome
搭配：帅哥 a handsome boy；帅气 handsome；动作很帅 a handsome action

例句：他的字写得真帅，估计练了好几年了。His writings are handsome. Maybe he had practiced for years.

他长得特帅，很受女孩子欢迎。He is very popular among girls for his handsome look.

405 顺便 shùnbiàn (副) (adv.) by the way
例句：你回来的路上顺便帮我买一份饭。Please buy a meal for me on your way home.

你去拿信的时候顺便帮我看看有没有我的信。On your way to pick up your letters, please help me check if I had any new letters too.

406 顺利 shùnlì (形) (adj.) smooth, successful
搭配：顺利结束 / 完成 to do sth successfully；一切顺利 everything goes smoothly；工作顺利 everything goes well with sb's work

例句：如果事情进行得顺利的话，我明天就回去了。If all things go smoothly, I'll be back tomorrow.

晚会顺利结束了，我们赶快回去休息吧。The evening party ended successfully. Let's go back to have a rest as soon as possible.

407 顺序 shùnxù (名) (n.) order, sequence
搭配：正确顺序 the right order；排列顺序 to put in order；先后顺序 sequencing

例句：把这道题的正确顺序写在答题纸上，然后交到我这。Write the correct order of this question on your answer sheet, and then hand it to me.

请大家按顺序排队，然后一个一个地进去。Please line up in sequence and come in one by one.

408 说明 shuōmíng (动/名) (v./n.) explain; instruction
搭配：说明情况 to explain a situation；说明书 an instruction；使用说明 a manual

例句：使用说明书在盒子里，你拿出来看看就会用了。The manual is in the box. You'll understand how to use it after reading the manual.

请具体说明一下你这么做的原因。Please explain specifically about your reasons for doing so.

实战练习（三十四）

一、听对话，选择正确答案

1. A. 四　　B. 五　　C. 六　　D. 九
2. A. 同事　B. 夫妻　C. 医生和病人　D. 顾客与售货员

二、选词填空

A 熟悉　B 顺利　C 数字　D 受不了　E 受到　F 售货员

1. 你猜猜我最喜欢的（　　）是几，猜对了我就请你吃饭。
2. A：我快（　　）了，经理怎么总是让我出差啊？
   B：那是经理看重你，出差虽然累，但能学到很多东西。
3. 希望这次我们都能够（　　）地通过考试。
4. 这个（　　）很负责，每件商品都记得很清楚。
5. A：没有（　　）经理的肯定，让我很难过。
   B：你表现得已经很不错了，不要伤心。
6. A：你对这里很（　　），经常过来玩吗？
   B：不是，偶尔过来一次。

A 数量　B 输　C 说明　D 顺便　E 帅　F 顺序

7. 我们虽然（　　）了比赛，但仍然很开心。
8. 他虽然长得很（　　），但个子不高。
9. 把昨天公司买的所有物品的（　　）统计一下。
10. 我昨天去逛街，（　　）交了电话费。
11. A：你要按排队（　　）卖票，这样才公平。
    B：好的，我知道了。
12. A：他送小红巧克力和花是什么意思啊？
    B：这（　　）他喜欢小红，想让小红做他的女朋友。

三、排列顺序

1. A. 这个售货员对超市的情况很了解
   B. 如果你不想输给她的话

C. 就尽快把超市的情况熟悉一下
2. A. 能很快把这些数字的正确顺序排列出来
   B. 还可以讲出这样排序的原因
   C. 他很聪明

四、完成句子

1. 把 请尽快 这次需要进货的数量 公司 整理好 _____
2. 说一声 顺便 向那个售货员 帮我 谢谢 _____
3. 走来 帅气的 正在 售货员 向这边 那个 _____
4. 鼓励 受到了 老师的 我 _____
5. 很顺利 这些数字 事情 说明 进行得 _____

五、看图，用词造句

1. 售货员

2. 帅

Unit 35

硕士　　　　　随着
死　　　　　　孙子
速度　　　　　所有
塑料袋　　　　台
酸　　　　　　抬
随便　　　　　态度

409 硕士 shuòshì (n.) master's degree, graduate

搭配：硕士学位 master's degree；硕士研究生 a postgraduate

例句：我们只招硕士和博士。We only recruited people with a master's degree or a doctor's degree.

李红不想读硕士。Li Hong doesn't want to pursue a master's degree.

410 死 sǐ (v./adj.) die; dead

搭配：怕死 to fear death；生与死 live or die；你死我活 a life and death struggle；死心眼儿 stubborn；死火山 extinct volcano; dead volcano；死水 dead water

例句：他一向都这么死心眼儿，你不要和他计较了。He has always been so stubborn and you should leave him alone.

这只小狗已经死了很多天了。The puppy has been dead for many days.

411 速度 sùdù (n.) speed

搭配：速度快/慢 at a fast/ slow speed；加快/减慢速度 to speed up/ to slow down

例句：要迟到了，我们得加快速度。We're about to be late so we should speed up.

现在的年轻人开车的速度都很快。Today's young people always drive fast.

412 塑料袋 sùliàodài (n.) plastic bag

搭配：使用塑料袋 to use a plastic bag；一只塑料袋 a plastic bag；环保塑料袋 a green plastic bag

例句：现在超市的塑料袋是收费的。We need to pay for the plastic bags in supermarkets now.

乱扔塑料袋会带来严重的环境问题。Throwing plastic bags away carelessly will bring severe environmental problems.

413 酸 suān (adj.) sour

搭配：酸甜苦辣 sweets and bitters of life；酸味 a sour flavor；酸菜 Chinese sauerkraut；酸奶 yogurt；心酸 to feel sad

例句：想买袋酸奶喝，可身上只剩一块钱了，我很心酸。I wanted to buy a bag of yogurt, but I only had one *yuan*, so I felt sad.

这种糖酸酸甜甜的，很好吃。The good-tasting candy is sweet and sour.

414 随便 suíbiàn (v./adj./conj.) feel free to; casual; anyhow

搭配：随便你 help yourself；随便说/写 to say/ write as you like；随便坐/看看 to sit anywhere you like; to see around by oneself

例句：来了这里就当自己家，随便坐吧。Please feel at home and sit anywhere you like.

不要紧张，随便说一说你对这件事的看法。Don't be nervous and express your opinions on the matter.

随便什么都行。Anything will do.

415 随着 suízhe 介 (prep.) along with

搭配：随着……的发展 along with the development of...；随着……的变化 change with...

例句：随着经济的发展，人们的生活发生了很大的变化。With economic development, people's life has undergone great changes.

随着子女一天天长大，父母也一天天老去。As the children grow up, parents also grow older day by day.

416 孙子 sūnzi 名 (n.) grandson

搭配：老王的孙子 Old Wang's grandson；爷爷和孙子 grandpa and grandson

例句：张爷爷和他孙子正在看电视。Grandpa Zhang and his grandson are watching TV.

你孙子都这么大了，该上大学了吧？ Your grandson is old enough to attend a university.

417 所有 suǒyǒu 形/名 (adj./n.) all; possessions

搭配：所有人 / 事 all people / issues；所有的东西 all items

例句：所有人必须在下午两点之前到这里集合。All people must gather here before two o'clock this afternoon.

他个子比其他所有人都高。He dominates everyone else by his height.

418 台 tái 量 (m.w.) (used for identifying the number of certain machinery, apparatus, etc.)

搭配：一台电视机 a television；一台洗衣机 a washing machine；一台戏 / 话剧 an opera/ a stage play

例句：妈妈决定买一台新的洗衣机。My mother decided to buy a new washing machine.

我们为这台戏准备了三个月。We have been preparing this drama for three months.

419 抬 tái 动 (v.) lift, carry

搭配：抬起来 to lift up；抬头 to raise head up；抬腿 to raise one's leg

例句：这个沙发很重，你抬得动吗？ Can you lift that heavy sofa?

别总低着头走路，抬头！ Don't lower your head too often, raise it up!

420 态度 tàidu 名 (n.) attitude

搭配：生活态度 attitude toward life；人生态度 a life attitude；态度不好 to behave badly

例句：他的人生态度很积极。His life attitude is positive.

你对这件事的态度非常重要。Your attitude to this matter is very important.

实战练习（三十五）

一、听对话，选择正确答案

1. A. 要检查身体　　B. 少用塑料袋　　C. 注意交通安全　　D. 城市生活方便
2. A. 想去旅游　　　B. 还没结婚　　　C. 心情不好　　　　D. 要搬出去住

二、选词填空

A 塑料袋　B 死　C 随着　D 速度　E 台　F 态度

1. 请把那（　　）电视机的使用说明书拿给我看看。
2. 经常使用（　　）对环境不利。
3. （　　）社会的发展，从事服务业的人越来越多了。
4. 他有一种积极的生活（　　），每天都在为美好的将来努力。
5. A：你开车的（　　）太快了，开慢点儿！
   B：再慢我们就要迟到了。
6. A：动物园里的老虎怎么会突然（　　）了呢？
   B：不知道，你快叫医生来看看吧。

A 抬　B 所有　C 酸　D 孙子　E 随便　F 硕士

7. 你怎么可以（　　）把妈妈送你的东西给别人呢？
8. （　　）起头来，让我好好儿看看你。
9. （　　）的人都走了，这时公司里的电话却响了起来。
10. 这道菜怎么这么（　　）啊？
11. A：大学毕业后你想做什么？
    B：我想读（　　）。
12. A：你今天怎么这么高兴啊？
    B：我（　　）考上北京大学了。

三、排列顺序

1. A. 最后关上灯就可以离开了
   B. 然后把地擦干净
   C. 你先把所有的塑料袋收起来

2. A. 这台洗衣机太重了
   B. 我们俩肯定不能抬到车上
   C. 我看还是找两个人帮忙抬一下吧

四、完成句子

1. 所有人 就算 我也要 都反对 和你在一起 ＿＿＿＿＿＿＿＿
2. 随随便便 你怎么能 就把 卖掉呢 这台洗衣机 ＿＿＿＿＿＿＿＿
3. 被 那个塑料袋 拿出去 他小孙子 玩了 ＿＿＿＿＿＿＿＿
4. 这种态度 对你 怎么是 你孙子 ＿＿＿＿＿＿＿＿
5. 没有人 几乎 这辆车 来 能抬得起 ＿＿＿＿＿＿＿＿

五、看图，用词造句

1. 酸

2. 塑料袋

Unit 36

谈	讨论
弹钢琴	讨厌
汤	特点
糖	提
躺	提供
趟	提前

Unit 36

421 谈 tán (v.) talk
- 搭配：谈话 to have a talk；谈心 to have a heart-to-heart talk；谈事情／工作 to talk about business / work；谈条件 to negotiate
- 例句：找个时间我们谈谈吧。Let's find a time to talk it over.
  一路上我们一直都在谈工作。We have been talking about work all the way.

422 弹钢琴 tán gāngqín play the piano
- 例句：有没有人说过你弹钢琴时的样子特别美？ Has anyone said you look particularly pretty when you play the piano?
  我从五岁开始学习弹钢琴，已经学了十三年了。It has been thirteen years since I began to learn playing the piano at the age of five.

423 汤 tāng (n.) soup
- 搭配：汤勺 soup ladle；做汤 to cook soup；菜汤 vegetable soup；绿豆汤 green bean soup
- 例句：我平时不喜欢喝汤。Usually, I don't like to drink soup.
  妈妈做的绿豆汤特别好喝。Mother's homemade green bean soup is especially tasty.

424 糖 táng (n.) sugar, candy
- 搭配：口香糖 chewing gum；巧克力糖 chocolate candy；红糖 red sugar；白糖 sugar；糖果 sweets；咖啡糖 coffee-tasted sweets；一勺糖 a spoonful of sugar
- 例句：我喝咖啡从不放糖。I drink sugar-free coffee.
  小孩子都喜欢吃糖果。Children all like sweets.

425 躺 tǎng (v.) lie
- 搭配：躺下 to lie down；躺在床上 to lie in bed；躺椅 deck chair
- 例句：很晚了，你快躺下休息吧，明天还要上班呢。It's getting late. Lie in bed and rest as soon as possible. You have to go to work tomorrow.
  这里很湿，你最好不要躺在这儿。It is wet and you'd better not lie here.

426 趟 tàng (m.w.) (used for a round trip)
- 搭配：走／跑一趟 to have a trip to；最后一趟火车 the last train
- 例句：如果我们错过了最后一趟公交车就只能打车回去了。If we miss the last bus, we have to take a taxi.
  他们都没能把李文请过来，看来只能让你亲自走一趟了。They couldn't invite Li Wen anyway. It seems you'll have to go to invite her by yourself.

427 讨论 tǎolùn (v.) discuss
- 搭配：讨论事情／问题 to discuss business / problems；进行讨论 to have a discussion of；一场讨论 a discussion

例句：这件事情我需要和你妈妈讨论一下再做决定。I need to discuss with your mother about this and then make my decision.

我们班昨天进行了一场关于食品安全的讨论。Yesterday, our class had a discussion on food safety.

428 讨厌 tǎoyàn (形/动) (adj./v.) hateful, disgusting; dislike

搭配：讨厌的人 / 事 a hateful person/ thing；讨厌的食物 / 天气 abominable food/weather

例句：我最讨厌的事不是做饭，而是洗碗。I prefer cooking to washing dishes.

我讨厌一边写作业一边听音乐。I don't like listening to music while doing homework.

429 特点 tèdiǎn (名) (n.) characteristic, feature

搭配：写作特点 writing features；个人特点 a personal feature

例句：这篇文章的写作特点很鲜明。This article has a vivid and distinguished writing feature.

她最大的特点不是聪明，而是认真。Her greatest feature is not being smart, but being careful.

430 提 tí (动) (v.) carry, lift, mention, bring

搭配：提意见 to give sb some suggestions；提问题 to raise question；提要求 to make a demand；提高 to improve

例句：一提起她，我就生气。At the mention of her name, I got angry.

他向我提了几个意见。He offered me a word or two of advice.

我去提水。I'll go fetch water.

431 提供 tígōng (动) (v.) provide

搭配：提供服务 to lend one's services；提供奖学金 to offer a scholarship；提供帮助 / 信息 to provide help/ information

例句：这里都是提供吃住的，你不用带被子过来。We provide bed and food here, and you needn't carry a quilt.

公司给员工提供春节回家的车票。The company provides employees with homeward tickets for Spring Festival.

432 提前 tíqián (动) (v.) advance, be ahead of schedule / time

搭配：提前出发 to set out early；提前完成 to finish in advance；提前到达 to arrive in advance

例句：他们提前三天就完成了这项任务。They completed the task three days ahead.

明天大家要提前半个小时到公司门口集合。Tomorrow, we should gather in front of the company entrance half an hour earlier.

实战练习（三十六）

一、听对话，选择正确答案

1. A. 生病了　　B. 想上班　　C. 很高兴　　D. 喜欢锻炼
2. A. 少喝汤　　B. 认真复习　　C. 早点休息　　D. 练习弹钢琴

二、选词填空

A 躺　B 弹钢琴　C 提供　D 讨论　E 汤　F 糖

1. 公司为每位员工（　　）一次到上海学习的机会。
2. 先不要（　　）下，把这些药喝了再睡。
3. 科学证明，吃饭前喝（　　）对身体有好处。
4. （　　）和盐都不能吃得太多，不利于健康。
5. A：你在家喜欢做什么？
   B：听听音乐，弹（　　），总之不会闲着。
6. A：你一会儿回去和大家（　　）一下，下午把你们的决定告诉我。
   B：好，我知道了。

A 特点　B 讨厌　C 谈　D 趟　E 提　F 提前

7. 今天我买了好多水果，都（　　）不动了。
8. 你快点去一（　　）医院，小华被车撞了。
9. 这台钢琴最大的（　　）是材料好。
10. 这么多工作，你还能（　　）完成，真让人吃惊。
11. A：我（　　）到人多的地方来，我们还是回家吧。
    B：好，我到那边买双袜子，然后就回去。
12. A：与人（　　）话时最好看着别人的眼睛，这表示对人的尊重。
    B：知道了，我以后会注意的。

三、排列顺序

1. A. 夏日的午后
   B. 突然回忆起去年我们一起学弹钢琴的日子
   C. 我躺在草地上

2. A. 但是你们也必须答应提前把商品给我们运过来
   B. 经过讨论
   C. 我们决定接受你们提出的条件

四、完成句子

1. 和孩子一起讨论　躺在床上　我喜欢　事情　学校发生的 _____
2. 讨论一下　大家　他们　是否可行　提出的条件 _____
3. 最大的　是　特点　这篇文章　用词很美 _____
4. 足够的钱　我会给你　弹钢琴　到北京　提供　去学习 _____
5. 提前两天　你还是　去一趟吧　到分公司 _____

五、看图，用词造句

1. 讨论

2. 躺

Unit 37

提醒	通知
填空	同情
条件	同时
停	推
挺	推迟
通过	脱

433 提醒 tíxǐng (v.) remind

搭配：提醒注意 to call one's attention of sth ；提个醒 to remind sb of sth

例句：请提醒大家明天多穿点衣服。Please remind everyone to wear more clothes tomorrow.
你知道他要出事，怎么不给他提个醒呢？Why didn't you remind him first since you had already known he'll run into a trouble?

434 填空 tiánkòng (v.) fill a vacancy/ blank

搭配：选词填空 a cloze test ；填空题 filling in the blanks

例句：这道填空题的答案是"理想"。The correct answer for this blank is "ideal".
选词填空这类题比较容易。The questions such as "filling in the blanks" are relatively easy.

435 条件 tiáojiàn (n.) condition

搭配：提条件 to propose a condition ；生活条件 living condition ；前提条件 prerequisite ；经济条件 economic condition

例句：这里的工作条件很好，收入也不错。The working condition here is very good.
小王家里的条件不错。Xiao Wang's family condition is good.

436 停 tíng (v.) stop, halt, stay

搭配：停电 the failure of electricity ；停水 to cut off water supply ；停下脚步 to stop walking

例句：他跑得太快了，一下子停不下来。He was running so fast that he couldn't stop himself.
他讲了一半突然停了下来。He stopped short in the middle of his story.

437 挺 tǐng (adv.) very, quite

搭配：挺好 pretty good ；挺难 quite difficult

例句：他这个人还是挺不错的。He is a very good person.
这本书挺好看的，你有时间可以看看。This book is very good, and you can read it when you have time.

438 通过 tōngguò (prep./v.) by means of; pass

搭配：举手通过 to pass by a show of hands ；通过考试 to pass a test

例句：大家一般是通过中介买房子。People usually buy houses through agents.
通过这件事我明白了一个很重要的道理。I learned an important lesson from this thing.
他通过了 HSK 六级考试。He has passed the HSK 6.

439 通知 tōngzhī (v./n.) inform; notice

搭配：接到通知 to receive a notice ；口头通知 oral notice

例句：你快通知大家比赛要提前一个小时开始。You should notify everyone that the match will start an hour earlier.
大家接到通知就马上出发了。We immediately set off on receiving the notice.

440 同情 tóngqíng (v.) pity, sympathize

搭配：值得同情 to deserve pity；表示同情 to show sympathy for；同情心 sympathy

例句：她三岁时就失去了父母，真让人同情。 She lost her parents when she was three years old and deserves lots of pity.

这是他自己的错，没必要同情他。It is his own fault. There's no need to feel sorry for him.

441 同时 tóngshí (conj./n.) at the same time, simultaneously, besides

搭配：同时发生 to coincide；同时出现 co-occur

例句：我同时听见两个人叫我。I was called by two persons at the same time.

见到老同学，我高兴的同时，又有点吃惊。I was both happy and surprised on seeing my old schoolmate.

442 推 tuī (v.) push

搭配：推车 a hand trolley；推出去 / 进去 to push out/ in；推开门 / 窗户 to open a window/ door

例句：你们快点把车推进来，把东西搬到房间里。You should hurry up and push the trolley in, then move the things into the room.

地铁人太多，我差点儿被推倒了。There're too many people in the subway and I was almost pushed to the ground.

443 推迟 tuīchí (v.) postpone

搭配：推迟比赛 / 会议 to postpone a match/ meeting

例句：比赛推迟三天，你去通知一下参赛运动员。The game is delayed for three days and you should notify the athletes about it.

由于经理有事，所以下午的会议推迟一个小时进行。As the manager has some other things to do first, the afternoon meeting is put off for an hour.

444 脱 tuō (v.) take off

搭配：脱掉 / 下 to take off；脱衣服 to take off clothes；脱袜子 to take off stockings

例句：请把鞋脱了再进来。Take your shoes off before you come in.

今天她实在是太累了，连衣服都没有脱就睡着了。She is too tired today and fell to sleep even before taking off her clothes.

实战练习（三十七）

一、听对话，选择正确答案

1. A. 医生　　B. 律师　　C. 老师　　D. 售货员
2. A. 轻松　　B. 难过　　C. 快乐　　D. 生气

二、选词填空

A 通过　B 推　C 通知　D 同时　E 脱　F 停

1. 快帮那位老奶奶（　　）一下车，她快骑不动了。
2. 把外套（　　）了，赶紧过来吃饭吧。
3. 师傅，请在前边（　　）车。
4. （　　）这个网站，我找到了很想买的那本书。
5. 你去（　　）大家，十五分钟后我们就出发去长城了，让大家做好准备。
6. A：认真学习的（　　），还要注意身体。
   B：谢谢您的关心。

A 同情　B 挺　C 推迟　D 条件　E 提醒　F 填空

7. 我要（　　）你一件事情，下午两点开会别迟到。
8. 下午的网球比赛要（　　）半个小时，你通知一下大家。
9. 我们对这个人不幸的命运表示（　　）。
10. 只有几个学生做对了这道（　　）题。
11. A：你有什么（　　）直接提出来吧。
    B：我希望提高收入。
12. A：这件事还（　　）麻烦的，估计结果要等几天才能出来。
    B：那我们就只能在这里等了。

三、排列顺序

1. A. 通过这个网站
   B. 还可以看到很多赛事的通知
   C. 大家可以看到最新的网球比赛

2. A. 为了准备 HSK 考试
   B. 李东进推迟了回国的时间
   C. 他希望能通过 6 级

四、完成句子

1. 通知　大家　学校　交学费 _____
2. 没有想到　我完全　我们会输　这场比赛 _____
3. 找到　都能　节目　全部的　在这个网站上 _____
4. 这辆自行车　请你把　我们家楼下　推到 _____
5. 挺让人同情的　这群　真的　失去健康的人 _____

五、看图，用词造句

1. 同情

2. 推

Unit 38

袜子 卫生间
完全 味道
网球 温度
网站 文章
往往 污染
危险 无

445 袜子 wàzi (名) (n.) socks
搭配：一双袜子 a pair of socks；厚袜子 thick socks; warm socks
例句：天冷了，你还是穿一双厚点儿的袜子吧。It's getting cold. You'd better wear a pair of thicker socks.
你的袜子都破了，还是再买一双吧。Your socks are all frayed. You'd better buy some new ones.

446 完全 wánquán (形)/(副) (adj./adv.) entire; totally
搭配：完全同意 totally agree；完全正确 be absolutely correct
例句：我完全不同意你的看法。I don't agree with you at all.
这些药对她的病完全没用。These drugs have none effects on her disease at all.

447 网球 wǎngqiú (名) (n.) tennis
搭配：网球比赛 a tennis match；网球公开赛 open tennis championship；网球场 tennis court；网球拍 tennis racket；网球鞋 tennis shoes
例句：他是一位著名的网球运动员。He is a famous tennis player.
我想约你一起去打网球。I want to invite you to play tennis.

448 网站 wǎngzhàn (名) (n.) website
搭配：建立网站 to make a website；打开网站 to open a website；网站管理员 a webmaster；免费网站 free website
例句：你到网站上查查这件衣服多少钱。You go to check the price of this dress on its website.
今天上网速度很慢，打开一个网站需要很长时间。Today's wire speed is very slow. It takes too much time to open a website.

449 往往 wǎngwǎng (副) (adv.) often
例句：事情往往不会向你想的方向发展。As often, things don't turn out as what people expect.
你越是希望某件事发生，它往往不会发生。Often the more you want something to happen, the smaller the chance will be.

450 危险 wēixiǎn (形)/(名) (adj./n.) dangerous; danger
搭配：危险动物 dangerous animal；冒生命危险 to risk one's life；减少危险 to lessen the danger of
例句：小孩子一个人在河边玩非常危险。Playing along the river is very dangerous for a child.
他冒着生命危险去河里救人。He jumped into the river and risked his life to save other people.

451 卫生间 wèishēngjiān (名) (n.) toilet, wash room, restroom

搭配：公共卫生间 public toilet；男 / 女卫生间 Men's/Ladies' (room)

例句：王东刚刚去卫生间了。Wang Dong went to the bathroom just now.

我喜欢带卫生间的卧室。I like a room with bath.

452 味道 wèidào (名) (n.) flavor, taste

搭配：味道好 / 坏 to taste delicious/ awful；各种味道 varied flavors；有味道 be tasty

例句：这家饭店的菜味道很好，有空我带你过去尝尝。This restaurant offers delicious foods. Let's go have a try when we're free.

别在教室里吃饭了，味道太难闻了。Don't eat your meal in the classroom since it smells.

453 温度 wēndù (名) (n.) temperature

搭配：温度高 / 低 a high/ low temperature；温度上升 / 下降 a rise/ drop of temperature

例句：今天的温度很低，你多穿点衣服。Today's temperature is very low. You'd better wear more clothes.

北极的温度非常低，很多植物都不能在那里生长。The temperature in Arctic regions is frigid, most of plants cannot grow there.

454 文章 wénzhāng (名) (n.) essay, article

搭配：写 / 看 / 读文章 to write/ read an article；一篇文章 an article

例句：这篇文章写得还挺不错的，我觉得可以发表。This article is not bad at all. I think it can be published.

把你昨天写的那篇文章改一下然后再拿过来。Take the article you wrote yesterday to me after revision.

455 污染 wūrǎn (动) (v.) pollute

搭配：污染环境 to pollute the environment；污染河流 to pollute a river；空气污染 air pollution

例句：这里的环境被严重污染了。The environment here is seriously polluted.

空气污染会使这些花变色。Air pollution will change the color of these flowers.

456 无 wú (动) (v.) not have, be without

搭配：从无到有 to grow out of nothing；无色无味 be colorless and odorless；无条件 without condition；无能 inability；无关 unrelated；无所谓 to make no difference；无心 not be in the mood for；无烟区 smokeless area

例句：科学证明，这种药对他的病是无效的。It has been scientifically proved that this drug is useless to him.

我不喜欢喝无色无味的水，你去给我换一杯咖啡。I don't like drinking a cup of colorless and tasteless water. Please change it for a cup of coffee for me.

这个老爷爷无儿无女，一个人很可怜。The childless old man was alone. What a pity.

实战练习（三十八）

一、听对话，选择正确答案

1. A. 解释原因　　B. 和她握手　　C. 请她吃饼干　　D. 学做巧克力
2. A. 很无聊　　　B. 放假了　　　C. 要做饭　　　　D. 在写东西

二、选词填空

A 危险　B 网站　C 文章　D 污染　E 往往　F 网球

1. 请先把这篇（　　）中的错字改过来，然后再打印。
2. 今天天气真好，下午我们一起去打（　　）吧。
3. 可能有（　　），大家一定要小心。
4. 听说这个（　　）上有很多便宜的衣服，我们也进去看看吧。
5. A：今天的报纸上有一篇文章是专门写水（　　）的，你看到了吗？
   B：看到了，我正想和你说这事呢。
6. A：你觉得现在的年轻人怎么样？
   B：我认为相对于外表，他们（　　）更注重知识。

A 袜子　B 卫生间　C 完全　D 温度　E 无　F 味道

7. 你（　　）不了解孩子的心。
8. 她现在还（　　）法面对你们，请你们快点离开这里。
9. 这家饭店的菜（　　）怎么样？你觉得好吃吗？
10. （　　）这么高，估计是发烧了，快带他去看看医生吧。
11. A：下午你去逛街顺便帮我买几双（　　）吧。
    B：好的，没问题。
12. A：请问附近有（　　）吗？
    B：前边有一个公共厕所。

三、排列顺序

1. A. 我看还是让小静陪你一起去吧
   B. 无论有没有危险
   C. 你都不能一个人去

2. A. 握手不仅可以拉近人们之间的距离
   B. 所以我们要多和身边的人握手
   C. 还能解除人们心中的误会

四、完成句子

1. 我　完全　打　不会　网球　_____
2. 真好　你　加的　往文章中　这几个词　_____
3. 出现　这些　往往不会　小误会　他们之间　_____
4. 是有味道的　错误地　认为　他们　水污染　_____
5. 网站　很　有些　危险　_____

五、看图，用词造句

1. 味道

2. 卫生间

Unit 39

无聊	现金
无论	羡慕
误会	相反
西红柿	相同
吸引	香
咸	详细

457 无聊 wúliáo (adj.) boring

搭配：非常无聊 be so boring；无聊的人 / 事 a bore

例句：无聊的时候我就听听音乐。When I feel bored, I like listening to some music.
工作太无聊了，我想辞职。This job is too boring and I want to quit.

458 无论 wúlùn (conj.) whatever

搭配：无论……都 / 也…… whatever... / however...

例句：无论我说什么，她都不听。Whatever I say, she just won't listen to me.
无论用什么方法，电脑就是开不了机。Whatever I do, the computer can't start up.

459 误会 wùhuì (v./n.) misunderstand; misunderstanding

搭配：有误会 to have a misunderstanding；减少误会 to reduce misunderstandings；产生误会 to produce a misunderstanding；小误会 minor misunderstanding

例句：我们都误会了他的意思。All of us misunderstood him.
误会解除了，他们的关系又正常了。They removed misunderstandings and recovered their relationship.

460 西红柿 xīhóngshì (n.) tomato

搭配：吃 / 洗 / 买西红柿 to eat/ wash/ buy tomatoes；西红柿蛋汤 tomato and egg soup

例句：我喜欢喝妈妈做的西红柿蛋汤。I like drinking tomato and egg soup cooked by my mother.
中午我们吃西红柿炒鸡蛋。We ate a dish of scrambled eggs and tomatoes as lunch.

461 吸引 xīyǐn (v.) attract

搭配：被……吸引住 be attracted by...；吸引……的目光 / 注意力 to take sb's attention；吸引力 attraction

例句：这里的美丽景色吸引了很多人。The beautiful scenery here attracts many tourists.
他被那个广告吸引住了。He was attracted by that advertisement.

462 咸 xián (adj.) salty

搭配：咸饼干 saltine；咸淡 degree of saltiness；咸水湖 a salt-water lake；咸菜 pickled vegetables；咸鸭蛋 a salted duck egg

例句：菜不要太咸，对健康不利。A salty dish is bad for your health.
他做的菜太咸了，快给我杯水喝。He made the dish too salty. Give me a glass of water to drink.
海水又苦又咸。Seawater tastes bitter and salty.

463 现金 xiànjīn (名) (n.) cash

搭配：付现金 to pay in cash；取现金 to draw some cash；准备现金 to prepare some cash；缺少现金 a shortage of cash; to run out of cash；现金管理 cash management

例句：她每天都把收入的现金存入银行。Each day she deposits the received cash in the bank.
如果收现金的话，要注意假钱。Be aware of the counterfeit money if you accept cash.

464 羡慕 xiànmù (动) (v.) admire, envy

搭配：羡慕成功 to envy sb's success；羡慕的目光 admiring looks

例句：他有一个让人羡慕的好姐姐。His sister is admired by other people.
她事业很成功，很多人都羡慕她。Many people envy her successful career.

465 相反 xiāngfǎn (形/连) (adj./conj.) opposite; on the contrary

搭配：相反意见 opposite view；相反方向 an opposite direction；正好相反 quite the reverse

例句：他们俩向着相反的方向出发了。They set out along the opposite direction.
我的看法跟她完全相反。My opinion is fully contrary to hers.

466 相同 xiāngtóng (形) (adj.) same

搭配：相同的爱好 the same hobby；相同的打算 the same plan；相同的决定 the same decision；相同的希望 the same hope

例句：我和同学们有着相同的打算。My classmates and I share the same wish.
我和姐姐的爱好相同。My sister and I share the same hobby.

467 香 xiāng (形) (adj.) aromatic, fragrant

搭配：香水 perfume；香味 fragrance；吃香 be popular

例句：昨天晚上我睡得很香，连梦都没有做。Last night I slept soundly and had no dream at all.
妈妈做的菜太香了。What a delicious dish my mother made!

468 详细 xiángxì (形) (adj.) detailed, specific

搭配：详细信息 detailed information；详细情况 the detail；详细地址 specific address；详细的研究 a detailed study；详细的材料 materials in detail

例句：关于这块地的详细信息，我已经放到你办公桌上了。I put the detailed information of this land on your desk.
经理详细询问了她的工作情况。The manager asked about her working conditions in detail.

实战练习(三十九)

一、听对话，选择正确答案

1. A. 很失望　　B. 不想出国　　C. 羡慕李刚　　D. 想申请辞职
2. A. 同事　　　B. 夫妻　　　　C. 师生　　　　D. 姐弟

二、选词填空

A 相反　B 无论　C 误会　D 香　E 无聊　F 西红柿

1. 如果你不和他解释清楚，(　　　)会越来越深的。
2. 请问(　　　)多少钱一斤？
3. 谁在做饭啊？怎么这么(　　　)呢？
4. 没什么事情可以做，真是(　　　)啊！
5. A：听说明天要下雪，你还出去锻炼吗？
   B：(　　　)明天下不下雪，我都会去锻炼的。
6. A：我不觉得这是个正确的决定，(　　　)我觉得你不应该这样做。
   B：那你说我该怎么办？

A 详细　B 咸　C 现金　D 羡慕　E 吸引　F 相同

7. 这道菜也太(　　　)了吧，不知道你到底放了多少盐。
8. 我们都被她的音乐才能深深地(　　　)了。
9. 我们有着(　　　)的爱好，那就是跑步。
10. 这个不能刷卡，只能付(　　　)。
11. A：我真(　　　)她的长头发！
    B：只要你一年不进理发店，你也可以有一头长发。
12. A：再把这个计划改一改，把方案写(　　　)一点。
    B：好的，经理。

三、排列顺序

1. A. 我不羡慕她的高个子
   B. 也不是很有吸引力
   C. 相反我觉得女孩子太高了

2. A. 说明书中都有详细的说明
   B. 洗衣机的使用方法很简单
   C. 你只要照着它上边的方法做就行了

四、完成句子

1. 所写的故事　实在是　太无聊了　那篇文章 _____
2. 变化　现代社会　发生着　正以　前所未有的　速度 _____
3. 你做的　太　西红柿鸡蛋汤　咸了 _____
4. 美景　现代旅游业的　具有吸引力的　促进了　发展 _____
5. 详细地　梦中的事情　记了下来　他把 _____

五、看图，用词造句

1. 无聊

2. 羡慕

Unit 40

响	笑话
橡皮	效果
消息	心情
小吃	辛苦
小伙子	信封
小说	信息

Unit 40

469 响 xiǎng 动/形 (v./adj.) make a sound; noisy

搭配：一声不响 be very quiet ；响声 a sound

例句：他一声不响地走掉了。He left without saying a word.
电视声音太响了。The TV is too noisy.
他手机铃声太响了，把我从梦中吵醒了。His mobile phone rang too loudly and woke me up.

470 橡皮 xiàngpí 名 (n.) rubber, eraser

搭配：橡皮泥 plasticine ；橡皮手套 rubber gloves ；一块橡皮 a rubber

例句：这几个字都写错了，用橡皮擦掉重写。Wipe out the misspelled words and write again.
我可以借你的橡皮手套用一下吗？Can I use your rubber gloves please?

471 消息 xiāoxi 名 (n.) news, information

搭配：好 / 坏消息 good/ bad news ；一条消息 a piece of news/ information ；内部消息 inside news ；最新消息 latest news

例句：这真是一个让人高兴的好消息，我们快去告诉妈妈。Let's tell mother about this pleasant news!
都两天了，还没有小丽的消息，她的家人都快急坏了。Xiaoli's family is very anxious since they haven't received her news for two days.

472 小吃 xiǎochī 名 (n.) snacks, refreshments

搭配：小吃店 snack bar ；地方小吃 local snacks ；经济小吃 cheap snacks

例句：他去医院对面的小吃店吃了碗面条。He had noodles in the snack bar on the opposite side of the hospital.
本店有各种各样的地方小吃。Various local snacks are served here.

473 小伙子 xiǎohuǒzi 名 (n.) lad, young fellow

搭配：帅小伙子 a handsome guy ；年轻小伙子 a young fellow

例句：他都六十多岁了，身体哪能跟小伙子比？He is over sixties. How can he be as strong as a young man?
前面那个小伙子就是我们的项目经理。The young fellow in front of us is our project manager.

474 小说 xiǎoshuō 名 (n.) novel, fiction

搭配：看小说 to read a novel ；写小说 to write a novel ；一部 / 本小说 a novel /a novelette ；长篇 / 中篇小说 a novel/novella ；网络小说 online novel

例句：他正在房间里看小说。He is reading a novel in the room.
我就是这本小说的作者，有什么问题可以直接问我。I'm the author of this novel. You can ask me any questions directly.

475 笑话 xiàohua （名/动）(n./v.) joke; jest

搭配：讲笑话 to tell a joke；一个笑话 a joke；笑话别人 to make a fool of sb

例句：他很幽默，爱讲笑话，所以我们都喜欢和他聊天。He is humorous and likes telling jokes. Therefore we all enjoy chatting with him.

笑话他人的缺点是不礼貌的行为。Laughing at other's defects is impolite.

476 效果 xiàoguǒ （名）(n.) effect

搭配：没有效果 to have no effect；取得效果 to get some effect；实际效果 practical effect；积极效果 positive result

例句：这些药对你的病没有效果。These drugs have no effects on your disease.

这则广告的效果很明显。This advertisement is very effective.

477 心情 xīnqíng （名）(n.) mood

搭配：心情好/坏 in a good/bad mood；心情激动/平静 in exciting/calm mood；心情复杂 to have mixed feelings；没心情 be not in the mood

例句：他现在心情很平静，已经不生气了。He is in calm mood now.

她心情不好的时候喜欢听听轻音乐。She likes listening to some light music when she feels bad.

478 辛苦 xīnkǔ （形）(adj.) hard

搭配：辛苦的工作 hard work；辛苦的生活 a hard life

例句：他们一天工作十二个小时，生活很辛苦。They work twelve hours a day and live a hard life.

谢谢你帮我把这些家具搬到楼下，辛苦你了。Thank you for taking all the troubles helping me bring the furniture downstairs.

能不能辛苦你跑一趟？May I trouble you to go and see about it?

479 信封 xìnfēng （名）(n.) envelope

搭配：买信封 to buy some envelopes；一个信封 an envelope；大信封 a big envelope

例句：信封里除了信，还有两张照片。Besides a letter, there are two photos in the envelope.

李红在信封上写上了自己的地址。Li Hong put her address on the envelope.

480 信息 xìnxī （名）(n.) information, message, news

搭配：一条信息 a piece of news；电子信息 electronic information；信息时代 information age；提供信息 to provide information；市场信息 market information

例句：我收到李红发来的信息，才知道王东生病了。It was only when I received the message from Li Hong that I knew Wang Dong was ill.

你是从哪儿知道的这条信息？Where did you get this information?

实战练习（四十）

一、听对话，选择正确答案

1. A. 科技　　B. 文学　　C. 自然　　D. 法律
2. A. 睡觉　　B. 请假　　C. 看比赛　　D. 吃早饭

二、选词填空

A 笑话　B 橡皮　C 心情　D 效果　E 消息　F 辛苦

1. 他要离开的（　　　）是假的吧，我怎么没听说过？
2. 这个字写错了，用（　　　）擦掉。
3. 没考好，我的（　　　）很差。
4. 我从来没有听过这么好笑的（　　　）。
5. A：小红的妈妈自己一个人带着两个孩子生活真是太（　　　）了！
   B：是啊，真是不容易。
6. A：昨晚的演出（　　　）怎么样？
   B：还不错，观众的反应很好。

A 响　B 小吃　C 信息　D 信封　E 小说　F 小伙子

7. 外面的（　　　）声很大，你出去看看孩子们在干什么？
8. 我喜欢美食，对各地的（　　　）很感兴趣。
9. 我忘记在（　　　）上贴邮票了。
10. 我已经老了，所以特别羡慕那些年轻的（　　　）。
11. A：边吃东西边看（　　　）是一个非常不好的习惯。
    B：我以后会注意的。
12. A：你对互联网有什么看法？
    B：它带来太多无用的（　　　）。

三、排列顺序

1. A. 哈哈大笑起来　　B. 大家都忘掉了难过的事情　　C. 这个笑话效果真是太好了
2. A. 我喜欢看小说　　B. 心情不好的时候就找一本读读
   C. 效果比看电影还好

四、完成句子

1. 能　橡皮　用用吗　你的　借 _____
2. 这个消息　带来了　好心情　给大家 _____
3. 这本　我有信心　写好　在一个月之内　小说 _____
4. 效果　这个　不好　笑话的 _____
5. 是　写小说　很辛苦的　一件　事情 _____

五、看图，用词造句

1. 辛苦

2. 小伙子

Unit 41

信心	性格
兴奋	修理
行	许多
醒	学期
幸福	压力
性别	牙膏

481 信心 xìnxīn （名）(n.) confidence

搭配：有信心 to have confidence in；信心十足 be very confident；充满信心 be full of confidence

例句：要对自己有信心，我相信你一定可以通过的。You should be confident and I believe you surely can pass the exam.

我对你充满了信心，快去面试吧，不要迟到了。I have confidence in you and don't be late for the interview.

482 兴奋 xīngfèn （形）(adj.) exciting, excited

搭配：感到兴奋 to feel excited；酒后兴奋 alcoholic excitement

例句：听到这个消息，大家都很兴奋。We all feel excited to hear this news.

知道这个消息后，我兴奋得觉都没睡。I couldn't fall asleep after hearing this exciting news.

483 行 xíng （动/形）(v./adj.) be right

例句：这怎么行呢，你还是找张医生来看看吧。This is no good and you'd better ask Doctor Zhang to have a look at it.

谁来都行。It doesn't matter who will come.

我的汉语口语不行。My oral Chinese is poor.

你真行，这么危险的动作也能完成。You're really terrific to finish this dangerous action.

484 醒 xǐng （动）(v.) wake up

搭配：叫醒 waken；醒来 to wake up

例句：她太累了，睡了一天才醒。She was too tired and slept for the whole day.

我睡醒的时候天还没有亮。I woke up when the sky was still dark.

485 幸福 xìngfú （名/形）(n./adj.) happiness; happy

搭配：个人幸福 personal happiness；幸福地生活 to live happily；幸福美满 perfect happiness；追求幸福 to pursue happiness

例句：小红结婚后，一直生活得很幸福。Xiaohong lives happily after getting married.

每个人都有追求幸福的权利。Everyone has the right to pursue happiness.

486 性别 xìngbié （名）(n.) gender

搭配：性别男/女 male/female；填写性别 to fill in the gender form；性别特征 gender traits

例句：填表时，常常要填"姓名、性别、年龄"等内容。The contents such as "name, gender, age, etc." are usually demanded when one fills in a form.

性别没有关系，重要的是要有能力。Compared with one's gender, one's capability is more important.

Unit 41

487 性格 xìnggé (名) (n.) nature, temperament

搭配：性格特点 personality；改变性格 to change sb's character；性格内向/外向 be introverted / extroverted

例句：他的性格非常好，很容易相处。He's a good-tempered and easy-going person.
我女朋友的性格十分开朗、活泼。My girlfriend is bright and cheerful.
他的性格不适合在办公室工作。Office work does not suit his temperament.

488 修理 xiūlǐ (动) (v.) mend, fix, repair

搭配：修理自行车 to fix a bike；修理电视 to repair TV；修理房屋 to fix the house；修理手表 to repair a watch

例句：王东正在修理电脑呢。Wang Dong is repairing the computer now.
我想把头发修理修理。I'd like to have my hair cut.

489 许多 xǔduō (数) (num.) many, much

搭配：许多事情 many things；许多水果 many fruits

例句：今天商场在做活动，里面有许多人。There are many people at the department store today since it is having a promoting session.
我今天买了许多菜，你等会儿来我家吃饭吧。I bought a lot of food today and you can come to my house to eat.

490 学期 xuéqī (名) (n.) term, semester

搭配：上学期 last term；下学期 next term；一学期 a term；学期结束 the end of the term

例句：这学期我们换了一个新的英语老师。We had a new English teacher this term.
下学期开始我就要实习了。Next semester I am going to work as an intern.

491 压力 yālì (名) (n.) pressure, stress

搭配：有压力 to have a pressure of ...；压力大/小 high / low pressure；减轻压力 to reduce pressure；心理压力 mental stress

例句：我不想在这里工作了，压力实在是太大了。I do not want to work under such a heavy pressure here.
现在大学生的就业压力越来越大。The pressure of getting employed is becoming heavier and heavier for college graduates today.

492 牙膏 yágāo (名) (n.) toothpaste

搭配：儿童牙膏 a children's toothpaste；药物牙膏 medicinal toothpaste；一支牙膏 a tube of toothpaste；牙膏和牙刷 toothpaste and toothbrush；挤牙膏 to be forced to tell sth bit by bit

例句：家里的牙膏没有了，我们一起去超市买吧。The toothpaste is used up, let's buy some new ones at the supermarket.
儿子，要把牙膏挤完才能扔掉。Son, you should throw away the toothpaste only after using it up.

实战练习（四十一）

一、听对话，选择正确答案

1. A. 幽默　　B. 漂亮　　C. 个子高　　D. 性格好
2. A. 经理　　B. 顾客　　C. 服务员　　D. 修车的

二、选词填空

A 性格　B 学期　C 修理　D 许多　E 牙膏　F 压力

1. 这只（　　）还没有用完，你怎么就把它扔到垃圾桶里了？
2. （　　）相同的故事却有着不同的意义。
3. 这（　　）一共五个月。
4. （　　）影响一个人的成功和失败。
5. A：我的手表怎么又不走了？
   B：一定是坏了，我来帮你（　　）一下。
6. A：你这两天怎么了？好像没有什么精神。
   B：没什么，就是感到学习（　　）很大。

A 醒　B 兴奋　C 信心　D 性别　E 行　F 幸福

7. 比赛结束后，赢得比赛的人都很（　　）。
8. 既然都睡（　　）了，就不要在床上躺着了。
9. 申请参加比赛的人有年龄、（　　）的限制。
10. 她的家庭非常（　　），真让人羡慕。
11. A：明天要去面试，我有点紧张。
    B：不用担心，我对你有（　　），你一定没有问题的。
12. A：今天大家这么高兴，你不喝怎么（　　）呢？来，我敬你一杯！
    B：干杯！

三、排列顺序

1. A. 听到这个消息　　B. 我非常兴奋　　C. 觉得自己成了最幸福的人
2. A. 换了工作之后　　B. 我感到很幸福　　C. 因为压力减轻了不少

四、完成句子

1. 很受欢迎　牙膏　水果味的　这种　_____
2. 这么兴奋　你　刚睡醒　怎么就　_____
3. 一个　我女朋友　我想找　性格　活泼的　女孩　当　_____
4. 对　考试　很有　这学期的　信心　我　_____
5. 修一修　你把　这棵树上的　树枝　去请人　_____

五、看图，用词造句

1. 兴奋

2. 修理

Unit 42

亚洲	眼镜
呀	演出
严格	演员
严重	阳光
研究	养成
盐	样子

493 亚洲 Yàzhōu (名) (n.) Asia

搭配：亚洲第一 No.1 in Asia；全亚洲 all over Asia；亚洲各国 Asian countries

例句：他是全亚洲最有名的演员。He's the most famous actor in Asia.

亚洲是世界七大洲中面积最大的洲。Among the seven continents around the world, Asia is the largest one.

494 呀 ya (助) (part.) (a syllable ending)

例句：原来是你呀，我都认不出来了。It turns out to be you! I even can't recognize you.

呀，你怎么来了？ Wow! Why do you come here?

495 严格 yángé (形) (adj.) strict

搭配：严格的老师 a strict teacher；严格的标准 exacting standard；严格控制 to control strictly

例句：王华对孩子们的要求很严格，孩子们都很怕他。Wang Hua is very strict with the children and they are all afraid of him.

我们一定要严格遵守学校的规章制度。We must strictly abide by the rules and regulations of our school.

496 严重 yánzhòng (形) (adj.) serious, critical

搭配：情况很严重 a serious situation；严重的病情 be seriously ill；严重后果 serious consequences；严重问题 serious problem

例句：这件事的后果很严重，你必须负责。You must take the responsibility for this serious consequence.

你犯了一个很严重的错误。You made a serious mistake.

497 研究 yánjiū (动) (v.) study, research

搭配：研究工作 research；基础研究 fundamental studies；研究方法 research method

例句：他对这个问题进行了认真的研究。He engaged in a serious study of the problem.

领导们研究该怎么解决这件事。The directors discussed as to what should be done to settle the matter.

498 盐 yán (名) (n.) salt

搭配：一斤盐 a half kilo of salt；咸盐 salt

例句：你做的菜实在是太咸了，一定是盐放多了。The dish you made is too salty. You must have put in too much salt.

食盐是人们的生活必需品之一。Salt is one of the life necessities to people.

499 眼镜 yǎnjìng (名) (n.) glasses

搭配：戴眼镜 to wear glasses；换眼镜 to change glasses；新眼镜 new glasses；太阳眼镜

sun glasses；一副眼镜 a pair of glasses

例句：我的眼睛很好，不用戴眼镜。I have a good eyesight and don't need to wear glasses.
夏天到了，我想买一副太阳眼镜。Summer is coming, I want to buy a pair of sun glasses.

500 演出 yǎnchū 动 (v.) perform, show
搭配：精彩演出 a wonderful show；演出场地 a performing place；一场演出 a performance；观看演出 to watch a performance；公开演出 an open performance；现场演出 to perform live
例句：昨天他们的演出很精彩，你没有去看确实很可惜。They put on a great performance last night and it was really a pity that you didn't come.
今天是他第一次公开演出，所以他很紧张。He feels very nervous about today's first open show.

501 演员 yǎnyuán 名 (n.) actor; actress
搭配：著名演员 a famous actor；当演员 to become an actor；男/女演员 an actor/actress
例句：成为一名演员，是她一生的梦想。Her dream of life is to become an actress.
这个演员的感情非常丰富。This actor is full of emotions.

502 阳光 yángguāng 名/形 (n./adj.) sunshine, sunlight
搭配：阳光充足 be full of sunlight；温暖的阳光 warm sunlight；在阳光下 under sunlight
例句：一连下了好几天的雨，今天终于见到阳光了。After several days of rain, today we finally see some sunlight.
中午的阳光是最强烈的。The sunshine at noon is very strong.
这个小伙子很阳光。The young fellow is full of energy.

503 养成 yǎngchéng 动 (v.) cultivate, form
搭配：养成好习惯 to form a good habit；慢慢养成 to slowly form；长期养成 to form a habit through a long time
例句：我们从小就要养成爱看书的好习惯。We should develop the good habit of reading books from a young age.
这些坏习惯都是长期以来逐渐养成的。These bad habits form gradually through a long period of time.

504 样子 yàngzi 名 (n.) appearance
搭配：样子很漂亮 a good-looking appearance；温柔的样子 a gentle appearance；看样子 it seems like ...
例句：我非常喜欢她开心的样子。I like her happy looking.
我还记得他以前的样子。I still remember what he was like in the past.
她不像有病的样子。She doesn't look sick.

实战练习（四十二）

一、听对话，选择正确答案

1. A. 吃惊　　B. 高兴　　C. 骄傲　　D. 伤心
2. A. 理想　　B. 演员　　C. 演出　　D. 生活

二、选词填空

　　　　A 呀　B 眼镜　C 亚洲　D 严格　E 严重　F 盐

1. 中国在（　　）是个大国。
2. 我（　　）找不到了，现在什么都看不见。
3. 这个菜怎么一点味道都没有，你一定是忘记放（　　）了吧。
4. 他们的生活真幸福（　　），每天都可以去公园散步。
5. A：你觉得他的文章写得怎么样？
   B：（　　）来说，许多地方用词不准确。
6. A：你爸爸现在的情况怎么样？
   B：流了很多血，医生说情况很（　　）。

　　　　A 研究　B 演出　C 演员　D 阳光　E 养成　F 样子

7. 他看见我了，却装作没有看见的（　　），我很生气。
8. 除了工资少得可怜，群众（　　）也是最辛苦的。
9. 儿童应该（　　）早睡早起的好习惯。
10. 今天的（　　）真好，我们一起出去散步吧。
11. A：明天的（　　）几点开始？
    B：八点，你要提前来啊。
12. A：我们学校今年招聘了多少（　　）生？
    B：十个左右吧。

三、排列顺序

1. A. 认真地修改修改　　B. 请你把报告拿回去
   C. 你的报告里有个比较严重的错误
2. A. 我终于迎来了演出的机会　B. 经过长时间的等待　　C. 我兴奋得不知道说什么才好

四、完成句子

1. 总是 很严格 妈妈 对我的 要求　＿＿＿＿＿＿＿＿＿＿＿＿＿＿
2. 坏习惯 儿子 我希望 养成 什么 不要　＿＿＿＿＿＿＿＿＿＿
3. 严重的 他 错误 一个 犯了　＿＿＿＿＿＿＿＿＿＿＿＿＿＿
4. 演出 要到 她 亚洲 参加　＿＿＿＿＿＿＿＿＿＿＿＿＿＿＿
5. 需要 才能够 花草 足够的 阳光 长大　＿＿＿＿＿＿＿＿＿

五、看图，用词造句

1. 演出

2. 眼镜

Unit 43

邀请	一切
要是	以
钥匙	以为
也许	艺术
叶子	意见
页	因此

505 邀请 yāoqǐng (动) (v.) invite

搭配: 发出邀请 to send an invitation；接受邀请 to accept an invitation；邀请信 an invitation letter；正式邀请 formally invite

例句: 下个星期三是我的生日，我想邀请你来参加。I want to invite you to my birthday party on next Wednesday.

张华被邀请去参加老同学的婚礼。Zhang Hua is invited to attend his classmate's wedding ceremony.

506 要是 yàoshi (连) (conj.) if, suppose, in case

例句: 这主意不错，但要是你妈妈发现了怎么办？It's a good idea, but what if your mother finds it out?

要是你不想去，我可以再安排其他人。I'll ask someone else to go if you do not want to.

要是你有时间，咱们就去医院看看他。Go to see him in the hospital if you have time.

507 钥匙 yàoshi (名) (n.) key

搭配: 一把钥匙 a key；汽车钥匙 car key；门钥匙 the door key

例句: 读书是打开智慧之门的钥匙。Reading is the key to opening the gate of wisdom.

我的钥匙不见了，你帮我找找。I lost my key and please help me to find it.

508 也许 yěxǔ (副) (adv.) perhaps, maybe

例句: 我觉得他的话也许是对的。I think his words are perhaps right.

你去找小红吧，也许她能帮助你。You can go to Xiaohong and maybe she can help you.

他也许会来。Maybe he will come.

509 叶子 yèzi (名) (n.) leaf

搭配: 一片叶子 a leaf；长叶子 to put forth leaves

例句: 秋天到了，树上的叶子全掉光了。In autumn the leaves of trees all fell down.

我喜欢把好看的叶子夹在书本里。I like clipping beautiful leaves in books.

510 页 yè (量) (m.w.) page

搭配: 第一页 page one；书的页数 pages of books；页边 margin；空白页 blank page

例句: 这本书的中间怎么少了几页？Why are the pages in the middle of this book missing?

请同学们把书翻到第三页。Please turn your book to page three.

511 一切 yíqiè (代) (pron.) all, everything

搭配: 一切办法 all means；所有的一切 all of；一切问题 all problems

例句: 妈妈把一切都安排好了。My mum has already arranged everything.

一切都有可能。Anything is possible.

Unit 43

512 以 yǐ (prep.) with, by

例句：以我们的标准，她不合格。By our standards, she is not qualified.
以他的能力，当经理都没问题。He is surely capable of being a manager.
中国队以 3:0 的比分获得了胜利。China won the match with a 3:0 score.

513 以为 yǐwéi (v.) think, consider

例句：我以为住在这儿很方便，其实并不方便。I considered it was convenient to live here at first, but the truth is contrary.
我以为这样做不行，其实可以。I thought it was impossible at first, but it is not.
你终于来了，我们还以为你不来了呢。There you are at last! We'd given you up.

514 艺术 yìshù (n.) art

搭配：领导艺术 the art of leadership；艺术家 artist；行为艺术 action art；艺术创造 art creation；艺术学院 an art college

例句：美有各种各样的艺术表现形式。Beauty has many artistic expressions.
巴黎是一座艺术之都。Paris is a city of art.

515 意见 yìjiàn (n.) view, opinion

搭配：准确意见 specific views；个人意见 personal opinion；提意见 to express a view；交换意见 to exchange views with sb；相反意见 a contrary view

例句：王东让我给他的文章提些意见。Wang Dong asked about my opinions on his article.
我经常跟同事们交换意见。I often exchange views with my colleagues.
我对她很有意见。I have a lot of complaints about her.
你老是有意见。You always have a bone to pick.

516 因此 yīncǐ (conj.) therefore

例句：我想让自己休息一下，因此就没有急着找工作。I want to have a rest, therefore, I don't set out to find a job in a hurry.
火车票买不到，因此我就去买了汽车票。I couldn't buy a train ticket, therefore I bought a bus ticket instead.
工作太忙，因此没有早点来看您。I was too busy to come to see you early.

实战练习（四十三）

一、听对话，选择正确答案

1. A. 超市　　B. 家里　　C. 医院　　D. 教室
2. A. 医生　　B. 演员　　C. 老师　　D. 经理

二、选词填空

A 邀请　B 也许　C 叶子　D 页　E 一切　F 钥匙

1. 这本书的（　　）码很乱。
2. 你看见我的车（　　）了吗？我找了半天都没有找到。
3. 这件事（　　）真的是我做错了。
4. 秋天到了，校园的地上满是飘落的（　　）。
5. A：你发会议（　　）信给张经理了吗？
   B：早就发过了，但他说要出差不能来参加会议了。
6. A：你觉得学校变化大吗？
   B：很大，这里的（　　）都和原来不一样了。

A 以为　B 以　C 艺术　D 意见　E 因此　F 要是

7. （　　）我看来，她现在这个样子就非常适合她。
8. 我给妈妈买了一件衣服，但是她不喜欢，（　　）我不得不把它退了回去。
9. 我喜欢（　　），特别是绘画。
10. 我（　　）今天会下雨，结果没下。
11. A：让张明当经理，你有什么（　　）？
    B：我完全赞成。
12. A：我（　　）请十天假去旅游，经理能同意吗？
    B：现在这么忙，最好别请。

三、排列顺序

1. A. 我以为她会接受我的邀请　B. 没想到她竟然拒绝了　C. 我的心情因此而变差
2. A. 就要多听取别人的意见　B. 要想赢得别人的尊重　C. 爸爸经常告诉我

四、完成句子

1. 艺术天分 一点 我 通过学习 才发现 自己没有 _____
2. 什么都 我 不知道 别以为 _____
3. 一切 来源于 生活 艺术 都 _____
4. 出门的 把 时候 钥匙 带上 _____
5. 没有 是 世界上 两片 叶子 完全相同的 _____

五、看图，用词造句

1. 钥匙

2. 意见

Unit 44

引起	优点
印象	优秀
赢	幽默
应聘	尤其
永远	由
勇敢	由于

Unit 44

517 引起 yǐnqǐ (v.) cause

搭配：引起注意 to draw attention；引起兴趣 to draw interests；引起误会 to cause misunderstanding；引起大火 to spark a fire

例句：这部电视剧在全国播出后，引起了不小的反响。This TV play produced a great reaction after being broadcasted.
她的出现引起了所有人的注意。Her appearance drew everyone's attention.

518 印象 yìnxiàng (n.) impression

搭配：留下印象 to leave an impression on sb；好/坏印象 a good / bad impression；第一印象 the first impression；改变印象 to change the impression

例句：北京人给我的印象是特别热情。Beijing people leave a passionate and cordial impression on me.
在人际交往中，第一印象是最重要的。The first impression is very important during interpersonal communication.

519 赢 yíng (v.) win

搭配：赢得比赛 to win a game/ match；输赢 lose and win；赢得冠军 to win the champion

例句：比赛输赢不重要，重要的是经历的过程。The experience is more important than the outcome of this contest.
第一次上台讲话，我就赢得了一片掌声。I won warm applauses on my first public speech.

520 应聘 yìngpìn (v.) apply for a job

搭配：应聘信息 job wanted；应聘结果 result of job application；应聘经验 job application experience

例句：他应聘到一家酒店做大堂经理。He was taken on as a lobby manger in a hotel.
应聘结果要三天后才能知道。The result of application will come out three days later.

521 永远 yǒngyuǎn (adv.) forever

例句：我希望永远不再看见你。I hope I've seen the last of you.
我们永远都不能忘记我们大学毕业的那一天。We will remember the day we graduated from the university forever.
害怕失败的人永远都不会成功。One who is always afraid of failures can never succeed.

522 勇敢 yǒnggǎn (adj.) brave

搭配：勇敢的民族 gallant people；勇敢的人民 a gallant people；勇敢的心 a brave heart

例句：年轻人要勇敢地面对挑战。Young people should face challenges bravely.
你要勇敢地面对现实。You should face the reality squarely.

523 优点 yōudiǎn / 名 (n.) / advantage, merit
  搭配：主要优点 main advantages；优点和缺点 merits and demerits；发现优点 to find merits
  例句：每个人身上都有优点和缺点。Everyone has merits and demerits.
    这个手机最大的优点是上网速度快。The biggest advantage of the mobile phone is its fast wire speed.

524 优秀 yōuxiù / 形 (adj.) / excellent
  搭配：优秀学生 top students；优秀作品 an excellent work；优秀人才 outstanding talents；成绩优秀 to get excellent results；表现优秀 to do well
  例句：当一名优秀的老师是我最大的理想。To be an outstanding teacher is my biggest dream.
    这名运动员非常优秀。He is a very excellent athlete.

525 幽默 yōumò / 形 (adj.) / humorous
  搭配：比较幽默 fairly humorous；幽默感 a sense of humor；幽默故事 a humorous story
  例句：这本小说的语言非常幽默。This novel features a high humorous language.
    王老师很幽默，很喜欢和别人开玩笑。Mr. Wang is humorous and likes playing jokes with others.

526 尤其 yóuqí / 副 (adv.) / especially
  例句：我很喜欢吃水果，尤其是苹果。I like eating fruits, especially apples.
    她对学外语很感兴趣，尤其是汉语。She is interested in learning foreign languages, especially Chinese.

527 由 yóu / 介 (prep.) / by
  搭配：由……引起 caused by；由内而外 from inside to outside；由上而下 from top to bottom；由坏变好 to transform from the bad into the good
  例句：比赛将要开始了，下面由我来宣布选手名单。The game will begin soon. Next let me declare the player list.
    由内到外，我们把房间检查了好几遍。We checked the room from inside to outside for several times.

528 由于 yóuyú / 介/连 (prep./conj.) / due to; because
  例句：由于这个病，他不愿意出来。He won't come out because of this sick.
    由于天气不好，比赛时间不得不推迟。We have to delay the match because of the bad weather.
    由于昨晚睡得太晚，她早上迟到了。She was late this morning because she slept too late last night.

实战练习（四十四）

一、听对话，选择正确答案

1. A. 继续工作　　B. 看书　　C. 买东西　　D. 看电影
2. A. 优秀　　　　B. 勇敢　　C. 浪漫　　　D. 严厉

二、选词填空

A 优秀　B 幽默　C 尤其　D 由　E 由于　F 优点

1. 学生很快（　　）几个人增加到七十多人。
2. 他一生有许多发明创造，是我国最（　　）的发明家之一。
3. （　　）比以前更忙了，我甚至没有时间给家里打电话。
4. 如果问他一个问题，（　　）是严肃的问题，他总喜欢先开个玩笑。
5. A：你理想中的女朋友是什么样的？
   B：她不需要很漂亮，但是一定要（　　）、活泼。
6. A：小王有什么（　　）？
   B：幽默、浪漫、能力强。

A 印象　B 赢　C 应聘　D 永远　E 勇敢　F 引起

7. 地球变暖已经（　　）全世界人们的关注。
8. 失去工作后，我到处（　　）。
9. 他给我的（　　）就是幽默、大方、真诚。
10. 海燕是（　　）的动物，面对海浪永远都不会害怕。
11. A：这样的错误希望以后（　　）都不要出现了。
    B：你放心吧，我会记住的。
12. A：想要（　　）得比赛，你就一定要坚持到最后。
    B：知道了，我一定不会放弃的。

三、排列顺序

1. A. 王华的优点很多　　B. 而且对人十分友好　　C. 他不但很幽默
2. A. 他是一个非常优秀的人　　B. 而且很勇敢　　C. 在我的印象里

四、完成句子

1. 要争取做　对社会　优秀人才　我们　有用的 _____
2. 这次会议　一定会　我们的友谊　增进 _____
3. 所有困难　面对　勇敢地　我们要　生活中的 _____
4. 留下　我想　给她　一个好印象 _____
5. 幸福的时光　真希望　我　能够　永远停留 _____

五、看图，用词造句

1. 赢

2. 幽默

Unit 45

邮局	与
友好	羽毛球
友谊	语法
有趣	语言
于是	预习
愉快	原来

529 **邮局** yóujú (n.) post office
搭配：一家邮局 the post office；邮局工作人员 staff in the post office
例句：他去邮局寄了一封信。He went to the post office to mail a letter.
刚才接到邮局的电话，让我去取包裹。A phone-call from the post office asked me to get my parcel.

530 **友好** yǒuhǎo (adj.) friendly, close friend
搭配：态度友好 a friendly attitude；关系友好 be on friendly terms with ...
例句：王经理对人十分友好，我很喜欢他。Manager Wang is very kind to others and I like him very much.
我们要学会与人友好相处。We should learn how to get well along with others.

531 **友谊** yǒuyì (n.) friendship
搭配：增进友谊 to promote friendship；友谊万岁 a longtime friendship；建立友谊 to build a friendship with
例句：愿我们的友谊长在！ May our friendship live forever.
小孩子之间的友谊最纯真了。The friendship among children is most innocent.

532 **有趣** yǒuqù (adj.) interesting, interested
搭配：有趣的书 an interesting book；有趣的消息 amusing story；觉得有趣 to feel interested
例句：王老师问了我一个有趣的问题。 Mr. Wang asked me an interesting question.
这个游戏非常有趣，大家都爱玩。We all like playing this interesting game.

533 **于是** yúshì (conj.) so, therefore
例句：麦克爱上了中国文化，于是决定来中国留学。Mike likes the Chinese culture, so he decided to study in China.
他们希望用音乐养活自己，于是他们决定到酒吧演出。They want to use their talents in music to make a living, so they decided to perform in the bar.

534 **愉快** yúkuài (adj.) happy, joyful
搭配：心情愉快 be very happy；愉快地工作 to work joyfully
例句：祝大家节日愉快！ I wish you all a happy holiday.
小红度过了一个愉快的下午。Xiaohong spent a happy afternoon.

535 **与** yǔ (prep./conj.) with, and
例句：与她谈话后，我感到很愉快。After talking to her, I feel very pleasant.
这事与我无关。It is none of my business.
我与她是非常好的朋友。She and I are very close friends.

Unit 45

536 羽毛球 yǔmáoqiú (n.) badminton
- 搭配：打羽毛球 to play badminton；羽毛球比赛 a badminton match；一只羽毛球 a badminton
- 例句：我们约好今天上午一起去打羽毛球。We planned to play badminton this morning.
  羽毛球运动开始逐渐在城市中流行起来。Playing badminton gradually becomes a popular game in the city.

537 语法 yǔfǎ (n.) grammar
- 搭配：语法关系 a syntactic relation；语法书 a grammar book；语法学 grammar；语法结构 grammatical structure；语法错误 grammar mistakes
- 例句：这种语法错误很常见。This syntax error is common.
  语法学家根据汉语词汇的语法特点，把它们分为十一类。According to the grammatical characteristics, grammarians divide vocabularies into eleven categories.

538 语言 yǔyán (n.) language
- 搭配：研究语言 to study a language；语言学 linguistics；语言交流 verbal communication；第二语言 second language
- 例句：他会说四种语言，确实很不简单。He speaks four languages and is really awesome.
  我对语言学很感兴趣。I'm interested in linguistics.

539 预习 yùxí (v.) preview
- 搭配：提前预习 to prepare lessons before classes；预习课文 to preview lessons
- 例句：上课前一天，要把课文预习一遍。You should preview the text the day before the class.
  预习是一个好习惯。Previewing is a good habit.

540 原来 yuánlái (adv./adj.) originally; original
- 搭配：原来的样子 original state；原来的校长 former principal of the school；原来的地方 the same place
- 例句：我原来是在中学工作，现在在大学当老师。I originally worked in a secondary school and now I am a university teacher.
  我说夜里怎么这么冷，原来是下雪了。No wonder I felt rather cold during the night, it was snowing outside.
  你还记得这个电影院原来的样子吗？Do you remember what this theater looks like originally?

实战练习（四十五）

一、听对话，选择正确答案

1. A. 书店　　B. 饭店　　C. 宾馆　　D. 教室
2. A. 不浪漫　B. 朋友很少　C. 经常迟到　D. 经常说假话

二、选词填空

　　　　A 语法　　B 语言　　C 原来　　D 预习　　E 友好　　F 羽毛球

1. 虽然双方没有共同（　　　），但是彼此却能够友好相处。
2. 他的研究方向是现代汉语（　　　）。
3. 要养成课前（　　　），课后复习的良好习惯。
4. 他惊讶地说："真没想到，（　　　）你们画家这么辛苦。"
5. A：我感觉张红对人不太（　　　），好像很难相处。
   B：其实她是个很热心的人。
6. A：你有什么爱好？
   B：我喜欢打（　　　）。

　　　　A 有趣　　B 友谊　　C 于是　　D 与　　E 愉快　　F 邮局

7. 一个人不可能孤独地生活在社会上，总是需要朋友，需要（　　　）。
8. 小孩子们都喜欢听一些（　　　）的故事。
9. 我喜欢学语言，（　　　）大学选了英语专业。
10. 能够天天（　　　）他一起上学，我感到很幸福。
11. A：哪儿可以买到信封呢？
    B：你去（　　　）看看。
12. A：看你今天心情很（　　　），有什么开心的事吗？
    B：是的，我儿子考上了博士。

三、排列顺序

1. A. 有利于学生掌握语法并提高语言的实际运用能力
   B. 这本书中的对话场景
   C. 与生活非常接近

2. A. 并且要学会预习和复习
   B. 必须要养成良好的阅读习惯
   C. 要学好一种语言

四、完成句子

1. 我要　寄信　邮局　去 ＿＿＿＿＿＿＿＿＿＿＿＿＿＿＿＿
2. 是有原因的　小红　原来　我发现　这样做 ＿＿＿＿＿＿＿＿
3. 要学的　预习一下　把下节课　请大家　语法知识 ＿＿＿＿＿
4. 打羽毛球　他们　去公园　都是　每次约会 ＿＿＿＿＿＿＿＿
5. 重点　这节课的　语法　是 ＿＿＿＿＿＿＿＿＿＿＿＿＿＿

五、看图，用词造句

1. 友好

2. 愉快

Unit 46

原谅　　　杂志
原因　　　咱们
约会　　　暂时
阅读　　　脏
云　　　　责任
允许　　　增加

Unit 46

541 原谅 yuánliàng (v.) forgive, pardon

搭配：得到原谅 to obtain a pardon；无法原谅 unforgivable；请求原谅 to ask for / beg sb's pardon

例句：没有得到他的原谅，我很不开心。I felt bad because he didn't forgive me.
我很后悔当时没有原谅张东。I regret that I didn't forgive Zhang Dong at that time.

542 原因 yuányīn (n.) reason

搭配：主要原因 the main reason (of)；找到原因 to find the reason；大概原因 a possible reason；解释原因 to explain the cause of

例句：是什么原因让他做出这么可怕的事情？What's the reason for his terrible action?
他这样做的原因到底是什么？What on earth is the reason for his action?

543 约会 yuēhuì (n./v.) date; make an appointment

搭配：安排约会 to arrange for an engagement；重要约会 an important appointment

例句：别忘了明天还有个约会。Don't forget tomorrow's appointment.
小红终于答应和我约会了。Xiaohong finally accepted to go on a date with me.

544 阅读 yuèdú (v.) read

搭配：阅读与写作 reading and writing；阅读习惯 a reading habit；阅读文章 to read an article

例句：我养成了每天阅读文章的好习惯。I have a good habit of reading everyday.
在学习时，注意力越集中，阅读速度就越快。During the process of study, the more you concentrate, the faster you read.

545 云 yún (n.) cloud

搭配：白云 a white cloud；多云 cloudy；一片云 a cloud

例句：天上有很多白云。The sky is full of white clouds.
今天天气不太好，多云。The weather is not good enough—it is cloudy today.

546 允许 yǔnxǔ (v.) allow

搭配：口头允许 verbally permit；允许竞争 to permit competition；得到允许 to obtain permission

例句：学校不允许学生迟到和早退。Schools do not permit students to arrive late or leave early.
如果时间允许的话，我想去看看老师。If time allows, I want to visit the teacher.

547 杂志 zázhì (n.) magazine

搭配：一本杂志 a magazine；阅读杂志 to read a magazine；科学杂志 scientific journal

例句：我经常到图书馆去看杂志。I often go to library to read magazines.
张明经常在《笑话》杂志上发表作品。Zhang Ming often publishes his works on the *Joke* Magazine.

548 咱们 zámen 代 (pron.) we, us

例句：咱们家的米吃光了，出去买点吧。Our rice is eaten up. Go and buy some.

咱们一起到公园散散步吧。Let's have a walk in the park.

客气什么，咱们都是一家人。Please don't stand on ceremony, we're all one family.

549 暂时 zànshí 名 (n.) temporary

搭配：暂时的放松 a temporary relaxation；暂时休息 a temporary rest；暂时的困难 temporary difficulties；暂时停课 to suspend school classes

例句：辞职后，我暂时在家休息了一段时间。After resignation, I rested at home for some time.

老房子要拆了，我们一家暂时住在亲戚家。Our old house will be pulled down, so we're temporarily living with our relatives.

550 脏 zāng 形 (adj.) dirty

搭配：脏东西 dirty thing；脏衣服 dirty clothes；说脏话 to speak dirty words

例句：你这衣服多少天没有洗了，真脏！Your clothes are so dirty! How long haven't you wash them?

把你的脏手洗干净再去拿东西吃。Wash your dirty hands before picking up any food!

551 责任 zérèn 名 (n.) responsibility, duty, obligation

搭配：负责任 to take an obligation；社会责任 social obligation；法律责任 a legal obligation；责任重大 to feel much responsibility；责任感 a sense of duty

例句：照顾好父母是子女的责任。Taking good care of parents is children's duty.

我们不应该把这次事故的责任都推到他身上。We cannot shift all blames of this accident to him.

552 增加 zēngjiā 动 (v.) increase

搭配：增加信心 to increase confidence；增加数量 to increase total number of；增加工资 to increase salaries；增加词汇量 to increase vocabularies；要求增加 to demand an increase

例句：中国是世界上人口最多的国家，近四十年增加了一倍。Chinese population has been doubled during recent 40 years, has the largest number of population in the world.

工作以后，我的体重增加了许多。I have gained a lot of weight after work.

实战练习（四十六）

一、听对话，选择正确答案

1. A. 想休息　　B. 公司太远　　C. 工资很低　　D. 公司环境不好
2. A. 女的很不满　B. 男的是研究生　C. 考研究生的人少　D. 女的在准备考试

二、选词填空

A 咱们　　B 暂时　　C 脏　　D 责任　　E 云　　F 增加

1. 我胖了，体重（　　）了30斤。
2. 他笑着对我说："别急，（　　）还没有适合你的工作，你慢慢等吧。"
3. 作为一个有社会（　　）心的科学家，爱因斯坦受到了各国人民的尊敬。
4. 明天（　　）要不要一起去参加学校的招聘会？
5. A：天上那是飞机吗？
   B：那是（　　）朵。
6. A：赶快把你的书桌整理一下，这些（　　）东西都扔到垃圾桶里去。
   B：好的，我这就收拾。

A 原因　　B 约会　　C 原谅　　D 阅读　　E 允许　　F 杂志

7. 为了能和那个女孩（　　），小明想尽了办法。
8. 不知道是什么（　　），小红今天没来上课。
9. 请（　　）我向您表达最诚挚的敬意。
10. 我喜欢躺在床上看各种（　　）。
11. A：请你（　　）我吧，我真不是故意把花瓶打破的。
    B：那你以后一定要小心。
12. A：怎样才能扩大我的知识面呢？
    B：你要大量地（　　）各种书籍。

三、排列顺序

1. A. 这样会给别人留下一个好印象
   B. 你就应该穿得整齐一点
   C. 如果你要去参加招聘会

2. A. 你的房间真是太脏了
   B. 在吃晚饭之前
   C. 咱们一起整理一下吧

四、完成句子

1. 责任　他　有　去　我　帮助 _____
2. 又窄　门前的　又脏　我家　这条路 _____
3. 增加　我们　都在　每年　公司的　人数 _____
4. 此次　上课　将暂时　给我们　招聘的　两个老师 _____
5. 杂志　妈妈　躺在　阅读　不允许我　床上 _____

五、看图，用词造句

1. 原谅

2. 阅读

Unit 47

占线	正好
招聘	正确
照	正式
真正	证明
整理	之
正常	支持

553 **占线** zhànxiàn (v.) the line is busy

搭配: 电话占线 a busy line；对方占线 the line is engaged

例句: 我给他们公司打过几次电话，可是对方一直占线。I tried to call their company several times, but the line was always busy.

你刚才和谁打电话呢？手机一直占线。Who are you talking with on the mobile? Your line was engaged all the time.

554 **招聘** zhāopìn (v.) recruit

搭配: 招聘会 a recruitment fair；人才招聘 personnel recruitment；招聘新人 to recruit new members；招聘广告 a job advertisement

例句: 学校经常举行人才招聘会。Schools often hold job fairs.

根据需要，我们决定招聘一些专业人才。We decided to recruit some professionals to meet our demands.

555 **照** zhào (v.) illuminate, light up, reflect, mirror, take a picture

例句: 冬天太阳光照在身上真暖和。It's warm in the sunshine even in winter.

她在镜子面前照了又照。She glanced at herself in the mirror.

这张照片照得很好。This photo is well taken.

556 **真正** zhēnzhèng (adv./adj.) really; real

搭配: 真正的幸福 real happiness；真正的乐趣 real interests；真正的爱情 true love

例句: 不学汉字很难真正地了解中国文化。It is difficult to understand the Chinese culture without learning Chinese characters.

一个真正勇敢的人，敢于面对各种困难。A true brave man dares to face difficulties.

557 **整理** zhěnglǐ (v.) tidy up

搭配: 整理房间 to put a room in order；整理书本 to tidy up books；整理行李 to arrange luggage；整理材料 to sort out materials；整理头发 to fix one's hair

例句: 在搬家的时候，我把所有的书都整理了一遍。I tidied all books up when we moved to a new house.

你赶紧把行李整理一下，我们就要出发了。You should quickly sort out the luggage since we are to depart in no time.

558 **正常** zhèngcháng (adj.) normal

搭配: 情况正常 in a normal condition；一切正常 everything goes normally；生活正常 to lead a normal life；表现不正常 to behave far from normal；精神不正常 to be out of one's mind

例句: 人类的正常体温是36度多。The normal body temperature of a person is a little more than 36 degrees.

他的行为极不正常。His behavior is far from normal.

559 正好 zhènghǎo (形/副) (adj./adv.) just in time; happen to

搭配：正好相反 just in the opposite；来得正好 to come in just in time

例句：这件衣服我穿着正好，颜色我也很喜欢。This shirt fits me nicely and I like its color very much.

我等车的时候，张东正好开车路过。When I was waiting for the bus, Zhang Dong happened to drive by.

现在天气不冷不热，正好出去旅游。It's neither too hot nor too cold, just the right weather for travel.

560 正确 zhèngquè (形) (adj.) right

搭配：正确与错误 right and wrong；正确的方法 the right methods

例句：你的发音方法不正确。Your method of pronunciation is not correct.

我们要正确对待别人的批评。We should treat others' criticism rightly.

561 正式 zhèngshì (形) (adj.) formal

搭配：正式开始 a formal beginning；正式通知 a formal notification；正式道歉 official apology

例句：三个月试用期后你就是正式职员了。You'll become a formal employee after this three-month probationary period.

我今天要参加面试，所以穿得很正式。I have an interview today and dressed up formally.

562 证明 zhèngmíng (名/动) (n./v.) certificate; prove

搭配：研究证明 research shows that ...；收入证明 an income certificate；学历证明 education certification；证明材料 certificate；健康证明 health certificate

例句：找工作时要向用人单位提供学历证明。We should provide academic qualifications when we look for jobs.

吸烟有害健康早已得到实验证明。The harm of smoking has long been proved.

563 之 zhī (代) (pron.) this or that

搭配：之一 one of ...；之上 all above；之前 before；总而言之 in brief；取而代之 to replace；言外之意 the hidden meaning between the lines

例句：他先去了趟图书馆，之后又去了教室。He first went to the library, and then went to the classroom.

总而言之，你以后要多加小心。All in all, you have to be careful.

564 支持 zhīchí (动) (v.) support

搭配：支持和反对 support and against；公开支持 an open support；大力支持 to support strongly；在……支持下 under the support of；赢得支持 to gain support

例句：妈妈非常支持我的事业。My mom strongly supports my career.

如果你是对的，我就支持你。I stand by you if you're right.

实战练习（四十七）

一、听对话，选择正确答案

1. A. 夫妻　　B. 师生　　C. 父子　　D. 同事
2. A. 职业　　B. 学习　　C. 生活　　D. 知识

二、选词填空

　　　　A 正好　　B 正确　　C 正式　　D 证明　　E 支持　　F 之

1. 在北温带和南温带地区，四季的出现（　　）相反。
2. 当比赛（　　）开始后，我们才到会场。
3. 你如果不（　　）我，那我只好去找张红帮忙了。
4. 你回来（　　）前，我已经去过你家两趟了。
5. A：你怎么知道这道题是正确的？
   B：下面我来（　　）给你看。
6. A：班上没有一个人知道这道题的（　　）答案。
   B：这道题真是太难了。

　　　　A 占线　　B 招聘　　C 真正　　D 整理　　E 照　　F 正常

7. 我们公司只（　　）一个打字员，应聘的有上百人。
8. 电话打不通，一直（　　）。
9. 你看你的床这么乱，你把它（　　）一下。
10. 你要多关心她，她最近有点不（　　）。
11. A：你觉得什么是（　　）的幸福？
    B：天天开心就是幸福。
12. A：你今天怎么穿得这么漂亮？
    B：公司下午要拍（　　）。

三、排列顺序

1. A. 有家公司在招聘　　B. 我给他们打电话　　C. 却一直在占线
2. A. 你的选择是正确的　　B. 只要你能够证明　　C. 我就支持你

四、完成句子

1. 是正确的　请你　证明　这道判断题　为什么 _____
2. 把男朋友　家人　什么时候　正式地　打算　介绍给　你 _____
3. 我的　王东　证明了　话 _____
4. 上海　哥哥　离开家之后　去了 _____
5. 决定　我　支持　你们的　正确　永远都 _____

五、看图，用词造句

1. 整理

2. 支持

Unit 48

知识	只要
直接	指
值得	至少
职业	质量
植物	重
只好	重点

565 知识 zhīshi (名) (n.) knowledge
  搭配：文化知识 cultural knowledge；知识水平 knowledge level；知识丰富 to have a wide range of knowledge；掌握知识 to master knowledge；科学知识 scientific knowledge
  例句：知识可以改变命运。Knowledge can change one's fate.
  李红的知识面很广。Li Hong has a wide range of knowledge.

566 直接 zhíjiē (形) (adj.) direct, immediate
  搭配：直接原因 direct reasons；直接和间接 direct and indirect；直接结果 immediate result
  例句：请把答案直接写在书上。Please write your answers directly in the book.
  我又问了一遍，他还是不肯直接回答我的问题。I asked him again, but he refused to answer me directly.

567 值得 zhíde (动) (v.) be worthy, deserve
  搭配：值得尊重 to deserve admiration；值得表扬 to deserve commendation；值得讨论 to deserve discussion；值得重视 to deserve attention
  例句：这件事不值得我去努力。This issue doesn't worth my efforts.
  他的学习经验值得我们学习。His study experience is worth learning.

568 职业 zhíyè (形/名) (adj./n.) professional; occupation
  搭配：职业教育 vocational education；职业运动员 professional athletes；职业演员 professional actors；危险职业 dangerous occupation；第二职业 second occupation
  例句：教师这个职业很受尊重。To work as a teacher is respectable.
  我很喜欢医生这个职业。I like working as a doctor.

569 植物 zhíwù (名) (n.) plant
  搭配：植物生长 growth of plants；绿色植物 green plants；水生植物 water plants
  例句：花园里有很多种植物。There are many plants in the garden.
  动植物能够适应自然环境的变化。Plants and animals can adapt to changes in natural environment.

570 只好 zhǐhǎo (副) (adv.) have to
  例句：小明生病了，只好躺在床上休息。Xiaoming was sick and had to lie down for some rest.
  教室里没有座位了，我只好站着听课。All seats in the classroom are taken and I have to stand there to listen to the lecture.
  我等了半天，他还没回来，只好先走了。I waited for a long time, but he failed to turn up. I had to leave.

571 只要 zhǐyào 连 (conj.) as long as

搭配：只要……就…… as long as

例句：只要认真学习，就一定能考出好成绩。As long as we study hard, we will gain good test results.

只要敢正视失败，就有成功的机会。As long as we directly face the previous failure, we will have the chance of success in the future.

572 指 zhǐ 名/动 (n./v.) finger; point at

搭配：手指 a finger；指出错误 to point out an error

例句：用手指着别人是很不礼貌的行为。Pointing at others is impolite.

小红指出了我文章中的几处错误。Xiaohong pointed out several errors in my article.

573 至少 zhìshǎo 副 (adv.) at least

例句：从这里坐车到中山路至少要一个小时。It takes at least an hour to go to Zhongshan Road from here by car.

商场里的一双鞋至少要500块钱，太贵了。A pair of shoes costs at least 500 *yuan* in the mall. How expensive!

574 质量 zhìliàng 名 (n.) quality

搭配：质量好 a good quality；提高质量 to promote quality；保证质量 to guarantee the quality of ... ；质量问题 quality problem

例句：我们一定要保证产品的质量。We must ensure the quality of the products.

我昨天从网上买了一件衣服，价格高，但质量不好。Yesterday I bought a dress on the Internet. Its price is high but its quality is not good enough.

575 重 zhòng 名/形 (n./adj.) weight; heavy, deep, serious

例句：这箱苹果有多重？What's the gross weight of the carton of apples?

她病得很重，但仍然继续工作。She is very ill, but she still keeps around.

抬那个重箱子要小心！Be careful lifting that heavy box!

576 重点 zhòngdiǎn 副/名 (adv./n.) with focus; point

搭配：学习重点 main points of study；工作重点 focal points of work；抓住重点 to catch the main points；重点学校 key school

例句：请你把这本书的重点内容告诉我。Please tell me the main points of this book.

经理开会时强调了这次工作的重点。The manager emphasized the focus of our work at the meeting.

实战练习（四十八）

一、听对话，选择正确答案

1. A. 沙发不好看　　B. 沙发太小了　　C. 没有发工资　　D. 不想买这个沙发
2. A. 很漂亮　　　　B. 很浪漫　　　　C. 不看重外表　　D. 男朋友很帅

二、选词填空

A 只要　　B 指　　C 至少　　D 重　　E 质量　　F 只好

1. 因为忘记带钱包了，我（　　）向同学借了钱买书。
2. 他（　　）着远处的那栋楼对我说："我新买的房子就在那儿，有空过来玩吧。"
3. 这个手机（　　）要一千块钱，我还是不买了。
4. 这些书太（　　）了，我拿不动。
5. 女：你觉得这个电脑怎么样？
   男：虽然外观不好看，但是（　　）很好。
6. 男：我想买这块手表，你觉得怎么样？
   女：（　　）你觉得好就行。

A 直接　　B 值得　　C 职业　　D 植物　　E 重点　　F 知识

7. 我们班这个星期天要举行有奖（　　）竞赛，你参加吗？
8. 这节课的（　　）是词语，回去要认真复习。
9. 别在楼下等我了，（　　）上去吧。
10. 王老师为人很真诚、热情，是（　　）我们尊敬的好老师。
11. 女：听说你很喜欢（　　）。
    男：是的，我家院子里有各种各样的花和草。
12. A：你女朋友的（　　）是什么？
    B：她是一名医生。

三、排列顺序

1. A. 但是我好像缺少这方面的能力
   B. 小时候我的理想是当作家
   C. 我只好放弃了这个理想

2. A. 于是我决定努力学习
   B. 在我的周围全是成绩好的学生
   C. 我感到压力很大

四、完成句子

1. 阅读能力　学中文的　自己的　都很　学生　重视 _____
2. 质量　我们　产品的　都很　重视　工厂的工人 _____
3. 中文知识　文章　至少　写好　要懂得　一点　要想 _____
4. 职业　教师　尊重的　是　值得　一个 _____
5. 直接　我　植物园　去　了 _____

五、看图，用词造句

1. 植物

2. 质量

Unit 49

重视	专业
周围	转
主意	赚
祝贺	准确
著名	准时
专门	仔细

577 重视 zhòngshì (动) (v.) pay attention to

搭配：引起重视 to draw attention from；得到重视 to receive attention；重视能力 to attach importance to capabilities

例句：经理对新来的小王很重视。The manager pays more attention to the newcomer Xiao Wang.

现在学生和家长都很重视外语学习。Nowadays students and parents attach great importance to the study foreign languages.

578 周围 zhōuwéi (名) (n.) circumference, environment, surroundings

搭配：周围环境 surroundings；周围地区 surrounding area

例句：夜深了，屋子周围一片冷寂。It's cold and still around the house at late night.

我家周围的环境很好。The surrounding environment of my house is very good.

579 主意 zhǔyi (名) (n.) idea

搭配：出主意 to give an advice；好主意 a good idea；改变主意 to change one's view；主意多 resourceful

例句：大家有什么好的主意尽管说出来。Please feel free to speak out your ideas.

张华没有什么主见，遇事总是拿不定主意。Zhang Hua is weak-minded and always can't make a decision when she runs into troubles.

580 祝贺 zhùhè (动) (v.) congratulate sb (on sth)

搭配：电话祝贺 a congratulatory call；表示祝贺 to express one's congratulations；热烈的祝贺 a warm congratulation

例句：祝贺你在这次比赛中获得了冠军。Congratulations on your championship in this competition.

祝贺你们演出成功！Congratulate you on your successful performance!

581 著名 zhùmíng (形) (adj.) famous

搭配：著名作家 a famous writer；著名演员 a famous actor

例句：陈道明是中国最著名的演员之一。Chen Daoming is one of the most famous actors in China.

姚明是中国最著名的运动员之一。Yao Ming is one of the most famous athletes in China.

582 专门 zhuānmén (形/副) (adj./adv.) special

搭配：专门研究 to specialize in；专门负责 to be responsible for；专门技术 an expertise

例句：我们公司特别需要电脑方面的专门人才。Our company needs computer professionals badly.

我今天是专门来祝贺你的。Today I go out of my way to congratulate you.

Unit

583 专业 zhuānyè (adj./n.) professional; special field of study

搭配：专业技术人才 professional and technical personnel；热门专业 a popular specialty；中文专业 Chinese major；本科专业 bachelor's degree

例句：那位专家的话太专业了，根本听不懂。The expert talked too professionally to be understood.
有很多电脑专业技术人才来参加这次的招聘会。Many computer professionals and technical personnel attended the job fair.
现在中文专业的毕业生不太好找工作。Graduates majored in Chinese are hard to find a job recently.

584 转 zhuǎn (v.) change, shift, transmit, transfer

例句：他转过头，打量着我。He turned his head and looked across at me.
下午天气转冷了。It turned chilly in the afternoon.

585 赚 zhuàn (v.) make a profit, gain

搭配：赚钱 to make money

例句：你今年赚了不少钱。You've made a lot of money this year.
他很会做生意，一年就把本钱赚回来了。He is good at doing business and gained the capital back only in one year.

586 准确 zhǔnquè (adj.) accurate

搭配：准确答案 an accurate result；准确无误 be sure of it；表达准确 a precise expression；准确数字 exact figures

例句：请你把这道题的准确答案告诉我。Please tell me the accurate answer to this question.
这些数字计算得不太准确，你重新算一遍吧。These figures are inaccurate and you'd better recalculate them.

587 准时 zhǔnshí (adj.) on time, punctual

搭配：准时参加 to take part in on time；准时到达 to arrive as scheduled

例句：我们明天八点半准时出发。Tomorrow we will start at half past eight as scheduled.
他一向都很准时，约会从来都不迟到。He has always been very punctual and is never late for an appointment.

588 仔细 zǐxì (adj.) careful

搭配：仔细检查 to have a careful check；仔细阅读 to read carefully；仔细研究 a careful study

例句：同学们一定要仔细检查自己的作业。Students must carefully examine their own homework.
你以后做事一定要仔细一点，不要这么马虎了。You must be more careful next time and don't be so sloppy.

实战练习（四十九）

一、听对话，选择正确答案

1. A. 想找工作　　B. 是学数学的　　C. 不懂计算机　　D. 想买电脑
2. A. 很准时　　　B. 很仔细　　　　C. 很严厉　　　　D. 是经理

二、选词填空

    A 重视　　　B 主意　　　C 祝贺　　　D 著名　　　E 专门　　　F 专业

1. 现在的中国父母非常（　　　）子女的教育。
2. 关于是找工作还是考研究生，他一直都拿不定（　　　）。
3. 他是中国最（　　　）的歌唱家。
4. 前几天我（　　　）到上海去看望了一个老朋友。
5. A：（　　　）你终于可以出国留学了。

  B：谢谢你。
6. A：你为什么会选择物理（　　　）？

  B：因为我从小就比较喜欢物理。

    A 赚　　　B 周围　　　C 准确　　　D 准时　　　E 仔细　　　F 转

7. 考试的时候，你们要（　　　）检查你们的答案。
8. 出门左（　　　）就是厕所。
9. 我的理想不是（　　　）大钱而是找一个好工作。
10. 你能不能在最短的时间内（　　　）地回答我所有问题？
11. A：你怎么一点时间观念都没有，开会总是不（　　　）。

  B：对不起，今天确实有点事情。
12. A：学校（　　　）有专业的医院吗？

  B：没有。

三、排列顺序

1. A. 总是自己拿主意　　　B. 因此周围没什么朋友　　　C. 他从不重视别人的意见
2. A. 王明也不清楚　　　　B. 什么专业适合自己　　　　C. 大家为他出出主意吧

四、完成句子

1. 祝贺你　这所　考上了　著名的大学　真心地 _____
2. 老师的问题　在课堂上　积极主动地　你一定要　回答 _____
3. 给出的　非常　他　数字　准确 _____
4. 祝贺　他　表示　向你　最真诚的　让我 _____
5. 当　一个　长大后　作家　儿童文学　我想　著名的 _____

五、看图，用词造句

1. 祝贺

2. 准时

Unit 50

自然	左右
自信	作家
总结	作用
租	作者
最好	座
尊重	座位

Unit 50

589 自然 zìrán (adj./n.) natural; nature
- 搭配：自然科学 natural science；自然条件 natural conditions；自然保护 conservation of nature
- 例句：你先别问，到时候自然就明白了。Don't ask now. You'll understand in due course.
  我喜欢亲近大自然，感受大自然的美。I like getting close to nature and enjoy her beauty.

590 自信 zìxìn (v./n./adj.) believe in oneself; self-confidence; be confident
- 搭配：自信心 confidence；缺乏自信 lack of confidence；充满自信 full of confidence
- 例句：听到大家对自己工作的肯定，王东更加自信了。On hearing the positive comments, Wang Dong became more and more confident.
  自从那次比赛之后，她就失去了自信。She lost her confidence ever since that match.

591 总结 zǒngjié (n./v.) summary; summarize
- 搭配：总结报告 a summary；做总结 to make a summary；工作总结 a work summary；总结情况 to summarize the situation
- 例句：你知道工作总结怎么写吗？Do you know how to write a work summary?
  王校长对这次会议进行了总结。Principal Wang made a summary of this meeting.

592 租 zū (v.) rent
- 搭配：租房子 to rent a house；租车 to rent a car；房租 rent money；租金 rental
- 例句：如果你觉得房租很贵，可以考虑和别人合租。If you think the rent is too expensive, you can share the room with others.
  租这套房子一个月要三千块。The house rent is three thousand *yuan* per month.

593 最好 zuìhǎo (adv.) best, had better
- 例句：你最好还是先做个自我介绍吧。You'd better begin by introducing yourself.
  你最好不要租这间房子，环境太差了。You'd better not rent this room. The environment here is too bad.
  天就要下雨了，你最好还是别走了。It looks like to rain and you'd better stay.

594 尊重 zūnzhòng (adj./v.) respectful; respect
- 搭配：尊重老师 to respect teachers；互相尊重 mutual respect；尊重人才 to respect talented people；尊重知识 to respect knowledge
- 例句：我非常尊重我的妈妈。I respect my mum very much.
  人与人之间要互相尊重。Peoples should show respects to each other.

595 左右 zuǒyòu (n.) about, or so
- 例句：可能需要一个小时左右。It will take an hour or so.
  她总是在九点钟左右上床睡觉。She always goes to bed at about nine o'clock.

596 **作家** zuòjiā 名 (n.) writer
搭配：一位作家 a writer；专业作家 a professional writer
例句：他是一名很受欢迎的作家。He is a very popular writer.
这位作家最近几年写了很多部作品。This writer got several works published in recent years.

597 **作用** zuòyòng 名 (n.) affect, action, function
搭配：起作用 to take effect；积极作用 positive effect；副作用 side effect
例句：可惜他们的计划完全不起作用。Unfortunately their plan misfired badly.
药已经开始起作用了。The medicine has begun to do its work.

598 **作者** zuòzhě 名 (n.) author
搭配：书的作者 the author of the book；一位作者 an author；作者介绍 an introduction of an author
例句：《围城》的作者是钱钟书。The author of *The Surrounded City* is Qian Zhongshu.
下面我们先把这篇课文的作者介绍一下。Next, let's introduce the author of this article.

599 **座** zuò 量/名 (m.w./n.) (for mountains, buildings and other similar immovable objects); seat
搭配：一座大山 a mountain；一座桥 a bridge；一座城市 a city
例句：画上的这座山真漂亮。The mountain in this picture is really magnificent.
我喜欢上了这座城市。I begin to like this city.
请帮他找个座儿。Please find a seat for him.

600 **座位** zuòwèi 名 (n.) seat
搭配：前面的座位 a front seat；一个座位 a seat；好座位 a good seat；安排座位 to arrange seats；留个座位 to preserve a seat
例句：他突然从座位上站起来走出去了。He suddenly stood up from his seat and went out.
在公交车上我们要主动给老人让座位。We should offer our seats to the elderly when we take a bus.
这个演出大厅一共有一千个座位。There are 1,000 seats in all in the performing hall.

实战练习（五十）

一、听对话，选择正确答案

1. A. 想租房子　　B. 房子不好　　C. 不想买房　　D. 房子价格高
2. A. 怕迟到　　　B. 怕堵车　　　C. 朋友在等她　D. 想坐前排座位

二、选词填空

　　　　　A 总结　　B 租　　C 自信　　D 左右　　E 作家　　F 最好

1. 听说你已经把房子都（　　）出去了，怎么这么快？
2. 张东每个月的生活费在 3000 元（　　）。
3. 他是最好的翻译，对自己很有（　　）。
4. 今天有雨，你（　　）带把伞。
5. 女：你有什么爱好？
   男：我喜欢看小说，以后想当（　　）。
6. 男：你的工作（　　）写好了没有？经理让你马上送过去。
   女：好的，就快写完了。

　　　　　A 作用　　B 尊重　　C 作者　　D 座　　E 座位　　F 自然

7. 我热爱大（　　）。
8. 这次比赛幸亏有李红参加，她起了很大（　　）。
9. 我家前面有一（　　）漂亮的小山。
10. 妈妈，我不想去这家公司上班，请你也（　　）一下我的意见，好吗？
11. 女：不好意思，你坐的好像是我的（　　）。
    男：真对不起。
12. 男：你见到这本书的（　　）了吗？
    女：见到了，原来他就是我们学校的王华教授。

三、排列顺序

1. A. 可以正确认识工作中的优点和缺点
   B. 工作总结很重要
   C. 通过它

2. A. 张明做生意很重视诚信
   B. 是一位值得我们尊重的生意人
   C. 也很重视商品的质量

四、完成句子

1. 这次 我们来 现在 活动的 经验 总结 ＿＿＿＿＿＿＿＿＿＿
2. 最后一次 我们 是 在去年的春节 见面 ＿＿＿＿＿＿＿＿＿＿
3. 最 我 他是 尊重 一位 的 老师 ＿＿＿＿＿＿＿＿＿＿
4. 座位了 时候 到 教室的 我 已经没有 ＿＿＿＿＿＿＿＿＿＿
5. 大自然 热爱 我 对 充满了 ＿＿＿＿＿＿＿＿＿＿

五、看图，用词造句

1. 座位

2. 尊重

Keys & Listening Script
答案及听力文本

实战练习（一）

一、1. D 2. B

听力文本

1. 男：李经理下午两点下飞机，安排了谁去机场接他？
   女：我正准备去和李明说呢，让他去接。
   男：你也去吧，接到人后先让他在宾馆里休息一下，会议结束后我再过去。
   女：好的，我现在就去。
   问：谁去接李经理？

2. 女：爸，你早上的药又没吃吧？
   男：本来是记得的，可吃完饭接了一个电话，我又给忘了。
   女：出院的时候医生是怎么说的，按时吃药，可你总是不放在心上，你得好好儿注意身体才行啊。
   男：好，我保证以后一定按时吃。
   问：关于男的，可以知道什么？

二、1. C 2. A 3. E 4. B 5. D 6. F   7. F 8. B 9. D 10. E 11. C 12. A

三、1. BCA 2. ACB

四、1. 安全带可以起到保护的作用。
2. 我保证提前二十分钟到公司。
3. 我觉得你应该向他说一声抱歉。
4. 王红对经理的这种安排不太满意。
5. 你怎么抱着一个篮球来了？

五、1. 他们的爱情故事很感人。
2. 你们的表演真是太棒了！

实战练习（二）

一、1. B 2. A

听力文本

1. 女：真是抱歉，李经理，本来我们王总是打算到机场来接您的，可有一个重要的会议，必须要他参加，所以安排我来接您。
   男：王总真是太客气了，张小姐来接我，我也很高兴啊。
   女：那我先送您去宾馆休息一下，明天再去公司，可以吗？
   男：不用了，我不累，现在去吧。
   问：男的现在在什么地方？

2. 男：你带小王跑新闻有两个月了吧？觉得他怎么样？
   女：工作很认真，安排给他的事情能按时完成，新闻报道也写得不错，我们组的人都很喜欢他。
   男：一个刚毕业的大学生能得到你的表扬，可不容易啊，他现在干什么去了？

女：下午有个会议，他帮着打扫会议室去了。

问：根据对话，可以知道什么？

二、1. F　2. C　3. D　4. A　5. E　6. B　　7. E　8. D　9. F　10. A　11. B　12. C

三、1. BAC　2. BCA

四、1. 这次活动报名昨天就已经结束了。

2. 他希望能得到老师的表扬。

3. 我觉得这个饼干太甜了。/ 这个饼干我觉得太甜了。

4. 点头一般表示同意或满意。

5. 我正在学习怎么做电子表格。

五、1. 他最喜欢吃这种饼干。/ 这种饼干一定好吃极了。

2. 她的表演非常精彩。

实战练习（三）

一、1. D　2. D

听力文本

1. 男：李红，结婚的东西准备得怎么样了？

女：也没什么可准备的，需要买的东西都买好了，这两天我在忙着打扫房子。

男：什么时候安排我们去参观一下你的新房啊？

女：只要大家有兴趣，什么时候去都可以。

问：女的主要是什么意思？

2. 男：赵玲，你明天有什么安排吗？

女：我本来想在家好好儿睡一觉的，不过赵强打算买笔记本电脑，让我和他一起去看看，你有什么事情吗？

男：我买了两张明天的电影票，想请你去看电影呢。

女：抱歉，等下次有机会吧。

问：女的原来打算明天干什么？

二、1. D　2. F　3. A　4. B　5. E　6. C　　7. F　8. C　9. A　10. E　11. D　12. B

三、1. BAC　2. BCA

四、1. 现在离参观时间还有二十分钟。

2. 他在上海还有一部分朋友。

3. 她把妈妈的鞋子擦得干干净净。

4. 我猜小王现在一定在回家的路上。

5. 王玲不得不留在家里照顾妹妹。

五、1. 她认真地擦着电脑。/ 她把电脑擦得干干净净。

2. 她利用休息的时间去博物馆参观。/ 她在参观的时候拍了很多照片。

实战练习（四）

一、1. C　2. B

听力文本

1. 女：我做了妈妈爱吃的菜，你尝尝怎么样？
   男：太甜了，糖放得有点多，医生说妈妈不能吃太甜的东西。
   问：他们现在最可能在哪儿？

2. 男：你明天有没有时间？
   女：明天有个重要的会议要参加，怎么了？
   男：丽丽让我明天带她去爬长城，可我感冒了，想让你带她去呢。
   女：后天再去吧，我后天有时间。
   问：男的为什么不想带丽丽玩？

二、1. C 2. F 3. B 4. E 5. D 6. A   7. C 8. D 9. E 10. F 11. A 12. B

三、1. BCA 2. BAC

四、1. 他的身高已经超过了两米。
2. 小王到北京工作差不多有半年了。
3. 我们要乘坐飞机去海南吗？
4. 这家餐厅的经理非常诚实。
5. 我觉得这场比赛很没意思。

五、1. 她很想尝尝这块饼干。
2. 他相信自己一定会成功！

实战练习（五）

一、1. D 2. C

听力文本

1. 男：小王，你见到我桌子上的那本汉语词典了吗？
   女：没有啊，我今天上午都在这儿整理材料呢。
   男：真是奇怪，我昨天下午还看到在桌子上呢。
   女：你去问问李红，她上午在你桌子那儿好像拿走一样东西。
   问：女的主要是什么意思？

2. 女：王东可真是粗心，昨天他是最后一个走的，这边的窗户都没关。
   男：不是吧，我昨天和王东一起下班的，当时李刚还在办公室里没走，他说有点儿材料要重新写一下。
   问：忘了关窗户的人最可能是谁？

二、1. A 2. D 3. F 4. B 5. E 6. C   7. D 8. E 9. C 10. F 11. A 12. B

三、1. ACB 2. CBA

四、1. 老师从来都没有表扬过他。
2. 我猜李明可能是明天出发。
3. 李丽喜欢早上起来就把窗户打开。
4. 王东生气的时候特别爱抽烟。/ 生气的时候王东特别爱抽烟。
5. 这个答案并不能让他满意。

五、1. 他非常吃惊地看着我。/ 这个消息让他极为吃惊。
   2. 她要到外地出差。

实战练习（六）

一、1. B   2. B
   听力文本
   1. 女：抱歉，小王，我今天要先走一会儿，等李红回来，你帮我把这些材料交给她，让她打印出来。
      男：怎么了？家里有事？
      女：我女儿昨天晚上就发烧了，我得带她去打针。
      男：那你快去吧。
      问：女的要去哪儿？
   2. 女：你看，这个帽子漂不漂亮？只要二十块钱。
      男：怎么这么便宜？
      女：商场现在正在进行打折活动，我觉得女儿戴大红色的帽子一定好看。
      男：如果是个黑色的，她会更喜欢。
      问：男的是什么意思？

二、1. F   2. A   3. D   4. E   5. B   6. C   7. B   8. D   9. E   10. A   11. C   12. F

三、1. BCA   2. CBA

四、1. 她从来都没有这样打扮过。
   2. 你的想法是错误的。
   3. 经理安排我把这些材料打印出来。
   4. 他去大使馆办了签证。
   5. 孩子一直不愿意去打针。

五、1. 他非常害怕打针。
   2. 她把自己打扮得很漂亮。/ 她特别爱打扮。

实战练习（七）

一、1. D   2. B
   听力文本
   1. 女：这次和女朋友去海南旅游，感觉怎么样？
      男：如果只说当地的风景的话，那当然是不错的。
      女：有其他让你不高兴的事情吗？
      男：导游啊，老是带我们去商店买东西，不买她就不高兴。
      问：男的主要是什么意思？
   2. 男：今天开会的时候经理表扬王东那一组了，你看王东得意的。
      女：上个月他们确实做得不错。
      男：我们也得努力，等到月底的时候要超过他们。

女：根据我们现在完成的情况，我估计应该差不多。

问：女的是什么意思？

二、1. E   2. C   3. A   4. B   5. F   6. D   7. D   8. E   9. B   10. A   11. F   12. C

三、1. ACB   2. BAC

四、1. 房间里到处都是衣服。

2. 你到底还要我等多长时间？

3. 王红觉得当一名导游很不错。

4. 小李当时并不知道这件事情。／这件事情小李当时并不知道。

5. 你不觉得你应该向她道歉吗？

五、1. 他带了礼物来向女朋友道歉。

2. 她的手里拿着一把刀。

实战练习（八）

一、1. D   2. B

听力文本

1. 男：你知道李红家的地址吗？

   女：不太清楚，你要干什么？

   男：王东说她生病了，所以这几天才没来上班，我想下午下班以后去看看她。

   女：张明可能知道，我去问问他，等一会和你一起去。

   问：根据对话，可以知道什么？

2. 女：前面怎么了？

   男：像是堵车，现在正是下班的时间。

   女：都是你，刚才让你早点儿出发，你还说时间早呢，这下怎么办？

   男：十二点的飞机，应该不会晚。

   问：女的可能是什么心情？

二、1. D   2. A   3. C   4. F   5. B   6. E   7. A   8. E   9. B   10. D   11. F   12. C

三、1. CBA   2. ACB

四、1. 政府正在对这起事故进行调查。

2. 地球是人类的母亲。

3. 他把钱包丢了。

4. 你这几个动作都做错了。

5. 我把李红家的地址给了王东。

五、1. 几个硬币从钱包里掉了出来。

2. 他的动作非常优美。

实战练习（九）

一、1. B   2. C

听力文本

1. 男：明天有时间吗？我想请你吃顿饭。

女：怎么，又想让我给你介绍女朋友？
男：给我介绍女朋友当然好了，不过，不是因为这个。你知道的，我的英文不怎么样，有一部分材料，想请你帮我翻译一下。
女：没问题，拿过来就是了。
问：根据对话，可以知道什么？

2. 女：小王，你周五忙吗？
男：周五？那天该我休息，在家没什么事，打算去看电影呢。
女：那天是儿童节，我女儿让我带她去动物园。我想和你换个班，行吗？
男：电影哪天看都行，孩子的节日可就那一天，你带她去玩儿吧。
问：男的主要是什么意思？

二、1. D 2. F 3. E 4. C 5. B 6. A 7. C 8. A 9. B 10. E 11. F 12. D

三、1. BAC 2. ACB

四、1. 他在那个公司不会有什么大的发展。
2. 以后再遇到法律上的问题都可以来找我。
3. 我要去公司看看发生了什么事。
4. 王东觉得肚子疼得厉害。
5. 他看到李红站在马路对面。

五、1. 这些书对做好翻译工作有很大的帮助。/ 我要把这些书都翻译成汉语。
2. 路上又堵车了。/ 堵车在大城市很常见。

实战练习（十）

一、1. D 2. C

听力文本

1. 男：还有一个星期就放暑假了，你有什么打算吗？
女：我正为这事烦恼着呢。
男：怎么了？
女：本来都和王东说好了，假期不回家了，在这儿找份工作，可是我爸妈都反对，让我一定回家。
问：谁让女的感到烦恼？

2. 女：真是抱歉，我可能不能按照原计划去旅游了。
男：怎么了？
女：刚刚经理打电话说，安排我去北京学习，然后还要去上海参加一个会议，明天就得出发，怎么办呢？
男：去学习的机会当然不能放弃了，我们等"十一"放假的时候再去桂林好了。
问：女的明天要去哪儿？

二、1. C 2. F 3. D 4. B 5. E 6. A 7. A 8. F 9. B 10. C 11. E 12. D

三、1. BCA 2. BAC

四、1. 超过三分之二的同学都反对这个决定。

2. 他放弃了这次出国的机会。
3. 我不知道哪个方向是去火车站的。
4. 这不过是他单方面的想法。
5. 放暑假的时候他不想回家。/ 他不想放暑假的时候回家。

五、1. 超市里的商品丰富多样。
2. 她正在为工作烦恼。

实战练习（十一）

一、1. D　2. C

听力文本

1. 女：昨天你儿子带回家的女朋友，李红满意吗？
   男：除了身高还符合她的标准之外，其他条件都不能让她满意。
   女：只要他们互相喜欢，感情好就行了，让李红别想那么多。
   男：是啊，我昨天也是这样和她说的。
   问：男的和李红是什么关系？

2. 男：现在感觉怎么样？
   女：比刚才好多了，医生怎么说的？
   男：说你太累了，得好好儿休息几天，这些药要按时吃。
   女：那么多材料还没看，怎么休息？等把这些忙完，我保证在家休息一段时间。
   问：女的主要是什么意思？

二、1. C　2. F　3. A　4. E　5. D　6. B　　7. B　8. D　9. A　10. E　11. C　12. F

三、1. BAC　2. ACB

四、1. 你感觉不到他的改变吗？
2. 父亲感动得说不出话来。
3. 李红是个感情丰富的人。
4. 我负责把这部分材料打印出来。
5. 王东已经知道了事情的复杂性。

五、1. 王东在教李红怎么使用复印机。
2. 为我们的友谊，干杯！

实战练习（十二）

一、1. A　2. C

听力文本

1. 男：你总是在网上购物，安全吗？
   女：没事的，你看我刚刚买的这双鞋，才一百八十块，专卖店里要三百多呢。
   问：女的选择网上购物的主要原因是什么？

2. 女：你现在在公司吗？
   男：没有，我去机场接一个客户。有什么事？

女：李红家的地址你有吧？发到我手机上，我刚才听李明说她生病了，想去看看她。

男：这样吧，等晚上我和你一起去。

问：男的打算和女的去干什么？

二、1. B 2. F 3. A 4. D 5. E 6. C   7. B 8. F 9. A 10. D 11. E 12. C

三、1. BAC   2. ACB

四、1. 他刚从图书馆回来。

2. 感谢各位老师这些年来对我的帮助。/ 感谢这些年来各位老师对我的帮助。

3. 他各方面的条件都不能让李红满意。

4. 王东身上的钱刚刚够吃这一顿饭。

5. 她用一个月的工资买了一件衣服。

五、1. 他正在学习中国功夫。/ 他是一个功夫高手。

2. 她生病了，感觉很难受。

实战练习（十三）

一、1. C 2. C

听力文本

1. 男：经理是因为上午的事情把李红叫到办公室去的吗？

   女：我估计是的，当时那个顾客吵得很厉害。

   男：到底是怎么回事啊？

   女：不是李红的错，是那个顾客自己点错了菜，非说是李红记得不对。

   问：李红最可能在什么地方工作？

2. 女：今天在学校发生了什么事，你这么高兴？

   男：老师开班会的时候表扬了我，说我把班里的卫生管理得很好，还让全班同学都为我鼓掌呢。

   女：你真是太厉害了，我相信你以后要是再努力一些，会比现在做得更好呢。

   男：我一定会的。

   问：根据对话，可以知道什么？

二、1. B 2. D 3. E 4. A 5. C 6. F   7. B 8. E 9. C 10. F 11. A 12. D

三、1. BCA   2. ACB

四、1. 他感觉自己的头发快要掉光了。

2. 我刚刚不是故意这样说的。

3. 谁把衣服挂在这儿？

4. 我估计明天很有可能会下雨。

5. 他对我说了很多鼓励的话。

五、1. 她每次购物都会买很多东西。

2. 墙上挂着一个钟。

实战练习（十四）

一、1. B 2. D

听力文本

1. 女：你明天休息，和我一起去商场逛逛吧？
   男：我得写一份材料，这两天就要交给经理，你找李红和你一起去吧。
   女：又不是让你逛一整天，你上午写材料，下午上街购物，不就行了？
   男：明天再说吧。
   问：男的主要是什么意思？

2. 女：李经理是今天上午八点的飞机吗？
   男：是的，我安排了小王去机场接他。
   女：今天的风这么大，航班不会晚点吧？
   男：没有，小王刚刚打电话来说，他们已经在回来的路上了。
   问：根据对话可以知道什么？

二、1. B 2. D 3. A 4. C 5. F 6. E   7. C 8. B 9. F 10. E 11. A 12. D

三、1. ACB/CAB   2. BAC

四、1. 他满头大汗地从外面跑进来。
    2. 李红不太喜欢逛商场。
    3. 她的寒假作业已经做完了。
    4. 经理规定我们上班不准玩游戏。
    5. 妈妈不让我一个人过马路。

五、1. 她们逛了一下午，买了不少东西。
    2. 她有些害羞，紧紧抱住了妈妈的腿。

实战练习（十五）

一、1. A   2. B

听力文本

1. 男：你上午给我的手机号码好像不对。
   女：不是李红的手机号吗？
   男：不是，我打过去的时候，对方说我打错了，你看看这个号。
   女：不好意思，这是我朋友的手机号，我给你发错了。
   问：根据对话，可以知道什么？

2. 男：妈妈，小猴子后来怎么样了？它后悔没听妈妈的话吗？它能找到回家的路吗？
   女：当然后悔了。后来，猴妈妈找到了它，把它带回了家。好了，今天就到这儿吧，你该睡觉了。
   问：女的在干什么？

二、1. C 2. F 3. A 4. D 5. E 6. B   7. C 8. E 9. A 10. D 11. F 12. B

三、1. ACB   2. BAC

四、1. 李红好像没来上班。
    2. 你别忘了多带些厚衣服。
    3. 我想把那个盒子拿下来。

4. 这样做对你有什么好处？
5. 通过这次考试才算合格。

五、1. 雪下得很大，地上已是厚厚的一层。
2. 护士正在给她打针。

实战练习（十六）

一、1. D　2. C

听力文本

1. 女：你快下班了吧？
   男：还有半个小时，等下了班我去接你。
   女：不用，我今天不回家吃饭了，我们经理说上次那个活动很成功，晚上他要请大家吃饭。
   男：好，我知道了。
   问：女的为什么给男的打电话？

2. 女：李明今天没来上班，说他身体不舒服，请一天假。
   男：他昨天还好好儿的，今天怎么就忽然不舒服了？我怀疑他不是身体不舒服，而是心里不舒服。
   女：什么意思？
   男：他一直想去北京参加这次会议，昨天经理说让小王去，估计他是心里不高兴才没来上班的。
   问：男的是什么意思？

二、1. B　2. F　3. C　4. A　5. D　6. E　　7. E　8. B　9. F　10. A　11. D　12. C

三、1. BAC　2. CAB

四、1. 我们不应该互相怀疑。
2. 你让他再好好儿回忆一下。
3. 李红表现得非常积极。
4. 王东获得了大多数人的支持。
5. 她报名参加了这次活动。

五、1. 他代表学校参加这次比赛，获得了好成绩。／他在这次比赛中获得了冠军。
2. 她听到自己获得成功的消息后，激动得跳了起来。

实战练习（十七）

一、1. D　2. B

听力文本

1. 男：你明天还要继续加班吗？
   女：本来明天是有个会议要参加的，不过，既然王东来上海了，那我们就一起去看看他吧。
   问：女的明天去干什么？

2. 男：你告诉李红明天几点集合？

女：九点啊，王东对我说是半个小时的集合时间，九点半出发。
男：刚刚大家又商量了一下，计划改变了，出发时间提前了一个小时。
女：那我打电话告诉李红。
问：出发时间改到了几点？

二、1. B　2. C　3. E　4. A　5. F　6. D　　7. C　8. D　9. B　10. E　11. A　12. F

三、1. ACB　2. CAB

四、1. 我们到加油站休息一下再走吧。
2. 我想把这本工具书寄给李红。
3. 当记者要经常加班。
4. 我估计李红不知道集合时间。
5. 王东计划明年开一家家具店。

五、1. 她从早上起来就在擦家具。
2. 经理交给她的材料太多了，她不得不加班。

实战练习（十八）

一、1. C　2. B

听力文本
1. 男：这个周末你不会再继续加班了吧？
女：材料已经交上去了，这个星期会正常休息。
男：那明天我们一起去看看家具吧，现在大部分商家都在做活动，价格还是很合适的。
女：我已经和李红说好了要去医院看王东，后天再去家具市场吧。
问：根据对话可以知道什么？

2. 男：你觉得医学院怎么样？
女：我不想报医学院。
男：为什么？一个女孩子将来当个医生或护士，多好。
女：好什么啊，李红的妈妈是医生，几乎没有休息的时间，还得经常加班，我才不想像她那样呢。
问：女的不愿意当医生的主要原因是什么？

二、1. B　2. E　3. C　4. D　5. F　6. A　　7. C　8. B　9. E　10. D　11. A　12. F

三、1. CBA　2. ACB

四、1. 坚持减肥不是一件简单的事。
2. 只有坚持到底才能获得成功。
3. 他一直坚持用汉语和我交流。
4. 王东把奖金全都交给了妻子。
5. 超市里的人减少了。

五、1. 他的交通工具就是这辆自行车。
2. 经理正在跟客户进行交流。

答案及听力文本

实战练习（十九）

一、1. A   2. B

听力文本

1. 男：李红，你现在去王教授家了吗？
   女：正在路上呢，王教授刚刚打电话让我早去一会儿帮她包饺子。
   男：李强突然来上海了，我现在要去机场接他，可能要晚一点才能过去，你帮我向王教授解释一下。
   女：好，我知道了。
   问：男的让女的解释什么？

2. 男：你怎么吃得这么少？
   女：我这两天感冒了，一直不想吃饭。
   男：我还以为你也在减肥呢，我们公司里的那些女孩子，都在比着看谁瘦，结果都把身体弄坏了。
   女：我从来不减肥的。
   问：根据对话，可以知道什么？

二、1. F   2. A   3. C   4. E   5. D   6. B   7. B   8. E   9. A   10. C   11. D   12. F

三、1. CBA   2. BAC

四、1. 谁也想不到事情的结果会是这样。
2. 你得把这个事给我解释清楚。
3. 这么多的观众让他很紧张。
4. 六月一日是孩子们的节日。
5. 这个计划怕是进行不下去了。

五、1. 先生，这里禁止抽烟！
2. 他向大家解释了这样做的好处。

实战练习（二十）

一、1. B   2. C

听力文本

1. 男：你究竟怎么了？看起来这么没精神，一路上也不说话，是身体不舒服还是公司发生了什么事情？
   女：你先去做饭吧，让我一个人安静一会儿，好吗？
   问：根据对话，可以知道什么？

2. 女：先生，这儿有镜子，您看您穿这件衣服多精神。
   男：大小还算合适，不过我不喜欢这个颜色，还有其他颜色吗？
   女：不好意思，这是最后一件了，如果您要的话，我可以给你打八折。
   男：算了，我还是再看看别的吧。
   问：男的现在最可能在哪儿？

二、1. C   2. B   3. F   4. E   5. A   6. D   7. D   8. C   9. E   10. B   11. A   12. F

三、1. ACB 2. BAC

四、1. 这一面镜子竟然这么贵？
2. 他究竟为什么拒绝参加这次会议？
3. 警察拒绝了王东的要求。
4. 我的竞争对手是一个有留学经历的博士生。
5. 他一说到京剧就来了精神。

五、1. 他发现一辆警察的车跟在后面。
2. 一位京剧演员正对着镜子仔细地化妆。

实战练习（二十一）

一、1. D 2. B
听力文本
1. 男：这里距离张教授家很远，走路要一个多小时呢。
   女：我开玩笑的，当然不能走着去了，我们坐公共汽车去。
   问：他们打算怎么去张教授家？
2. 男：张小姐，能谈谈新作品的主要内容吗？
   女：这部小说主要写了一个可怜的小女孩成长的故事。
   男：那您对这个故事有什么看法吗？
   女：我觉得虽然人们之间的距离是看不见的，但是感情是可以用心感受的。
   问：女的可能是做什么的？

二、1. B 2. F 3. C 4. A 5. D 6. E   7. E 8. D 9. A 10. F 11. B 12. C

三、1. ABC 2. BAC

四、1. 他在认真地考虑一个科学问题。
2. 北京烤鸭很受欢迎。
3. 世华公司拒绝举办这次活动。
4. 请把您对他的看法说出来。
5. 我喜欢和爱开玩笑的人在一起。

五、1. 她开心得跳了起来。
2. 她正在考虑明天穿什么衣服。

实战练习（二十二）

一、1. D 2. D
听力文本
1. 男：困死了！
   女：以后别这么晚睡觉，电视有什么好看的？
   问：关于男的，下面哪项正确？
2. 男：那个老人一直在咳嗽，真可怜。
   女：是啊，她的子女不在身边，生病了都没人照顾。
   问：关于那位老人，下面哪项正确？

二、1. B 2. A 3. E 4. D 5. C 6. F   7. B 8. C 9. F 10. D 11. E 12. A

三、1. ABC   2. BAC

四、1. 这里的空气肯定很新鲜。
   2. 可怜的孩子一直在咳嗽。
   3. 我现在困得不得了。
   4. 真是太可惜了。
   5. 客厅距离厨房非常近。/ 厨房距离客厅非常近。

五、1. 她咳嗽得很厉害。
   2. 这里有树有水，空气非常清新。

实战练习（二十三）

一、1. D   2. D
   听力文本
   1. 男：你尝一下我刚刚做的菜辣不辣。
      女：不辣，但是有点咸。
      问：女的觉得男的做的菜怎么样？
   2. 男：快点起床，再不起恐怕要迟到了。
      女：现在才六点半，时间还来得及，让我再睡十分钟。
      男：现在都七点五分了，快来不及吃早饭了。
      女：手表又坏了，我马上起床。
      问：现在几点了？

二、1. F 2. C 3. B 4. D 5. E 6. A   7. F 8. B 9. C 10. E 11. A 12. D

三、1. BAC   2. CBA

四、1. 再大的困难都有解决的办法。
   2. 浪漫常常会带来浪费。
   3. 我还没来得及说话他就走了。
   4. 这个垃圾桶恐怕不能用了。
   5. 请把这条路修宽一点儿。

五、1. 他在学习上遇到了困难。
   2. 请把垃圾扔进垃圾桶。

实战练习（二十四）

一、1. D   2. A
   听力文本
   1. 男：下午陪我去浪漫发屋理个发吧。
      女：可是我和小丽要去看王奶奶，你还是自己去吧。
      问：女的主要是什么意思？
   2. 男：你冷静点儿，小华不会有事的。
      女：可是都等了两个小时了，医生怎么还没出来？

265

男：虽然小华这次病得很厉害，但我相信一定不会有事的。

女：希望小华能早点好起来。

问：他们现在可能在哪儿？

二、1. C　2. D　3. F　4. E　5. A　6. B　　7. C　8. B　9. E　10. F　11. D　12. A

三、1. ACB　2. BCA

四、1. 王东对人很有礼貌。

2. 她连自己的妈妈都不关心。

3. 老虎是一种很厉害的动物。

4. 请把你的理想写在纸上。

5. 我不能理解他为什么会这样做。

五、1. 她通过电话与父母联系。

2. 十号理发师正在为这个小男孩理发。

实战练习（二十五）

一、1. D　2. C

听力文本

1. 男：小姐，今年很流行这种衣服，你穿着也很好看，买一件吧。

   女：我不喜欢这个颜色，帮我换一件绿色的，谢谢。

   问：女的可能在哪儿？

2. 男：昨天张静联系我说她来北京了，明天我们一起请她吃个饭吧。

   女：这两天太热，还是找个凉快的天儿再请吧。

   男：好啊。另外她生日快到了，别忘了给她准备生日礼物。

   女：知道了，先这样吧，我要工作了。

   问：他们现在正在做什么？

二、1. E　2. D　3. A　4. C　5. B　6. F　　7. B　8. A　9. E　10. C　11. F　12. D

三、1. BCA　2. ACB

四、1. 这是找您的零钱。

2. 换房子非常麻烦。

3. 今年特别流行这种毛衣。/ 这种毛衣今年特别流行。/ 今年这种毛衣特别流行。

4. 你另外得准备一些零钱。

5. 怎样才能说一口流利的汉语？

五、1. 李红喜欢去各地旅行。

2. 垃圾桶里扔满了垃圾。

实战练习（二十六）

一、1. D　2. B

听力文本

1. 男：家里还有好几条毛巾，你怎么又买了？

   女：这是买衣服的时候送的，免费。

问：关于这条毛巾，可以知道到什么？

2. 男：小静，你这么马虎，以后会遇到很多麻烦的。
女：不管我有什么麻烦，你都会想办法解决的。
男：如果我不在你身边呢？所以你要改掉这个坏习惯。
女：知道了，我以后会注意的。
问：男的希望女的做什么？

二、1. C 2. F 3. B 4. D 5. A 6. E   7. F 8. D 9. E 10. C 11. B 12. A

三、1. BCA 2. CBA

四、1. 这个国家的教育是免费的。
2. 马虎的小红忘记了笔记本电脑的密码。
3. 昨晚我梦到了一个美丽的地方。
4. 他的目的是把毛巾洗干净。
5. 难道是迷路了吗？

五、1. 这位小姐穿上这件美丽的衣服之后变得更美丽了。
2. 用银行卡取钱得先输入密码。

实战练习（二十七）

一、1. C 2. A

听力文本

1. 男：难道你不知道李明就是我们的新经理吗？
女：不知道，不过他这么有能力，当上经理我一点也不觉得奇怪。
问：他们可能是什么关系？

2. 男：这些小孩子太难教了，我现在特别难受，不知道该怎么和他们交流。
女：你要耐心点，刚开始教都这样。
男：你平时都是怎么做的，给我指点一下。
女：你可以增加教学内容的趣味性，课后多与他们谈心。
问：女的可能是做什么的？

二、1. B 2. F 3. D 4. A 5. E 6. C   7. A 8. C 9. D 10. F 11. B 12. E

三、1. ACB 2. CBA

四、1. 请你耐心地把这些内容看完。
2. 以你的能力翻译好这篇文章肯定没有问题。
3. 难道你不知道他们谈话的内容？／他们谈话的内容难道你不知道？
4. 弄丢了妈妈送的手机我心里特别难受。
5. 中国朋友陪着我去办签证。／我陪着中国朋友去办签证。

五、1. 看到她这么难受，我心里也很不好受。／听到这个坏消息，她难受得不得了。
2. 王总您好，今天由我来陪您参观工厂。

实战练习（二十八）

一、1. A 2. A

听力文本

1. 女：我的袜子破了，你陪我去买几双新的吧。
   男：好，等我做完这几道判断题就陪你去。
   问：男的正在做什么？

2. 男：下午我们约小米一起去打乒乓球吧。
   女：还是不要叫他了，刚才他被王教练批评了，估计没心情去。
   男：王教练脾气这么好，很少批评人，怎么回事啊？
   女：他这个星期迟到了六天。
   问：王教练为什么批评小米？

二、1. C 2. F 3. B 4. D 5. A 6. E   7. C 8. B 9. D 10. A 11. E 12. F

三、1. ACB   2. CAB

四、1. 骗子永远不会说自己是坏人。
2. 那个漂亮的瓶子里有很多彩色的乒乓球。
3. 这是一篇批评乒乓球运动员的文章。
4. 他从来不在这么多人面前发脾气。
5. 平时都是小红陪我去看乒乓球比赛的。

五、1. 她打乒乓球的动作非常标准。
2. 面对经理的批评，李红很难过。

实战练习（二十九）

一、1. C 2. B

听力文本

1. 女：小张，飞机快起飞了，你怎么还没到啊？
   男：我把签证忘在办公室里了，现在正往机场赶呢，就快到了。
   问：他们可能是什么关系？

2. 女：祝你生日快乐！这是我送你的巧克力蛋糕。
   男：谢谢，很高兴你来参加我的生日晚会，快进来吧。
   女：其他同学都来了吗？
   男：早就来了，他们在屋里吃水果呢。
   问：关于男的，可以知道什么？

二、1. B 2. D 3. A 4. F 5. C 6. E   7. E 8. F 9. C 10. A 11. B 12. D

三、1. BCA   2. CAB

四、1. 千万不要把签证丢在家里。
2. 这种巧克力看上去很像一座小桥。
3. 我的亲戚不喜欢这里的气候。
4. 请在飞机起飞前把手机关上。
5. 墙上的那些相片都是妈妈照的。

五、1. 心情不好的时候可以吃点儿巧克力。
2. 小李敲了敲张经理办公室的门，发现里面没有人。

实战练习（三十）

一、1. C 2. D

听力文本

1. 男：你觉得我把这个任务交给李平怎么样？
   女：这确实是一个正确的决定。李平是这群人中最有能力的一个。
   问：女的主要是什么意思？

2. 男：我上午在超市入口处看到王静了，她正要和一群朋友去买东西。
   女：怎么可能，她去上海出差了，你肯定是认错人了。
   男：我确实没有看错，她还和我问好呢！
   女：估计是工作任务完成了，她提前回来了。
   问：关于王静，可以知道什么？

二、1. A 2. E 3. B 4. D 5. F 6. C   7. D 8. A 9. F 10. E 11. B 12. C

三、1. ABC 2. CBA

四、1. 经理交给我们的任务确实很难。
2. 他仍然记得那个热闹的生日晚会。
3. 任何事情都难不住这群年轻人。
4. 他的缺点是缺少耐心。
5. 昨天我给你的那些人民币确实是真的。

五、1. 大家在一起喝酒非常热闹，每个人都很开心。
2. 小男孩要把香蕉皮扔进垃圾桶里。

实战练习（三十一）

一、1. B 2. D

听力文本

1. 男：你打算考研究生还是直接找工作？
   女：我和我男朋友已经申请到了一所美国的大学，明年六月我们会一起出国。
   问：女的决定做什么？

2. 男：妈，你和爸商量好把沙发放在哪个房间了吗？
   女：你爸想放在卧室，但我觉得放在客厅更好一些。
   男：难道你们都没有考虑过放在我的房间吗？
   女：你的房间太小，根本放不下。
   问：他们在讨论什么？

二、1. C 2. E 3. F 4. A 5. D 6. B   7. D 8. F 9. C 10. B 11. E 12. A

三、1. ACB 2. CBA

四、1. 小红正坐在沙发上写申请书。
2. 我觉得颜色稍微深一点儿会更好看。
3. 李红养成了写日记的习惯。
4. 他们最后也没商量好买哪个沙发。

269

5. 你陪我去那片森林散散步吧。

五、1. 每天下午她们都会带着自己的孩子来这里散步。

2. 秋天到了，森林变成了一片黄色的海洋。/ 这片森林里有很多大树，空气很清新。

实战练习（三十二）

一、1. A 2. C

听力文本

1. 男：小红，一会儿爸爸带你去动物园，你想看什么动物啊？

   女：我想看狮子、猴子，还有大象。

   男：好，那你先把饭吃完，吃完饭我们就出发。

   问：他们现在可能在哪儿？

2. 女：王师傅，给我来碗面条。

   男：实在是不好意思，店里的面条卖完了，只剩下米饭和包子了。

   女：啊？那我要四个包子吧。

   男：好，我马上给你拿。

   问：女的最后决定吃什么？

二、1. B 2. D 3. C 4. A 5. F 6. E   7. C 8. F 9. A 10. B 11. D 12. E

三、1. CAB 2. ABC

四、1. 教室里就剩我一个人。

2. 实际上每个人对张师傅都很失望。

3. 生活就是一部现场直播的电影。

4. 把剩下的东西都拿到李静的车上去吧。

5. 失败并不是一件可怕的事情。

五、1. 这次活动失败了，我受到了经理的批评。

2. 她对吵架的父母很失望，所以离家出走了。

实战练习（三十三）

一、1. B 2. C

听力文本

1. 男：这里离首都机场很远，你快点儿收拾，我们快来不及了。

   女：知道了，我穿好上衣就出来，你先拿着行李下去叫辆出租车吧。

   问：他们现在可能在哪儿？

2. 男：我觉得公司必须适应市场要求做一些改变。

   女：你有什么想法直接说出来吧。

   男：我想招几个销售方面的人才。

   女：这个想法很好，你负责开个招聘会吧。

   问：男的想要做什么？

二、1. B 2. E 3. F 4. D 5. A 6. C   7. B 8. F 9. D 10. A 11. E 12. C

三、1. BAC 2. ACB

四、1. 香蕉不适合在北方生长。/ 香蕉不适合生长在北方。
2. 你收到世纪公司的复试信息了吗？/ 世纪公司的复试信息你收到了吗？
3. 我已经把你这个月的收入打到银行卡里了。
4. 你必须在一周之内适应这里的一切。/ 在一周之内你必须适应这里的一切。
5. 你是否适应首都的生活？

五、1. 他们收入很高，刚买了一辆好车。/ 这辆车花了他们一年的收入。
2. 客人走了，宾馆的服务员正在收拾房间。

实战练习（三十四）

一、1. C 2. A

听力文本

1. 男：我已经告诉你我电脑开机密码的五个数字了，剩下的一个数你自己猜吧。
   女：难道是四？要不就是九。
   问：男的电脑开机密码总共有几位数字？

2. 男：请按照顺序把这些材料整理好，下午拿给我。
   女：好的，我马上就做。
   男：天冷了，明天给公司的每个售货员发一套厚衣服。
   女：好的，那我先出去了。
   问：他们可能是什么关系？

二、1. C 2. D 3. B 4. F 5. E 6. A 7. B 8. E 9. A 10. D 11. F 12. C

三、1. ABC 2. CAB

四、1. 请尽快把公司这次需要进货的数量整理好。
2. 顺便帮我向那个售货员说一声谢谢。
3. 那个帅气的售货员正在向这边走来！
4. 我受到了老师的鼓励。
5. 这些数字说明事情行得很顺利。

五、1. 这个可爱的女售货员在帮客人拿东西。
2. 他认真工作的时候特帅。/ 穿西装的这个男人很帅。

实战练习（三十五）

一、1. B 2. B

听力文本

1. 男：经常使用塑料袋不但对自己的身体不好，也对城市的环境不好。
   女：知道了，我再也不用了。
   问：男的主要是什么意思？

2. 男：我们的事你父母是什么态度？
   女：我和他们谈了，他们说只要我高兴，不反对我们在一起。
   男：真是太好了，我一定会让你成为世界上最幸福的新娘的。
   女：谢谢你，我感到很幸福。

问：关于女的，可以知道什么？

二、1. E 2. A 3. C 4. F 5. D 6. B 7. E 8. A 9. B 10. C 11. F 12. D

三、1. CBA 2. ABC

四、1. 就算所有人都反对我也要和你在一起。
2. 你怎么能随随便便就把这台洗衣机卖掉呢？
3. 那个塑料袋被他小孙子拿出去玩了。
4. 你孙子对你怎么是这种态度？
5. 几乎没有人能抬得起这辆车来。

五、1. 这个苹果不好吃，太酸了。
2. 用塑料袋买菜很方便，但是不利于环保。

实战练习（三十六）

一、1. A 2. C

听力文本

1. 男：我讨厌整天躺在床上，你问问医生我可不可以提前出院啊？
女：你只要养好身体，很快就可以回家了，不要着急。
问：关于男的，可以知道什么？

2. 男：明天就要比赛了，今晚你最好提前睡觉，不要再弹钢琴了。
女：那怎么行，我一定要弹两个小时的琴才能睡。
男：好，再喝点汤，练完琴就赶紧睡觉。
女：知道了，爸爸，我已经吃饱了。
问：男的希望女的做什么？

二、1. C 2. A 3. E 4. F 5. B 6. D 7. E 8. D 9. A 10. F 11. B 12. C

三、1. ACB 2. BCA

四、1. 我喜欢躺在床上和孩子一起讨论学校发生的事情。
2. 大家讨论一下他们提出的条件是否可行。
3. 这篇文章最大的特点是用词很美。
4. 我会给你提供足够的钱到北京去学习弹钢琴。
5. 你还是提前两天到分公司去一趟吧。

五、1. 他们正在讨论一件很重要的事情。
2. 我躺在草地上看着蓝天，想着自己美好的将来。

实战练习（三十七）

一、1. D 2. B

听力文本

1. 女：先生，对不起，这里的手推车不能推到超市外面去。
男：不好意思，我马上放回去。
问：女的可能是干什么的？

2. 男：你是怎么知道张丽丈夫去世的消息的？

女：通过公司的网站知道的。大家都很同情张丽，才结婚丈夫就死了。
男：谁也没想到会出这样的事故啊，找时间我们去看看她吧。
女：要不明天去吧。
问：女的现在心情怎么样？

二、1. B 2. E 3. F 4. A 5. C 6. D 7. E 8. C 9. A 10. F 11. D 12. B

三、1. ACB 2. ABC

四、1. 学校通知大家交学费。
2. 我完全没有想到这场比赛我们会输。
3. 全部的节目都能在这个网站上找到。
4. 请你把这辆自行车推到我们家楼下。
5. 这群失去健康的人真的挺让人同情的。

五、1. 我很同情她，没想到她的病这么严重。
2. 两位女士推着购物车在超市选购东西。

实战练习（三十八）

一、1. C 2. D

听力文本

1. 男：既然误会都解除了，那我们就握握手，和好吧。
   女：好啊，但是你要请我吃好吃的，我要吃巧克力味儿的饼干。
   问：女的希望男的做什么？

2. 女：喂，小明，我好无聊啊，你干吗呢？
   男：我正在写一篇文章的读后感。你今天不用上班吗？
   女：我今天放假，你一会儿来我这儿吃饭吧。
   男：好啊，马上就过去找你。
   问：关于小明，可以知道什么？

二、1. C 2. F 3. A 4. B 5. D 6. E 7. C 8. E 9. F 10. D 11. A 12. B

三、1. BCA 2. ACB

四、1. 我完全不会打网球。
2. 你往文章中加的这几个词真好！
3. 他们之间往往不会出现这些小误会。
4. 他们错误地认为水污染是有味道的。
5. 有些网站很危险。

五、1. 这道菜的味道一定好极了。
2. 请问卫生间怎么走？

实战练习（三十九）

一、1. C 2. A

听力文本

1. 男：我们公司的李刚申请到出国深造的机会了，这个消息真让人兴奋。

女：是啊，也很让人羡慕。

问：女的主要是什么意思？

2. 男：我觉得张亮在会上提出来的计划很好，你觉得呢？

女：我不这样认为，相反我觉得这个计划会限制公司的发展。

男：你是不是有什么新的想法？

女：是的，等我把详细的计划写好就拿给您看。

问：女的和张亮可能是什么关系？

二、1. C　2. F　3. D　4. E　5. B　6. A　　7. B　8. E　9. F　10. C　11. D　12. A

三、1. ACB　2. BAC

四、1. 那篇文章所写的故事实在是太无聊了。

2. 现代社会正以前所未有的速度发生着变化。

3. 你做的西红柿鸡蛋汤太咸了。

4. 具有吸引力的美景促进了现代旅游业的发展。

5. 他把梦中的事情详细地记了下来。

五、1. 她很无聊，现在都想回房间睡觉了。

2. 李红的礼物那么大，真让人羡慕。

实战练习（四十）

一、1. B　2. A

听力文本

1. 男：你读过巴金的小说《家》吗？

女：还没有，不过我正打算从网上买一本看看呢。

问：他们正在谈论哪方面的事情？

2. 女：快醒醒，快七点了，上班要迟到了。

男：最近经理心情好，给我们放了两天假。

女：难怪你昨晚兴奋地看比赛看到十二点多！

男：不要烦我了，让我再睡会儿。

问：男的想要做什么？

二、1. E　2. B　3. C　4. A　5. F　6. D　　7. A　8. B　9. D　10. F　11. E　12. C

三、1. CBA　2. ABC

四、1. 能借你的橡皮用用吗？

2. 这个消息给大家带来了好心情。

3. 我有信心在一个月之内写好这本小说。

4. 这个笑话的效果不好。

5. 写小说是一件很辛苦的事情。

五、1. 这份工作很辛苦，但她还在坚持。

2. 这个小伙子正在打电话。

实战练习（四十一）

一、1. D   2. C

听力文本

1. 女：听说你有女朋友了，漂亮吗？
   男：我不看重外表，她是一个活泼、开朗、积极向上的女孩。
   问：男的的女朋友怎么样？

2. 女：请问你们经理在吗？
   男：他不在，有什么事？
   女：我昨天才给儿子买的玩具汽车，今天就坏了，我想换一个。
   男：拿给我看看，我帮你修修。
   问：男的是做什么的？

二、1. E   2. D   3. B   4. A   5. C   6. F   7. B   8. A   9. D   10. F   11. C   12. E

三、1. ABC   2. ABC

四、1. 这种水果味的牙膏很受欢迎。
   2. 你刚睡醒怎么就这么兴奋。
   3. 我想找一个性格活泼的女孩当我女朋友。
   4. 我对这学期的考试很有信心。
   5. 你去请人把这棵树上的树枝修一修。

五、1. 听到弟弟考上大学的消息，她非常兴奋。
   2. 这位师傅在修理汽车的时候遇到了一点麻烦。

实战练习（四十二）

一、1. A   2. A

听力文本

1. 男：你怎么穿成这个样子？这样能出门吗？
   女：怎么了？我觉得很好看。
   问：男的是什么语气？

2. 女：我最想当演员，你呢？
   男：我原来一直想当个医生，但是现在又想当老师了。你为什么想当演员呢？
   女：因为可以到处去演出呀。
   男：那可是非常辛苦的。
   问：他们在讨论什么？

二、1. C   2. B   3. F   4. A   5. D   6. E   7. F   8. C   9. E   10. D   11. B   12. A

三、1. CBA   2. BAC

四、1. 妈妈对我的要求总是很严格。
   2. 我希望儿子不要养成什么坏习惯。
   3. 他犯了一个严重的错误。
   4. 她要到亚洲参加演出。

5. 花草需要足够的阳光才能够长大。

五、1. 这次演出的人数很多，差不多有一百个人。/ 这次演出非常精彩。

2. 她戴着一副新眼镜。

实战练习（四十三）

一、1. A 2. C

听力文本

1. 男：哪种饮料的口感比较好？
   女：这种饮料口感好，很甜，很多顾客都喜欢买这种。
   问：他们最可能在哪儿？

2. 男：你和你男朋友是怎样认识的？
   女：我们是在医院里认识的，那天他正好带学生去看病。
   男：你觉得你男朋友怎么样？
   女：他给我的第一印象不是很好，但是后来才发现他有很多优点，比如幽默、勇敢等。
   问：女的男朋友可能是做什么的？

二、1. D 2. F 3. B 4. C 5. A 6. E   7. B 8. E 9. C 10. A 11. D 12. F

三、1. ABC   2. CBA

四、1. 通过学习我才发现自己没有一点艺术天分。/ 我通过学习才发现自己没有一点艺术天分。

2. 别以为我什么都不知道。

3. 一切艺术都来源于生活。

4. 出门的时候把钥匙带上。

5. 世界上没有两片叶子是完全相同的。

五、1. 车钥匙在我手里，你想要的话就过来拿吧！

2. 他对我很有意见。

实战练习（四十四）

一、1. A 2. A

听力文本

1. 男：听说《狗和猫》这部电影很有趣，今晚我们一起去看吧？
   女：今晚不行，由于工作没做完，晚上得加班。
   问：女的晚上要做什么？

2. 男：王华真是个了不起的人，样样都行。
   女：是的，他优点确实很多，不但学习成绩好，而且篮球打得也很好。
   男：他还很幽默、友好，性格也很开朗，很容易与人交往。
   女：我们都很喜欢他。
   问：王华是个什么样的人？

二、1. D 2. A 3. E 4. C 5. B 6. F   7. F 8. C 9. A 10. E 11. D 12. B

三、1. ACB   2. CAB

四、1. 我们要争取做对社会有用的优秀人才。
2. 这次会议一定会增进我们的友谊。
3. 我们要勇敢地面对生活中的所有困难。
4. 我想给她留下一个好印象。
5. 我真希望幸福的时光能够永远停留。

五、1. 听到国家足球队赢了的消息，他大叫起来。
2. 麦克非常幽默，和他在一起很开心。

实战练习（四十五）

一、1. A 2. D

听力文本

1. 男：这个月的《世界地理》杂志到了没有？
   女：还没有，你明天再来看看吧。
   问：他们可能在哪儿？

2. 男：你知道我无法原谅你的原因是什么吗？
   女：是因为我约会总是不准时吗？
   男：不是的。你经常对朋友说些不真实的话。
   女：对不起，我以后会尽量注意的。
   问：关于女的，可以知道什么？

二、1. B 2. A 3. D 4. C 5. E 6. F 7. B 8. A 9. C 10. D 11. F 12. E

三、1. BCA 2. CBA

四、1. 我要去邮局寄信。
2. 我发现小红这样做原来是有原因的。/ 我发现原来小红这样做是有原因的。
3. 请大家把下节课要学的语法知识预习一下。
4. 他们每次约会都是去公园打羽毛球。
5. 这节课的重点是语法。/ 语法是这节课的重点。

五、1. 大家虽然来自不同的国家，但相处得很友好。
2. 收到朋友的礼物，她愉快极了。

实战练习（四十六）

一、1. A 2. D

听力文本

1. 男：工作干得好好儿的，你为什么突然离开了公司？
   女：因为感觉很累，我想暂时放松一段时间。
   问：女的为什么要离开公司？

2. 男：昨天的招聘会你参加了没有？人可多了。
   女：我现在不想找工作，所以没去。
   男：听说你准备考研究生，我觉得考研究生要比找工作简单些。

277

女：其实也不是，现在考研究生的人数每年都在增加。

问：根据对话，可以知道什么？

二、1. F　2. B　3. D　4. A　5. E　6. C　　7. B　8. A　9. E　10. F　11. C　12. D

三、1. CBA　2. ABC

四、1. 我有责任去帮助他。

2. 我家门前的这条路又脏又窄。/ 我家门前的这条路又窄又脏。

3. 我们公司的人数每年都在增加。

4. 此次招聘的两个老师将暂时给我们上课。

5. 妈妈不允许我躺在床上阅读杂志。

五、1. 女孩并不想原谅她的男朋友。

2. 阅读报纸让我们获得更多信息。

实战练习（四十七）

一、1. A　2. A

听力文本

1. 男：今天下午我要开会，你到学校去接儿子吧。

   女：行，正好下午我没有事。

   问：他们可能是什么关系？

2. 男：你觉得当老师怎么样？

   女：挺好的呀，一年能有两个假期。不过我不想当老师，我从小就想成为一名演员。

   男：我支持你，但是当演员是很辛苦的，你要做好准备。

   女：我知道很不容易，但它是值得我付出努力的。

   问：他们在谈论什么？

二、1. A　2. C　3. E　4. F　5. D　6. B　　7. B　8. A　9. D　10. F　11. C　12. E

三、1. ABC　2. BAC

四、1. 请你证明这道判断题为什么是正确的。

2. 你打算什么时候把男朋友正式地介绍给家人？

3. 王东证明了我的话。

4. 哥哥离开家之后去了上海。

5. 我永远都支持你们的正确决定。

五、1. 服务员在整理房间。

2. 我们都支持李明做部门经理。/ 我的建议得到了大家的支持。

实战练习（四十八）

一、1. D　2. C

听力文本

1. 男：你看这个沙发怎么样？很漂亮吧。

   女：还是看看别的吧，这个沙发至少要花掉我们一个月的工资。

   问：女的是什么意思？

2. 男：听说你男朋友是个中文老师，人长得帅吗？
   女：我不重视外表，只要他人好就行了。
   男：我和你不一样，我找女朋友比较看重外表。
   女：那你的女朋友一定很漂亮。
   问：关于女的，可以知道什么？

二、1. F　2. B　3. C　4. D　5. E　6. A　　7. F　8. E　9. A　10. B　11. D　12. C

三、1. BAC　2. BCA

四、1. 学中文的学生都很重视自己的阅读能力。
2. 我们工厂的工人都很重视产品的质量。
3. 要想写好文章至少要懂得一点中文知识。
4. 教师是一个值得尊重的职业。
5. 我直接去植物园了。

五、1. 植物的生长离不开阳光。
2. 这台电脑的质量非常好。

实战练习（四十九）

一、1. B　2. A

听力文本

1. 男：电脑软件做得这么好，你一定是学计算机的专门人才吧？
   女：不是，我是数学专业的。
   问：关于女的，可以知道什么？

2. 男：经理今天表扬王红了，说她开会从来都不迟到。
   女：这是事实，准确地说，她上班也从没有迟到过。
   男：她真是了不起。
   女：此外，王红还很热心，经常主动去帮助有困难的人。
   问：关于王红，可以知道什么？

二、1. A　2. B　3. D　4. E　5. C　6. F　　7. E　8. F　9. A　10. C　11. D　12. B

三、1. CAB　2. ABC / BAC

四、1. 真心地祝贺你考上了这所著名的大学。
2. 在课堂上你一定要积极主动地回答老师的问题。
3. 他给出的数字非常准确。
4. 他让我向你表示最真诚的祝贺。
5. 长大后我想当一个著名的儿童文学作家。

五、1. 大家拿起酒杯一起祝贺李红的成功。
2. 他们准时来到了会议地点。

实战练习（五十）

一、1. D　2. D

听力文本

1. 男：我今天去看房子了，房子有三个卧室，环境也很好，就是有点贵，买不起。
   女：那我们就先租房子住吧，等过段时间再买。
   问：男的主要是什么意思？

2. 女：你怎么还不出发？讲座就要开始了。
   男：急什么，讲座不是八点半开始吗？现在才七点五十，还早呢。
   女：我想早点去，这样才能坐最前面的座位。
   男：那你先走吧，我等会儿再去。
   问：女的为什么要提前出发？

二、1. B 2. D 3. C 4. F 5. E 6. A   7. F 8. A 9. D 10. B 11. E 12. C

三、1. BCA 2. ACB

四、1. 现在我们来总结这次活动的经验。/ 我们现在来总结这次活动的经验。
   2. 我们最后一次见面是在去年的春节。
   3. 他是我最尊重的一位老师。
   4. 我到教室的时候已经没有座位了。
   5. 我对大自然充满了热爱。

五、1. 这里有很多空座位，你可以随便找一个坐下。
   2. 只有尊重自己，别人才会尊重你。